DATE DUE

D1446195

COMMUNICATION SKILLS FOR EXCEPTIONAL LEARNERS

Margaret S. Webber
Bloomsburg State College, Pennsylvania

AN ASPEN PUBLICATION®
Aspen Systems Corporation
Rockville, Maryland
London
1981

Library of Congress Cataloging in Publication Data

Webber, Margaret S.
Communication skills for exceptional learners.

Includes index.
1. Exceptional children—Education—Language
arts. 2. Communicative disorders in children.
3. Speech therapy for children. I. Title.
LC3973.W4   371.91'4   80-28094
ISBN: 0-89443-343-1

Library of Congress Catalog Card Number: 80-28094
ISBN: 0-89443-343-1

Printed in the United States of America

1 2 3 4 5

To Mary Ruth

Table of Contents

Acknowledgments

The author wishes to acknowledge the assistance of, and express a sincere word of appreciation to, professional colleagues who contributed to the preparation of this manual.

Mrs. Lamoine Fritz. Although there are many who deserve a note of recognition on the completion of this work, the first thank-you goes to Lamoine. As friend and secretary, her contribution cannot be measured.

Evelyn M. Duncan, M.Ed. Mrs. Duncan acted as materials adviser for this work. As Assistant Director of the Central Pennsylvania Special Education Resource Center, she selects and distributes educational materials on a daily basis. Her years of experience working with exceptional children and special educators made her service invaluable.

G. Donald Miller, Ph.D. Dr. Miller is Professor of Audiology, Department of Communication Disorders, Bloomsburg (Pennsylvania) State College, and acted as consultant and resource person for Chapters 2 and 3.

Richard M. Smith, M.S. Mr. Smith is a speech pathologist in private practice. His years of college teaching and field experience as a practitioner made his assistance of unlimited value in the preparation of the speech and oral language section.

And to my son *Glenn* and the many friends who gave support throughout the writing of this book; thank you.

Margaret S. Webber
February 1981

Overview

For most individuals, learning to listen, speak, read, and write is an easy developmental process. If the material is presented when the learners are ready, they acquire the ability to use a very sophisticated system of sounds and symbols with relative ease.

Unfortunately, there are those who are not developmental language learners. For the exceptional learner, language can be anything but natural and easy. It can be confusing and even frightening. Without language—that is, words or signs that represent objects, emotions, and conditions—individuals literally lack the ability to think. Without language, an acceptable manipulation of one's environment is virtually impossible, making day-to-day living a difficult task.

Learning to receive and send language symbols is one of the most important aspects of human development. Therefore, it is imperative that every effort be made to help exceptional learners acquire language to their fullest capacity.

This manual's express purpose is to assist in the language education of the exceptional learner. As a language arts guide, it is designed for use by all persons, professional and lay, involved with the education and well-being of the special child.

The aim is to present facts of a technical nature in such a way that the reader can readily assimilate information needed in helping exceptional learners. The material is basic information intended as both a starting point for individuals new to the education of exceptional learners and as a review resource for the experienced. It is designed as a practical source for dealing with language skills of the mentally and/or physically handicapped, the learning disabled, the socially and/or emotionally maladjusted, and the gifted and talented.

The manual is divided into four major topic areas: auding, speaking, reading, and writing. The theoretical basis of the specific language process under consideration is presented. For example, the section on auding contains information on sound waves and how the human ear and nervous system receive and transmit these vibrations, eventually converting them to meaningful stimuli referred to as language.

Also included are the normal development of the four language areas, frequently encountered problems, etiology of problems, and methods for identification of specific language disabilities. Methods and materials for developing skills in each of the topic areas are suggested.

Chapter 1

An Introduction to the Language Process and Communication

LANGUAGE, COMMUNICATION, AND THE EXCEPTIONAL CHILD

If you are, or will be, involved in the education and well-being of an exceptional child, you are aware of the importance of language development and the ability to communicate. Learning language and being able to communicate is a crucial factor in anyone's life, but for the atypical it may mean the difference between existence and living.

Being locked within human walls without the ability to say "I am," "I love," "I need" is a state difficult for normal persons to comprehend. Even a partial deterrent to total communication such as a misarticulated speech/sound difference or a reading problem can make life disappointing, confusing, and frustrating.

The ability to use language for communication can mean acceptance of self and acceptance by family and peers. Unfortunately, the opposite also is true. The inability to use language to communicate fully can cause self denial as well as rejection by family and those who should be peers.

It is critical that every effort be made to assist the exceptional child in developing language ability that will enhance communication. A basic understanding of the language process and communication will aid in achieving this goal.

THE LANGUAGE PROCESS

In American English, the singular noun *language* identifies a total process. For the purpose of this discussion, the four major abilities in the

---

Note: This book follows the practice of using the masculine pronoun whenever the pronoun refers to both males and females. Feminine pronouns appear only where the antecedents are exclusively female.

process—auding, speaking, reading, and writing—are considered. The ability to hear and comprehend (aude) is one facet of language. Auding is not language but is one component of the total process. Similarly, speaking, reading, and writing also are parts of the whole; they are interrelated elements that facilitate communication through language.

In the normally developing child, the acquisition of words—language—occurs with little attention to the interrelationships and intrarelationships of the system. With the exceptional individual, this may not be possible. Therefore, the teacher (educator, parent, relative, friend, etc.) must understand both the language and the process if the child is to learn to communicate.

Language can be visualized as a process core from which elements radiate and return for regeneration (Figure 1-1). The total process is both receptive (decoding) and expressive (encoding).

Auding is the apex element or the root function. In normal development it is the primary source from which all other process elements derive their

---

Figure 1-1 Language As an Interrelated Process

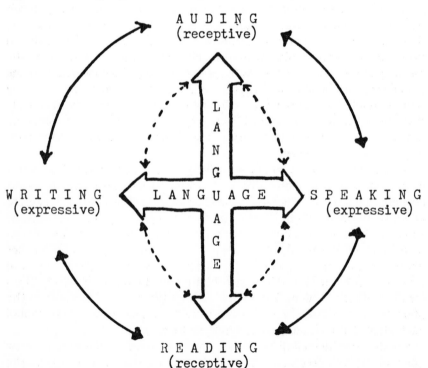

fundamental base. Auding is one of the two receptive elements (the other is reading). The auding element includes the ability to receive sounds, discriminate among sounds and sound patterns, and comprehend or interpret these sounds as symbols that have meaning.

Speaking, the expressive sound counterpart to auding, requires somewhat more complex abilities. Linguistically, this process element includes neurological integration that allows the user to retrieve meaningful sound patterns and to produce motorically (to articulate) the sound symbols that we call words. Beyond the ability to recall and produce specific sound symbols, the speaker also must have the intellectual capacity to comprehend and use linguistic structures such as phrases and sentences. The application of knowledge gained through a previous language experience in producing words and word order that conform to standard patterns requires instantaneous retrieval and synthesis of linguistic information. Reauderization, or the ability to hear one's self, acts as an expressive monitor. The interrelated elements of auditory language and oral language combine to form a miniprocess referred to as oracy. Fortunately for humankind, oracy can stand alone as a total communication system. Individuals can pursue and enjoy most life functions with aural-oral language.

Reading, the receptive written language element, in the normal developmental sequence is dependent upon prerequisite aural-oral abilities. Reading requires the ability to perceive the written symbol visually, to match or pair that symbol with a sound, and to determine the specific meaning of the set of symbols as they are ordered linguistically. Beginning reading instruction almost always is oral. Therefore, reading (or decoding written symbols) begins with the integration of two receptive elements that are aided and reinforced by the expressive element—speech. The initial visual receptive vocabulary is paired with an already existing auditory receptive vocabulary.

As the user of written language symbols matures, has additional experiences, and acquires more refined decoding skills, the reading process element may appear to be visual-visual. However, this is not an accurate appraisal of the function. Reading by an accomplished person at the most sophisticated level remains an integrative process. When encountering an unfamiliar written word, the reader relies on the recognition of smaller word parts (syllables) to which a sound symbol can be attached to achieve meaning. If this analysis fails, and if contextual clues do not help sufficiently for correct identification, the reader turns to the dictionary. The phonetic transcription or spelling indicated there elicits a sound symbol equivalent that facilitates completion of the process.

Reading, the decoding of written symbols, requires the user to draw upon an auditory receptive vocabulary for both sound and meaning. The retrieval of the sound and meaning is enhanced further through the motor-kinesthetic vocal expression of the word. Hearing, understanding, and using the word helps greatly in the visual retention of written symbols.

Writing, usually the last component of the language process to be developed, is the most complex of the four elements. Writing is a motoric-expressive language act. If speech development requires an auditory base, and reading needs both aural and oral abilities, it is logical to conclude that the written encoding element is dependent at least in part upon auding, speaking, and reading vocabulary and comprehension of these process elements.

To communicate through written expression, an individual must have the capacity to formulate thought patterns into motorically produced visual symbols that are comprehensible to others. The first step is to determine the intent of expression, to think of an idea. To accomplish this, a mental language that is an internalized oral process is used. An individual thinks silently in oral language, hearing words without creating sound. When the thought has been conceived, the writer must retrieve the written symbols that represent the verbal. Although words, to be meaningful, are produced as wholes, the written production requires the recall of separate symbols (letters) in a specific sequence called spelling. Correct spelling is an act of visual sequential memory that is related directly to sound symbol (phoneme) knowledge and to sound discrimination.

The ordering of written words into sentences and paragraphs requires an understanding of oral expressive patterns that have been refined and reinforced during visual experiences in reading. In reading what has been written, the correctness of expression often is determined by sound. That is, the writer reads either orally or silently and says, "Yes, that sounds right," meaning that the idea has been conveyed in acceptable language.

The application of symbols referred to as punctuation is learned auditorally and then visually. The language user hears a natural hesitation or pause in an utterance and translates it visually into an understanding of commas for junctures and periods for pauses. The reader recognizes rising intonation as indicated by a question mark and senses a feeling of excitement when encountering an exclamation point. The writer retrieves and applies these understandings gained from hearing, speaking, and reading experiences to produce written language that will have meaning to others.

The motor act, the physical production of written symbols, is a highly complex neural integrative function and the most difficult aspect of the language process. The production of written symbols requires the retrieval of specific and distinctively different forms that represent speech sounds. Auditory, visual, and kinesthetic memories are combined to produce the act of writing. The thought is produced in silent speech; the visual symbols are recalled in form, sequence, and pattern. Stored and matched proprioceptive data guide the hand and arm to manipulate the writing instrument in producing legible marks that convey meaning through the written language element.

Language, and particularly American English, is an integrated process initiated through the auditory channel. As depicted in Figure 1-1, language, when following the normal path, builds one element upon another. Understanding the reciprocal effect of the growth and development of one element upon another makes it possible for the teacher to help the exceptional learner. It is this back-and-forth reinforcement that improves the separate elements. Drawing on the strength of an intact element may increase the productivity of an impaired language learner in achieving maximum communication ability, or at least delineate a circuitous path to that goal.

COMMUNICATION

The word *communicate* is derived from the Latin communicatus, which is translated literally to mean *impart* or *participate*. More specifically, it means to share by all. When applied in American English it refers to the act of imparting information that can be understood by all who use the same language system. The meaning is intended to be common to the expressor(s) and receiver(s).

If it were as simple to communicate as the word implies, there would be far less confusion, conflict, and sorrow in life. Inherent in the use of the term is mutual understanding. This, unfortunately, is why communication often falls short of the intent. For the educator or parent interested in understanding fully the act of communicating, it is helpful to consider the involvement of psychological acceptance as well as the many modes that may be used for sending and receiving.

The difficulty with the act of communicating often is attributed to problems of psychological acceptance. Basically, this refers to an accurate perception of a situation. Psychological acceptance can be affected by emotional state, biological state, experience background, or a combination of these conditions. This can be illustrated best by a situation to which the reader may relate from similar experience:

The sender (S) is in a splendid mood. The receiver (R) has experienced a long line of petty annoyances and is in a black mood. They meet. S says, "Hi! You're looking great today." This is intended as a compliment, pure and simple. R is insulted. To R, the statement implies that on other days this individual's appearance was less than acceptable. The result of the brief encounter may have far-reaching effects and is an example of miscommunication due to psychological set differences.

Another consideration in understanding communication is the vehicle used for imparting the message. It can be a single mode such as sound alone or it may be multimodal, that is, sound and gesture.

A sender speaking over the telephone uses a sound symbol system to convey a message—the mode is audible. When the sender is visible to the receiver, the vehicle may become multimodal. For example, consider S, whose hands are placed about four inches apart, palms in. S says, "Did you see the b-i-i-ig fish that John caught?" The exaggeration and the intonation used on the word big, plus the size indicated by the placement of the hands, reverses the literal meaning. If R understands that the fish was quite small, S and R are communicating through a multimodal presentation of a sound symbol system and a gestural system with meaning common to both participants.

Generally, the more modes involved, the clearer the message. This is true at least for individuals who can integrate and match two or more messages. Consider the example of the fish story and a concrete thinker. A child who cannot think in the abstract will perceive two separate and incompatible sets of information. Children who react to words and not to intonation, facial expression, or gestures may be miscommunicating on a regular basis. Any adult who has attempted playfully teasing such a child will understand the condition readily.

Reaching the point of common understanding involves a complexity of factors. While the list of possible affecters is nearly endless, there are three factors of major importance: the symbol system, language learning ability, and opportunity.

The Symbol System

The symbol system, in this case American English, is a synthesis of many languages. The words that constitute the building blocks of the language are derived for the most part from a system other than American English. The correct pronunciation or spelling of a word is related to the system of its origin, such as grand prix, pronounced grahn pree as in French. This simply means that American English has an inconsistent morphological base and lacks systematic regularity of phoneme-grapheme correspondence.

A phoneme is said to be the most elemental speech sound in a language. Linguists cannot agree on the number of phonemes in American English. Generally, the count is 44; however, there is a stated range of 35 to 45.

A grapheme is a letter symbol for a phoneme. In American English, 26 graphemes are used to represent the 44 sounds. This is accomplished by assigning more than one elemental sound to a single letter, for example, the letter *e* as in *e*gg, *e*at, and *e*lephant.

To complicate the phoneme-grapheme situation further, the system employs more than one spelling for some sounds. This makes letters such as *f*, *c*, and *x* unnecessary. Consider, for example, the sound beginning the word fish. For the purpose of illustration, it is called *fa*. *Fa* may be written as *ph* in physical, or *ough* in enough. For that matter, why not *phish*?

American English, as a symbol system, is marked with inconsistencies that the language user must master if total communication is to occur. In addition to these examples, the teacher (educator, therapist, parent) should consider word form changes, tenses, parts of speech, word order, etc. This text touches on each of these language areas when appropriate for developing communication skills in exceptional learners.

Language Learning Ability

Language usage often is equated with intelligence. This may be an erroneous assumption. It can be the lack of language that causes a child to be labeled mentally retarded (MR). A child who cannot, or does not, answer the psychologist's questions scores low on measures of intelligence. As most intelligence tests are language oriented—that is, they are verbal measures—the child with delayed or impaired language is doomed to failure and the consequent low IQ score. It is a vicious cycle.

What may be more important than the child's failure to achieve on the intelligence test is what happens once the incorrect label has been applied. In many cases, because the child has been identified as mentally retarded, it is assumed that he lacks the ability to learn language. Unquestionably, intelligence plays a significant role in rate and sophistication of language acquisition. However, language learning ability is far more than just intelligence.

A child with delayed language development may be demonstrating maturational lag. The ability to learn language is not impaired; it is merely slowed down. Maturational lag may be manifested as no speech long beyond the age when the average child begins to talk. Other children may develop limited expressive vocabulary, retain immature syntax, converse in one-word sentences, or have severe misarticulations that make speech unintelligible. There is no single pattern other than a marked difference in their level of language development when compared to the norm.

Recognizing children with a maturational lag is complicated by the fact that there are no absolute signs. Some children will have concomitant problems such as retarded motor skills or short attention spans, or be difficult to toilet train. Others may be totally average in all areas except language. Occasionally these children are recognizable through medical examination when body functions, particularly reflex actions, are well within normal limits.

When language development is delayed, it is wise to assume maturational lag. The educator (therapist, parent) should begin steps to stimulate language development and should consider learning ability to be unimpaired. If worked with properly, children with maturational lag soon begin to demonstrate their language learning ability.

There are children who have at least average intelligence but who also have impaired language skills. Their overall learning ability is intact; they are not mentally retarded; they have a specific language disability. Educationally, they are classified as learning disabled.

A language disability may manifest itself as a problem in one or more of the language elements. The diagnosis of a specific language disability may be complicated because of the interrelationship between and among the language elements. For example, a problem with auditory discrimination (the inability to hear differences in speech sounds) may be noted as an articulation problem because an individual tends to produce what is heard. A problem in formulating thought for oral expression may be noted as a reading comprehension problem when the child cannot respond verbally to questions about the reading passage.

Unlike the children with maturational lag, individuals with specific learning disabilities may not catch up. A specific language disability is associated with central nervous system dysfunction. In such cases remediation is through a strong or unimpaired language element. A child who cannot retrieve the sound symbol that should be attached to a visual symbol need not fail to become a reader. If reading material is paired with a sound script and if the process is repeated a sufficient number of times, retrieval becomes automatic. Children with specific language disabilities may have a language deficit; however, their overall learning ability can be used effectively to master the symbol system and to learn to communicate on all levels.

Learning ability, as stated previously, is related to intellectual capacity. However, this does not mean that individuals with lowered mental capacity should not be expected to acquire language skills. In cases of severe mental retardation, the rate and degree of acquisition may be markedly less than the average, but in most situations language is possible for the purpose of communicating basic needs. It should be remembered that learning ability also is affected by expectancy. Teachers or parents who expect some degree of language development are rewarded more often than those who do not believe in success.

Opportunity

Language development and communication through language cannot occur without opportunity to learn. Every child's environment should abound with learning opportunities. It is the responsibility of the adults in the child's life to use and to create language learning opportunities.

The first opportunity occurs when a parent sees and speaks to the newborn infant. Although the infant is unable to respond linguistically, he can and probably will react.

Learning the symbol system begins at a surprisingly young age. The first step may be that of recognizing human voices. When the infant learns which voice is mother (or mother figure) he has begun the important behavior of attending to sound for purposes of discrimination and identification.

As the child grows, so does the number of situations that afford learning. When visual ability matures to the point that the child can discriminate visually, he undoubtedly will focus on facial features. The adult then has the opportunity to help the child note expressions that communicate emotions.

When the child reaches the developmental stage of sound experimentation (babbling), the parent should utilize moments of play to reinforce random sound production. The child will be fascinated if the parent repeats a sound the infant has made accidentally. If the child is being held and has the opportunity to see and hear the adult's production of the sound, the usual reaction is an attempt to mimic.

The child who has the opportunity to practice sound production repeatedly with an adult generally develops articulatory control at a more rapid rate than usual. On the other hand, when sound production is not reinforced, the natural inclination to make sounds may diminish and speech may be delayed.

Naming objects helps in building receptive and expressive vocabulary. For example, during feeding, the parent can identify utensils such as spoon and dish, when dressing the child name items of clothing, and during play periods describe toys as to color, size, and texture. Opportunities for this type of teaching-learning are nearly endless.

A child need not be at the speaking stage to begin appreciating written language. Reading to a child, even if he is too young to understand, gives the parent-teacher an opportunity to help develop tonal patterns, attention span, and visual discrimination.

At the point in development when the child is speaking, encourage him to ask questions. Create the behavior by modeling. Ask simple questions to which he can respond. However, should the child learn too well and the questions become incessant, the parent-teacher must remember that this is an integral part of creating an atmosphere for learning. The adult's behavior is the child's clue to continue learning or to withdraw.

Allowing a child to observe an adult reading a letter from (or writing to) a friend and discussing how pleasant letters can be promotes a desire for similar experiences. The child who has the opportunity to see someone read and enjoy it develops a desire to learn the written symbol system.

The opportunity to learn language is a natural part of every child's life. However, the opportunities for language practice may need to be increased when working with an exceptional learner. The examples in this book are but a few of the easily created but extremely important language learning opportunities.

BEGINNING LANGUAGE INSTRUCTION

The question now is how and where the teaching of language skills to exceptional learners begins. The answer is so simple that most teachers and parents never consider it an answer. The first step is to accept the child, the child's language, and the child's particular form of exceptionality.

Correct identification of the child's specific problems and level of functioning should be the next order of business. After accomplishing this, the wise teacher will use the child's strengths, build confidence, and gradually attack problem areas—if possible, the little problems first.

The material in Chapters 2 through 9 is presented in developmental order. Types of problems are discussed and teaching strategies and materials are suggested. While this book is not a panacea, it is believed that the seasoned professional, the beginning teacher, the paraprofessional, and the parent all will find information that can be of help when working with special children.

Chapter 2

Hearing

SOUND PRODUCTION AND MOVEMENT

When preparing to work with a deficit skill such as delayed language or auditory imperception, the educator should acquire knowledge related to the normal development of the affected learning. The following material is not intended as a technical explanation of acoustics, audiology, or the central nervous system. It is basic information that should help in understanding typical and atypical auditory ability.

Air Conduction

If any object is at rest in a medium such as air, and it has the properties necessary to vibrate, and if it receives a force sufficient to effect vibration, sound is produced.

That explanation of sound at first may appear confusing, but is not if an elementary science experiment that clearly demonstrated this phenomenon is recalled. A tuning fork was placed in a holder or held by hand, with prongs upward. When one of the prongs was tapped, or a force was exerted strong enough to set the prong in motion, the sound produced by the vibrating movement of the tuning fork was heard.

To hear the sound, two conditions were necessary: an exerted force and a conductive medium. In the experiment, the energy exerted on the prong was transferred and the moving prong became the force. The conductive medium, air, also was present.

In all natural settings, objects on this planet are surrounded by air. Air is a medium in which sound waves can propagate with relative ease and uniformity. One cubic inch of air contains billions of particles that, although they are in continuous random motion, do have a stable point. If one particle is *pushed* in a given direction, it will be returned to its original place by forces created by compression and rarefaction.

11

Consider the movements of three particles, *A, B,* and *C,* involved with the sound waves produced in the experiment. The right prong of the fork was set in motion. It moved toward particle *A,* sending it on its way toward *B.* The space between *A* and *B* decreased, or was compressed. Compression tends to create an outward force. Thus *B* was set in motion and *A* was pushed back toward the tuning fork, or *A*'s original position. In addition, during the time *A* had moved outward, the space between the prong and *A* had fewer particles and was rarefied. Rarefaction creates a force that pulls inward, or in the direction of the rarefied space. The creation of these forces by compression and rarefaction caused *A* to return to the original position.

In the meantime, *B* was moving toward *C,* causing compression between *B* and *C,* and rarefaction between *B* and *A.* As *B* approached *C,* compression forces started *C* in motion, and so on.

What occurred was a continual pattern of particles moving closer and then farther apart. The particles were displaced temporarily, then returned to their original position in space.

The sound wave created with the tuning fork was the movement or a disturbance through the medium (air) without permanently displacing the particles themselves. The movement can be visualized as a chain reaction continuing on until the particles of the medium end. Sound waves will continue propagation in the direction of the existing path until reaching a point where medium changes and/or forces diminish (Denes & Pinson, 1963).

The sound produced by an instrument, by a natural force, or by the vocal mechanism such as in speech, travels in much the same way. When someone speaks, the sound will travel through the air until it reaches an object with a density dissimilar to that of air. The movement or conduction then will change, depending upon the molecular structure of the object. Sounds may be heard as echoes as they rebound or they may be distorted as the original pattern is changed through obstruction or as the force diminishes.

In addition to understanding sound production and sound wave movement, readers should be familiar with several terms associated with sound. Understanding these terms will facilitate reading audiograms as well as discussing specific types of hearing loss and amplification devices such as hearing aids.

Cycle

Picture the tuning fork of the earlier experiment. The prongs of the fork were at rest. A force was exerted. One prong moved to the right, changed directions, passed through the rest position, moved an equal distance to the left, and returned to the original point. The complete motion was one *cycle* of oscillation.

Displacement and Amplitude

The distance *B* traveled in one direction, from the stable point toward *C,* is called *displacement.* The maximum displacement is referred to as the *amplitude* of the vibration.

Frequency and Hertz

The *frequency* of a sound wave is the number of air particle vibrations occurring in one second, and is the same as the frequency rate of the sound source. Frequency, or cycles per second (cps), is expressed in *hertz* and written as Hz.

Velocity

Velocity refers to the speed at which the vibrations move through the medium. At sea level, sound waves in air travel at about 1,130 feet per second, or 770 miles per hour. Velocity increases in media denser than gases, such as in liquids and solids.

Intensity and Decibel

To understand *intensity,* or the strength of a sound wave, return to the tuning fork experiment. When the prong created a force in the direction of particle *A,* the tuning fork *worked* or transferred energy to the particle. The energy then was transferred from particle to particle as the sound wave spread outward. The energy transferred to individual particles decreased as the number of particles increased. The measurement of the energy level along the direction of the sound wave movement is referred to as the intensity of the sound wave.

Sound wave intensity is measured in *decibels,* abbreviated dB. Decibels are not linear measures like ounces, pounds, or meters. A decibel is a ratio of two sounds. When the intensity of a sound is expressed in decibels, it indicates that an arbitrarily chosen standard or reference sound is *X* number of times greater or less than the sound being measured. For example, dB HL (hearing level) is referenced to the threshold of normal human hearing.

ANATOMY AND PHYSIOLOGY OF HEARING

Having reviewed the production of sound and how it moves through air, the next consideration is how the human ear receives and transmits sound to the cortical area of the brain that is involved in auding. Specifically, how is the human ear constructed to facilitate sound transmission?

The evolution of the human auditory apparatus had its beginning in the first stages of change from sea life to land existence (Jaffe, 1977). What has evolved in the process is a three-part sense organ that collects, amplifies, and transforms sound waves, or acoustic energy, into mechanical energy, then into hydromechanical energy, and finally into electrical energy receivable by the brain. The three parts of the hearing organ are referred to as the outer, the middle, and the inner ear (Figure 2-1).

The Outer Ear

The primary purpose of the hearing organ that evolved is to receive sound vibrations and to convert them into signals that can travel through the auditory system to the brain. The first step of the process occurs with the collection and direction of sound by the outer ear.

The outer ear, the most visible part of the hearing sense organ, serves a minor role in the auding process. The outer portion is called the pinna or auricle and is flesh-covered cartilage. The semiconical shape of the pinna may have greatly facilitated the gathering of sound waves during some stage of human evolution; however, it serves little purpose in the hearing process today. The ear canal (external auditory meatus) also is part of the outer ear.

The ear canal is an air-filled passageway. It generally is about one inch long, with the external end open at the pinna and the internal end closed by the eardrum (tympanic membrane). The ear canal acts as a resonator for certain sounds, depending on their frequency. The ability to amplify sound waves, with respect to which frequencies and to the amounts of amplification, is related to the size and shape of the ear canal cavity. This resonance, or amplification, makes it possible to hear sounds that otherwise would be less audible. In addition, the air-filled canal tends to maintain a more stable temperature and humidity condition for the middle ear. The wax-secreting glands and tiny hairs in the canal help protect the sensitive eardrum from foreign bodies.

The Middle Ear

The middle ear, where acoustic energy is changed into mechanical energy, is called the tympanum and somewhat resembles a drum. It is sepa-

Figure 2-1 The Ear

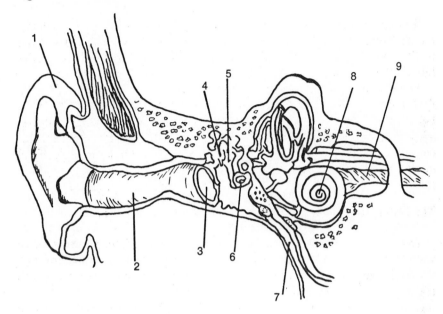

1. Outer ear, minor role in hearing; cosmetic.
2. External auditory canal, amplifies and directs sound; protects eardrum; stabilizes air temperature.
3. Tympanic membrane (eardrum) vibrates, carrying sound waves to ossicles.
4. Malleus (hammer), first ossicles.
5. Incus (anvil), second ossicles.
6. Stapes (stirrup), third ossicles; working with other bones, it vibrates, carrying sound.
7. Eustachian tube, supplies air to middle ear and controls pressure.
8. Cochlea, transforms sound to hydraulic energy and then to electrical impulses.
9. Auditory nerve, transmits impulse from inner ear to auditory portion of the brain.

rated from the outer ear by the eardrum and from the inner ear by a bony wall containing two openings, the oval window and the round window.

The Eustachian tube allows air into the middle ear and is an extension of the middle ear into the posterior nasal passage (nasopharynx). It serves as an air and/or pressure exchange pathway, keeping air pressure within the middle ear equal to the outside air pressure. When the Eustachian tube becomes blocked and external air pressure increases or decreases, the eardrum becomes distended or retracted. This condition can be both painful and damaging. If, for example, a person rises to a higher altitude and the Eustachian tube is blocked, preventing pressure equalization, the middle ear pressure soon will exceed the pressure in the ear canal, distending the eardrum, with resultant discomfort and possible damage to the membrane. The reverse pressure conditions occur when altitude decreases, causing retraction of the eardrum. These conditions can be encountered while driving through mountainous country, riding in an elevator, or flying in an airplane.

The ossicles, a series of three bones, span the middle ear cavity. The first of these, the malleus (hammer), is attached to the eardrum. The malleus extends into the area of the middle ear referred to as the attic (epitympanic recess), where it articulates with the incus (anvil). In turn, the incus connects to the head of the stapes (stirrup). The stapes is attached to the footplate by two crura, and the footplate is held in the oval window by a ligament. The round window is covered by a membrane.

The air-filled middle ear serves two primary functions directly related to hearing: (1) when the ossicles vibrate as a unit, they transmit the movements of the eardrum to the inner ear; (2) when the eardrum is stimulated by sounds of excessive intensity, the muscles of the middle ear act to impede the movement of the ossicular chain, thereby protecting the inner ear from damage.

The Inner Ear

The inner ear houses the end organ of hearing where sound waves are converted from mechanical energy into hydromechanical energy and finally into electrical pulses. The inner ear is in two parts, vestibular and auditory.

The vestibular portion is involved directly with equilibrium and balance. Because of the relationship of the vestibular and auditory portions, some types of hearing loss may be accompanied by equilibrium or balance problems. The vestibular portion otherwise is not related directly to hearing.

The auditory portion of the inner ear is the cochlea, where energy is transformed for hearing. The cochlea is divided into three scalas or ducts: the scala vestibuli, scala tympani, and the cochlear duct or cochlear partition.

If the cochlea, a snail-like cavity, were unrolled, it would be seen that the cochlear partition is a hollow duct that separates the scala vestibuli from the scala tympani (Denes & Pinson, 1963). Both scalas (vestibuli and tympani) contain viscous fluid called perilymph. This fluid is free to move from scala to scala through a valve-like connecting area known as the helicotrema.

The cochlear duct is filled with a denser fluid, encolymph. The cochlear partition, or duct, is separated from the scala vestibuli by Reissner's membrane and from the scala tympani by the basilar membrane. The basilar membrane is very narrow at the basal end of the cochlea and widest at the apical end. It is narrow and stiff near the oval window, and wider and progressively more flexible toward the helicotrema.

Motion of the stapes, transmitted through the oval window, excites the cochlear structure. When the window moves as a result of sound vibrations, pressure vibrations that are set up in the fluids of the cochlea cause the partition to vibrate. Because of the physical properties of the basilar membrane and sound waves, high frequency vibrations along the partition reach the point of maximum displacement near the oval window, where the membrane is narrow and stiff. At the apical end of the cochlea where the membrane is wider and more flexible, low frequency vibrations reach maximum displacement. When the vibrations reach maximum displacement as dictated by the sound waves and structures they are acting upon, the vibrations then move through the cochlear duct for additional processing. Critical dampening, or the essential elimination of sound waves, follows the point of maximum displacement and processing.

The vibration, or hydraulic action, is converted into impulses transmittable to the brain at the organ of Corti. The organ of Corti is a collection of minute supporting cells lying on the basilar membrane inside the cochlear duct. Hair cells are sensory receptors supported by the organ of Corti. On the end of the hair cells are extremely fine hairs that make contact with the tectal membrane. There are approximately 3,500 inner hair cells and 12,000 to 20,000 outer hair cells.

Nerve fibers from the auditory nerve (VIIIth cranial nerve) extend into the organ of Corti. When the basilar membrane vibrates responding to sound waves, the tiny hairs are subject to the sheer force from a delayed motion of the tectorial membrane. The result of the excitation is the production of electrical pulses that are transmittable along the nerve to the brain stem. When impulses enter the brain stem, they proceed through various paths to the cortex of the cerebrum. Fibers of the auditory nerve cross to the opposite side of the brain. By this movement, impulses from both ears reach both the left and right hemispheres of the brain.

Hearing by Bone Conduction

The process just described is termed air conduction hearing. There is another method of transmitting sound vibrations that is referred to as bone conduction hearing. Although the average listener is not aware of this process, it is occurring during normal hearing and in particular when receiving sounds of great intensity.

The inner ear, the end organ of hearing, is located within the bones of the skull. Because the crucial process of converting sound vibrations into electrical impulses occurs in the inner ear, and because the inner ear is housed within a bony structure, it is possible to receive and utilize sound vibrations that do not pass through the outer and middle ears.

Sound waves that cause the bones of the skull to vibrate can produce movement of the fluids of the inner ear. The process thereafter is much the same as with air conduction hearing. However, the bones of the skull are relatively insensitive to sound vibrations outside the body. Hearing through bone conduction requires much greater sound energies and therefore is much less efficient than hearing by air conduction.

AUDITORY SENSITIVITY

Auditory sensitivity is the ability to hear, or receive, sounds of various intensities, frequencies, and durations. The average human has potential auditory sensitivity far greater than that required for the development of oral language. A loss of sensitivity at extremely high or low frequencies often goes undetected because this ability seldom is used. In fact, when becoming aware of sounds in these ranges, individuals often react in a negative fashion because they perceive these unfamiliar sounds as being unpleasant noises.

For developing language skills, the learner should have the ability to hear sounds within the speech range. The critical speech range generally is stated as 500, 1000, and 2000 Hz, although 4000 and 6000 Hz may be included. Average conversational speech is produced at approximately 45 to 50dB HL. For the individual to process speech sounds at a comfortable level, the sounds should have thresholds for the speech frequency of approximately 20dB HL or better.

Hearing Loss

The loss of sound sensitivity may be inherited or acquired. Since the range of possible dysfunction spans from permanent deafness to a mild and temporary loss, only terms and conditions that would concern educators dealing with language development are discussed here.

The term *hereditary,* when applied to hearing loss, means that the abnormality, or dysplasia, was present in the fertilized egg. Conditions associated with genetic structures are not always noticeable at birth or in the early developmental stages. A child may be born with normal sensitivity and the hearing loss may occur later in life. The initial clue to the cause of this type of hearing loss may be first noted in the case history when the informant reports that a brother, uncle, grandmother, or some other relative has a similar hearing problem.

The age at which the loss occurs and the degree of severity depend on the specific cause and type of dysfunction. The hearing loss may be mild at first but, because of a degenerative process, may increase in severity. Otosclerosis is an example of this type of condition. It is a result of a pathological bony growth causing the footplate of the stapes to fixate in the oval window. Very few young children have a noticeable loss because of this condition. Loss of hearing usually is noted first in the late teens and early twenties. Initially, it is a conductive loss, but if not treated properly it may develop into a sensorineural loss. It is found most often in women, and a mother-daughter pattern is not uncommon.

In addition to inherited hearing problems, specific abnormalities may be the result of chromosomal aberrations. These conditions are not inherited, in the true sense of the word. The change in number and configuration of the chromosomes can occur as a matter of chance and not as an inherited pattern. Trisomy D is an example of chromosomal aberration and is known to cause hearing loss.

Conditions other than those caused by gene patterns are considered *acquired*. An acquired condition may occur in uterine, at birth, or at any time thereafter. Acquired hearing loss is caused by toxic agents, infection, or trauma.

The rubella baby is an example of an acquired hearing loss due to infection while in the uterus. Rubella, a type of measles, can have devastating effects on the fetus if contracted by the mother during the first trimester of the pregnancy. This disease, if it occurs during the crucial stages of fetal development, may cause other types of abnormalities as well. The stage of fetal development and severity of the diseases are the influencing factors.

The detrimental effects of rubella were established clearly in the early 1960s when thousands of expectant mothers were infected with the disease. Hearing loss was just one of the handicapping conditions reported among the children born to these women.

While other diseases are suspected of having similar effects on the developing fetus, the incidence of such occurrences has not been established so dramatically. It should be noted, however, that any illness during pregnancy that requires the use of drugs or is accompanied by high body temperatures may cause handicapping conditions, including hearing loss.

Maternally ingested drugs (toxic agents) are another well-established cause of acquired hearing loss. The type and degree of loss depends on the stage of fetal development when the drug was ingested, how much was taken, and its kind or composition. Perhaps the most widely known of the damaging drugs is thalidomide. The effects of this drug on the developing fetus are so profound that it no longer is prescribed during pregnancy (Katz, 1978).

Many other drugs have side effects of a less dramatic nature. For example, quinine is believed to have serious effects on hearing, both to a developing fetus and to adults, such as residents of the malaria belt, who need continual dosage (Katz, 1978). The best rule when considering drug ingestion is to suspect all drugs, even aspirin if taken in large amounts or over extended periods of time.

Acquired hearing loss that occurs after birth is found among children in both regular and special education classes. Many of these conditions are temporary but need to be considered when planning educational programs and should be of special concern in attempting to develop language skills in young children.

Impacted Cerumen

Cerumen is referred to as wax. Heavy secretions of this substance can obstruct the ear canal and cause a conductive hearing loss. If this condition is suspected, the proper procedure is immediate referral to an otologist (a medical hearing specialist). Properly cared for, the hearing loss generally is not permanent. However, if left untreated or improperly cared for, permanent damage to the sensitive tissue can occur.

Foreign Body

Insertion of a foreign body (a pea, a pebble, or an eraser) in the ear canal is not uncommon. Fortunately, an object large enough to cause a conductive loss usually is visible upon examination. Auditory ability returns to normal after the object is removed. However, if the object is wedged into the canal, it is best to have an otologist remove it. Depending upon the size and shape of the object, probing can force it farther into the ear canal, with possible damage to the tympanic membrane.

Otitis Externa

Otitis externa is a bacterial infection of the external canal skin. Although the term is incorrect, it often is called fungus of the ear. Severe cases of this condition where discharge and swelling occur can cause a conductive loss (Katz, 1978). Fortunately, the most common variety is nothing more serious than dry, scaling tissue that does not affect hearing.

Serous Otitis Media

Serous otitis media is the most common cause of conductive hearing loss in children of school age. It may result from anything from an infection to an allergy. When the Eustachian tube becomes infected or irritated so that it does not ventilate the middle ear properly, the middle ear begins to change and cannot function as it should. In fact, the condition can be considered cyclical: the Eustachian tube becomes blocked, the middle ear is not ventilated and produces a fluid, the fluid further disrupts the function of the Eustachian tube, and so on.

If the condition is recognized soon enough, decongestants can be effective. However, in long-term cases it is necessary to resort to myringotomy, a procedure in which tubes are inserted in the tympanic membrane to ventilate the middle ear. In effect, the inserted tube temporarily replaces the faulty functioning Eustachian tube. In most cases after the tubes have been in place for a sufficient period of time, the fluids are eliminated, the Eustachian tube functions properly, and hearing becomes normal again.

One of the perplexing aspects of this condition is that it may go undetected for months or even longer. A case in point: in September, Dee was given a routine audiological examination and found to have normal hearing. In October, she contracted chicken pox, a cold, and other accompanying little ills. The physician prescribed the usual medication, and the childhood disease ran its course. Unfortunately, the Eustachian tube remained infected, and the cycle began.

At first, the hearing loss was so slight that Dee never noticed. Eventually, she became accustomed to saying "Huh?", "What did you say?" and missing parts of conversations. She was baffled by her teacher's impatience. Her parents and her teacher said she was spoiled and trying to get attention.

When Dee's problem was discovered and the tubes were inserted, life changed markedly for her, her teacher, and her parents. Her grades improved, and the teacher could return to giving oral directions to the entire class. Phonics became fun, and even Dee's peers seemed to like her better.

Trauma

Conductive hearing loss may occur as a result of mechanical trauma. That is, a blow to the head, especially with an open palm over the ear, may cause a perforation (an opening in the tympanic membrane), a hemotympanum (blood in the middle ear), or even damage to the ossicular chain (Katz, 1978). The degree of involvement depends on the intensity of the blow, the frequency of such occurrences, and if and when proper treatment is received.

CENTRAL AUDITORY PROCESSING

In this chapter, the central nervous system is discussed in terms of auditory processing. However, the system operates fundamentally the same for all sensory processing. The point of origin may be different, that is, visual stimuli are received by the eye and pass along the optic nerve, but the process is the same. If the central nervous system (CNS) can be understood in relation to auditory sense performance, the information can be applied to any sense organ or perceptual process.

Central Nervous System

To understand the process involved in the central nervous system, it is helpful to draw an analogy between the nervous system and the electrical system in the home. The electrical system contains a source of power, or energy, that is transported or conducted along a pathway to a point where it is transformed into a product. For example, when a plug is inserted in a receptacle, energy in the form of electrical impulses travels along a cord to a light bulb, producing illumination.

In the electrical system, energy is produced by a generator that transforms one type of energy (such as water or atomic) into another form of energy (electricity). The electrical energy travels along a cord, which is a bundle of fine copper wires (conductors) encased in an outer insulating covering. When the energy reaches the bulb, it is received by tiny fibers or filaments that react and produce illumination. The resulting product, light, is dependent upon several factors.

The electrical system must have an active energy source. The cord must be intact—that is, there cannot be a break in the insulating covering or in the copper wires. The light bulb must be of proper strength to receive and utilize the energy, and the filaments must be whole and functional. Lastly, the size, shape, and color of the bulb affect the output of light; that is, a frosted or colored bulb appears to produce less illumination than a clear bulb receiving the same amount of energy.

If there is a break in the copper wires, it may produce a short circuit; that means the passage of electrical current is disrupted. In certain situations, the energy can be seen bridging the break; this is called arcing, and sparks can be seen. At other times, the wiring can be intact but there is either partial illumination or none at all. For instance, if a bulb is loose in the socket, it may flicker or not light at all. To correct this situation, a simple tightening of the bulb in the socket will produce illumination. At still other times, even though energy is flowing, the wires are intact, and the bulb is securely in place, there is no light. In such cases, the bulb may have burned out or may lack the capacity to use the energy transmitted.

The central nervous system can be considered in much the same way as the electrical system. The energy source in the auditory processing begins when sound is produced. A series of energy transformations occurs until the organ of Corti, located in the cochlea, transforms the hydromechanical energy into electrical energy transmittable through the auditory nerve.

The nerve is constructed much like the cord in the electrical system. It has a covering called a sheath that is composed of a fatty white substance, myelin. The myelin sheath (Figure 2-2) acts in the same fashion as the insulated covering of the cord to protect the fibers of the auditory nerve. Malformation or lack of myelin exposes the fibers to danger of damage and may impede process functions, as in the break in the electric cord cover.

Within the CNS are cells called neurons that have three parts: cell body, axon, and dendrite(s). Like all cells in the human body, the cell

Figure 2-2 Myelin Sheath Enlarged and Simplified

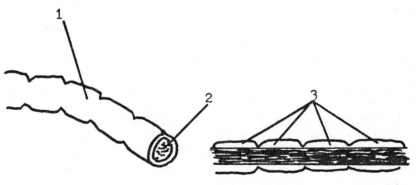

1. Sheath 2. Cytoplasm 3. Myelin, an indented sheath

body has a complex outer border or cell membrane, a substance called cytoplasm, and a dense oval-shaped central body or nucleus (Figure 2-3). A neuron has one axon but may have numerous dendrites. The axon and dendrites are elongations or fibers formed from the cytoplasm and cell membrane and are at each end of the cell body. The dendrites carry impulses toward the cell body, the axon carries them away. Neurons vary in size and in some places in the nervous system attain a length of several feet from the outer tip of a dendrite through the cell body to the opposing outer end of the axon.

There is a very minute space between the axon of one neuron and the dendrite of another neuron. This small space is called a synapse. The axon fiber has the ability to secrete the substance neurohormone. This chemical substance crosses the opening, or synapse, stimulating the dendrites of the next neuron, which in turn produces a new electrical impulse. Thus the auditory message travels on electrical impulses from the axon of one neuron to the dendrites and cell body of the next neuron.

Like the fine copper wires of the electrical system, the completeness and location of the neuron fibers facilitate the transmission of electrical impulses. A break or disruption of neuron fibers results in faulty flow of impulses. In addition, the physical or chemical condition of the cell must

---

Figure 2-3 Neuron, Enlarged and Simplified

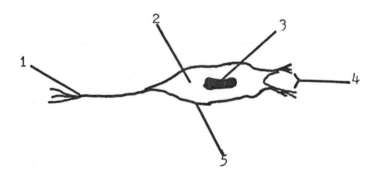

1. Axon   2. Cytoplasm   3. Nucleus   4. Dendrites   5. Cell membrane

The nerve impulse travels from right to left, going to the cell body from the dendrites, and moves toward synapse through the axon.

be basically healthy, capable of functioning, and of the proper chemical balance or composition for the transmission of impulses.

The pathway for processing auditory stimuli in the central nervous system begins with the auditory nerve, traveling to the brainstems, and into the temporal cortex. The system is not closed, that is, the impulses do not simply move from point of origin along a straight path to the cortex. Impulses carrying auditory information are acted upon at various points and, once processed, may elicit new impulses that continue on or return to the cochlear nerve.

In the developmentally normal individual, both hemispheres of the brain receive the auditory stimuli transmitted by the electrical impulses. The signal received by the left hemisphere is stronger coming from the right ear, and the signal to the right hemisphere is stronger from the left ear. It is believed that in most people the left hemisphere is dominant for the utilization of language stimuli and the right hemisphere for music and nonlanguage sounds. However, there is sufficient evidence suggesting receptive and retrieval ability by the subdominant hemisphere to warrant attempts to use this potential after severe damage to the dominant side. In other words, if there is massive damage to the language dominant hemisphere and loss of language ability, redevelopment of language skills may be possible by using the language potential of the subdominant hemisphere.

Perceptual Functions

Perception is a relatively common term in education. Its meaning often depends on the person using the term, or on the context in which it is being employed. Perception means awareness—in this case, awareness of sound, specifically speech sounds.

Perceptual processes occur in the central nervous system and range from initial or empty awareness to a highly developed cognitive process. The various levels or stages of perception are referred to by many names, again depending on the person using the terms. The levels are intradependent insofar as the development of one perceptual skill or process may need information from a higher skill to function correctly.

The lowest level skill or function within the processing hierarchy exists when individuals initially react to a sound. There is no meaning attached; it is an empty awareness. When the person's behavior includes at least minimal awareness of the tonal characteristics of the sound, he has begun to discriminate. For this function to occur, the central nervous system has begun to process or analyze the sound for differences such as frequencies and intensities.

Although sound discrimination is at first a low-level function, it does develop in sophistication as the individual's intellectual growth and sound experiences continue. The further development of discriminatory ability is dependent upon higher-level functions. Conversely, the development of higher-level functions is dependent to some extent upon the development of discrimination ability.

The next step in the hierarchy of functions is the level at which sounds are recognized or identified. In this stage of the process, the central nervous system has acted upon the sound to the degree that it has heard and noted that it is one that has been heard before. For example, a person is asleep and the telephone rings. The individual is startled by the sound (brain stem process), listens for a moment and hears other environmental sounds and mentally compares or discriminates among them (second-level function), then identifies the sound as a bell (third-level function). When the person begins to associate or specifically identify the sound as the telephone and not the doorbell, processing begins at the highest level.

If individuals fail to develop fully any one of the lower-level functions, they probably will be unable to operate adequately at a higher level. A child who does not process correctly at the discrimination level will be confused in attempting to identify and comprehend sounds. Consider, for example, the child who cannot hear the difference in the phonemes /p/ and /b/. The educator says "Pat Mary." The child thinks the words were "Bat Mary." If the child responds based on this perception and hits Mary, this unacceptable and antisocial behavior that to others appears unreasonable is explainable.

Yet another step in the process that must be considered is storing or imprinting auditory information for later retrieval. If an individual has an intact and functioning hearing organ and central nervous system, the person will have the potential ability to receive auditory stimuli that will leave a lasting impression on the cells of the cortex. The use of the storage and retrieval functions of the system is referred to as memory, which is considered as immediate recall or long-term recall.

Auditory processing that includes comprehension over a period of time is the highest level of functioning and, as it relates to language sounds, is the most complex. It occurs in the cerebral cortex, but its accuracy and efficiency depend upon lower-level functions, beginning in the brain stem areas.

In educational terms, processing dysfunctions are categorized as imperceptions. However, this does not describe either the dysfunction or the behavior. For the purpose of planning language development programs, the educator must consider specific abilities such as identification, discrimination, and memory.

Auditory processing by the central nervous system can be viewed as a series of small steps or intraprocesses in a very complex system. The ability of an individual to complete the auditory process beyond the hearing sense organ is dependent upon an intact and fully functioning CNS. The impulses received by the auditory nerve must travel without obstruction or break along the pathway to the brain stems and on to the cortex, as previously described. Upon their reaching the cortical area, there must be sufficient numbers of healthy cells and a proper chemical balance for imprinting to occur. A break or obstruction in the pathway may cause delayed or faulty processing. The lack of healthy, functioning cells in the cortex may produce delay in processing, incorrect processing, or inability to process.

AUDITORY EVALUATION

To this point, this chapter has dealt primarily with processes involved in hearing and perception. What follows is an overview of audiological measurement and perceptual skills evaluation. Understanding how auditory sensitivity is measured should assist educators in making referrals and in reading reports.

The discussion of perceptual skills testing, with a few exceptions, is intended as material usable by anyone working with language development who can read and follow directions. These measures often are referred to as teacher-administered tests and are not restricted in use to certified professionals.

Pure-Tone Audiometry

The measurement of sensitivity is considered the job of the audiologist (hearing testing specialist) or, as in many school districts, of the school nurse. There are two major purposes for sensitivity testing: (1) screening to identify possible hearing loss and (2) complete evaluation to determine threshold and type of loss.

There also are two types of screening procedures. The first is a rapid screening to identify possible loss, and the second establishes minimal level of hearing efficiency or threshold. The first type may be administered by persons who are familiar with an audiometer and the procedure for screening, but need not be audiologists. The second type should be performed by a trained specialist and often is the starting point for an in-depth evaluation.

Auditory sensitivity is measured by an electronic instrument called an audiometer. Testing should take place in a sound-treated room if possible.

A pure-tone audiometer emits a controlled sound (a pure tone) at various frequencies and intensities. Although there are numerous brands, the principles of function and the basic components of the audiometer are the same in all. A trained professional can administer either air conduction or bone conduction tests. The most common test for screening purposes, such as that routinely administered by the school nurse, is a pure-tone air conduction test.

The audiometer, a box-like apparatus containing dials, buttons, and bars, depending on make and model, is attached to a power source. Earphones are placed on the person to be tested. The earphones are marked right and left to correspond with the ear receiving the tone. The evaluator sets the controls to a specific frequency and decibel level and presses a bar that activates the device, sending a tone to the subject's ear. The required response is made by raising either the right or left hand indicating that the sound was heard in the corresponding ear.

During a pure-tone threshold evaluation, the charting of responses is done on a small card called an audiogram. The evaluator uses pencils of two different colors for plotting right and left ear. The audiogram, because of its simplicity, is read easily and indicates the intensity levels for each test frequency at which the subject indicated hearing the sound.

Sample air conduction response audiograms are shown in Figures 2-4 and 2-5. The right ear responses are indicated by the symbol O, the left ear by X. Figure 2-4 indicates normal hearing and Figure 2-5 a moderate bilateral hearing loss of 50-60dB HL at all frequencies.

Bone conduction threshold also can be measured with a pure-tone audiometer. For this type of testing the earphones are replaced by a vibrator that is positioned on the mastoid process of the temporal bone, an area just behind the outer ear, or placed in the center of the forehead.

The results of bone conduction testing when compared with, or used in conjunction with, the outcome of air conduction evaluations help identify specific dysfunctions. Bone conduction testing should be administered by either an audiologist or an otologist.

Sweep Test Screening

By school law, all children must receive an audiometric screening routinely. In many school districts the first measure is administered when the child enters school; testing thereafter occurs semiannually. In the meantime the child may have developed a mild hearing loss due to infection, swimming, or other factors. Therefore, it is helpful for the diagnostician or classroom teacher who suspects a hearing problem to administer a quick measure known as the sweep test.

Figure 2-4 Normal Hearing

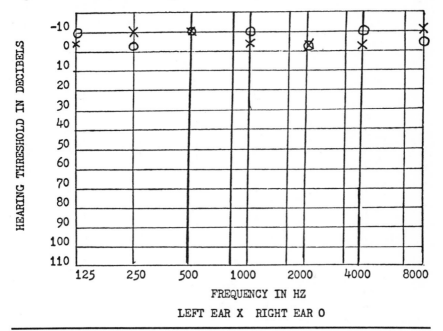

This procedure, as the name implies, is accomplished by quickly sweeping across frequencies. The only purpose is to identify children who should have additional audiological evaluation. If correctly administered, the test will indicate that the child did or did not respond to a specific sound or sounds in the speech range. The procedure does not establish threshold, and the findings should not be considered conclusive. They simply are an indication that the child may have a hearing problem.

Appendix A presents a complete step-by-step explanation of the procedure. The material is programmed in such a way that it can be mastered quickly, usually within an hour. However, caution should be exercised. An audiometer is a very delicate electronic device; misuse can disturb calibration and effectiveness of operation. Teachers should practice with all parts and steps in the procedure before testing and should not resort to on-the-job training on the child with whom they are working, or whom they suspect of having a hearing loss.

Speech Sound Audiometer

A pure-tone audiometer, while helpful in determining specific types of hearing loss, is somewhat limited in application to speech and language

Figure 2-5 Moderate Hearing Loss

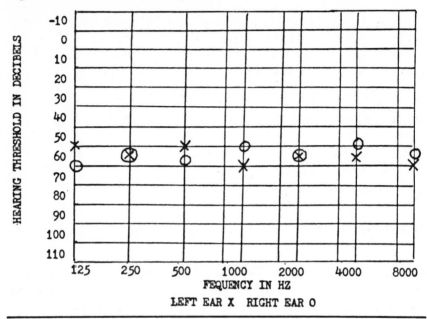

learning. Audiologists and otologists also use speech audiometry. This type of testing measures the loss of sensitivity for speech as well as the ability to identify or discriminate words and/or sentences. It is possible to be able to hear a tone but, because of a specific auditory processing dysfunction, be unable to use this ability in speech processing or discrimination.

The procedure may vary from clinic to clinic and specialist to specialist. Generally, subjects to be tested are seated so they can neither interpret facial expressions nor read lips. The evaluator begins with a simple series of words spoken into a microphone and delivered to the earphones. In this way frequency and intensity can be varied but controlled. The testing is continued on through more complex discriminatory material until a threshold for speech sensitivity and a suprathreshold measure for discriminatory ability are obtained for each ear.

Information obtained from speech audiometry can be extremely useful to the teacher or therapist in planning a remedial program. When a child demonstrates speech and/or language problems related to speech sound deficits, it is recommended strongly that an audiologist or a speech therapist interpret information from speech audiometry.

AUDITORY PERCEPTUAL MEASURES

As stated in the introduction to this section on measurement, the tests that are listed here do not require certification or long, involved training courses. The tests are ones with which the author is familiar and are included because of their usefulness to classroom teachers in identifying problems. They are but a small sample of the tests that are available. The age range is from preschool through adult and includes group screening measures as well as individually administered tests.

Auditory Discrimination Test (Rev. 1973)
   Joseph M. Wepman, Ph.D.
   Language Research Associates, Inc.
   Palm Springs, California

Purpose: auditory discrimination of speech sounds.

Population: ages 5- to 8-year-old.

Description: This 40-item test uses pairs of similar and dissimilar words and is very easy to learn and to administer. It is a one-to-one test. If the child is adequately prepared to respond, it takes about five minutes. The test comes in two forms. The discussion of perceptual development, especially the process of discrimination, can be helpful in understanding the importance of this skill.

   Although the author states clearly how to prepare the child to respond to the test items, this practice may not be sufficient. Many young children do not understand "same" and "different." This concept is extremely confusing when the pairs of words rhyme but are dissimilar. This caution is true for any measure that uses the same/different concept.

Auditory Skills Test Battery (1974)
   Ronald Goldman, Ph.D.; Macalyne Fristoe, M.S.; and Richard
      Woodcock, Ed.D.
   American Guidance Service, Inc.
   Publishers Building
   Circle Pines, Minnesota 55074

Purpose: Auditory discrimination, attention, memory, and sound symbol knowledge.

Population: Age three to adult.

Description: This extensive battery includes four separate tests that yield data independent of the other tests; when used collectively they can be

extremely helpful in planning remedial and developmental language programs. The subtests are: The Diagnostic Auditory Discrimination Test,
The Auditory Memory Tests, The Auditory Selective Attention Test, and
The Sound-Symbol Tests. Auditory stimulus is presented on a tape or
may be verbalized by the examiner. The subject responds by pointing to
the appropriate picture for discrimination, memory, and sequence.

This test is time consuming, and in the experience of the author of this
book, the classroom teacher seldom has the opportunity to use this test
battery in its entirety. The best results are achieved when testing is done
in a room free of distraction (no other children) and when administration
occurs over a period of several sessions.

Kindergarten Auditory Screening Test (1971)
Jack Katz, Ph.D.
Follett Publishing Company
1010 West Washington Boulevard
Chicago, Illinois 60607

Purpose: Figure-ground, sound blending, and discrimination.

Population: K–1st grade.

Description: This screening test can be administered in groups of six to
ten children. The testing material includes a record that improves uniformity of test administration and tends to eliminate speech variances
among administrators. The usual time needed to administer the battery is
about 20 minutes. When the results of this screening test are interpreted
correctly and applied to the training suggestions in the manual, this measure can be helpful in planning a developmental language program.

Language-Structured Auditory Retention Span Test (LARS) (1975)
Luis Carlson
Academic Therapy Publications
P.O. Box 899
San Rafael, California 94901

Purpose: Auditory memory for words and sentences.

Population: Mental age three years seven months through adult.

Description: LARS is a sentence recall test and is published in two forms;
both contain 58 test items ranging in length from one word to sentences
appropriate for adults. It is administered individually; directions for administration, scoring, and interpreting are clear and easy to follow. Beginning with item 6, in a somewhat random order, sentences contain

either a single nonsense word or regular word uncommon to the vocabulary being tested. The purpose of this distractor is to aid in the identification of persons who may have a specific language disability that becomes more apparent when working with unfamiliar material. The section on remediation and circumvention briefly but clearly outlines procedures for the education of persons who fail this measure.

Screening Test for Auditory Comprehension of Language (STACL)
(1973)
Elizabeth Carrow, Ph.D.
Learning Concepts
2501 North Lamar
Austin, Texas 78705

Purpose: Screening for grammar and syntax.

Population: Ages three–seven years.

Description: This is a 25-item screening test that can be given in groups of 4 to 30, depending on the age of the individuals. The directions are clear and easy to follow, and are in English and Spanish. The examiner says a word or words in a sentence, and the subjects respond by making a mark in an easy-to-use booklet. This is a quick screening procedure to identify children who should be seen by a language specialist. This test is extremely helpful as a preschool screening measure.

Screening Test for Auditory Perception (The STAP) (1969)
Geraldine M. Kimmell and Jack Wahl
Academic Therapy Publications
P.O. Box 899
San Rafael, California 94901

Purpose: Discrimination and identification of letter sounds and memory.

Population: Grades 2–6 and remedial classes.

Description: The STAP is a group test measuring several perceptual skills. It takes about 45 minutes but need not be completed in one session. The five subtests measure ability to perceive the differences in long and short vowels, initial single consonants and blends, rhyming and nonrhyming words, speech sounds in paired words, and memory of nonverbal rhythmic patterns. One advantage of this test is that it is appropriate for children over 8, the age where many perceptual measures end. Suggestions for the application of test results are helpful. The authors' remarks on the test's shortcomings help identify those for whom this test is, or is not, appropriate.

Test of Nonverbal Auditory Discrimination (Tenvad) (1975)
Norman A. Buktenica, Ph.D.
Follett Publishing Company
1010 West Washington Boulevard
Chicago, Illinois 60607

Purpose: Pure-tone discrimination.

Population: K through grade 3.

Description: Tenvad is a nonverbal measure of auditory discrimination that uses pure tones that are produced on the accompanying record. It measures pitch, loudness, rhythm, duration, and timbre. It is suggested that the use of tones rather than words eliminates confusion related to rhyming elements. It can be given to groups of 10 or fewer and, if directions are followed very carefully, may be used with entire classes if aides are available. The section in the manual that suggests the step-by-step development of auditory discrimination ability is useful in planning programs and in writing general behavioral objectives (Individualized Education Programs—IEPs).

Yellow Brick Road (1975)
Christine Kallstrom, Ph.D.
Learning Concepts
2501 North Lamar
Austin, Texas 78705

Purpose: Preschool screening procedures.

Population: Four years nine months to six years nine months.

Description: This preschool screening measure can be given to groups up to 20 with proper assistance. There are four subtests—motor battery, auditory battery, visual battery, and language battery. The auditory battery includes discrimination, How Many?, Copy Cat, Sequence, Association, and Guess What I Am? The format is based on the *Wizard of Oz* theme with children going down the yellow brick road and stopping at stations for testing along the way. It takes about one hour for a child to complete all phases. Children follow in line and one child finishes every five minutes, or 24 children in a two-hour period. This test is interesting and fun for the children as well as being helpful in identifying possible language and motor problems.

REFERENCES

Buktenica, N. A. *Test of nonverbal auditory discrimination (Tenvad)*. Chicago: Follett Publishing Company, 1975.

Carlson, L. *Language-structured auditory retention span test* (LARS). San Rafael, Calif.: Academic Therapy Publications, 1975.

Carrow, E. *Screening test for auditory comprehension of language (STACL)*. Austin, Tex.: Learning Concepts, 1973.

Denes, P. B., & Pinson, E. N. *The speech chain*. Bell Telephone Laboratories, Inc., 1963.

Goldman, R., Fristoe, M., & Woodcock, R. *Auditory skills test battery*. Circle Pines, Minn.: American Guidance Service, Inc., 1974.

_____ . *Test of auditory discrimination*. Circle Pines, Minn.: American Guidance Service, Inc., 1970.

Jaffee, B. F. *Hearing loss in children*. Baltimore: University Park Press, 1977.

Kallstrom, C. *Yellow brick road*. Austin, Tex.: Learning Concepts, 1975.

Katz, J. (Ed.). *Handbook of clinical audiology* (2nd ed.). Baltimore: The Williams and Wilkins Company, 1978.

_____ . *Kindergarten auditory screening test*. Chicago: Follett Publishing Company, 1971.

Kimmell, G. M., & Wahl, J. *Screening test for auditory perception* (The STAP). San Rafael, Calif.: Academic Therapy Publications, 1969.

Wepman, J. M. *Auditory discrimination test* (Rev. ed.). Palm Springs, Calif.: Language Research Associates, Inc., 1973.

Chapter 3

Auditory Skills

TEACHING AUDING

We live in a world of sounds, and we learn by hearing and understanding these sounds. The importance of listening in education has been recognized for many years. A study by Wilt in 1950 indicated that at least half of the average school day was spent in listening. With the advent of portable radios, stereo sets, and television, the total percent of time involved in auditory learning activities has increased. Unfortunately there are children who do not, or cannot, use their auditory sense modality fully. This means that for some children the main source of learning is closed or at best is available only partially.

In any classroom, either regular or special education, the types of auditory dysfunction and the degree of involvement may vary greatly. One child may have a mild problem with discrimination and another a moderate figureground problem. These children can be taught to improve their auditory skills. Therefore, the author believes that auding, like reading, should be included in all curriculum planning.

Planning an Instructional Setting

It is a rare occasion when a classroom teacher is given an opportunity to select or design the instructional environment. It is the fortunate teacher who is assigned an empty room and allowed to order desks, tables, and instructional materials. In most cases, however, the teacher can arrange or rearrange the room to facilitate maximum auditory efficiency. In so doing, the teacher should consider the composition of the group to be instructed, the specific auditory needs, and how sound is received and acted upon by the auditory system.

Traditional seating of children in neat rows is not conducive to good sound reception. Seats should be arranged so that every child has a direct and unobstructed path to the teacher (Figure 3-1). Do not seat one child behind another; stagger the desks so that neither the pupil's visual nor acoustic space is blocked by other students. Visual space is included here because visual contact, or being able to see the speaker's mouth, may be beneficial to the child with an auditory problem.

If a teacher is taught to stand during an instructional period, the individual may be literally speaking over the pupils' heads. When children are seated, especially small ones, and the teacher is standing erect with head held in an upward position, the sound is being directed over and not to the pupils. In addition, children who look up to see the teacher receive a distorted visual picture of the lip movement. A teacher who is speaking from a seated position may be far more effective than one who is projecting from several feet above the seated children.

If the intent of oral instruction is to have children listen and understand, then auditory attention is necessary. To prevent visual distraction that might affect attending behavior, consider what is behind or around the speaker. Place yourself, or a child who is speaking to the class, in a position that will facilitate holding the pupils' attention. Do not stand in front of a bulletin board with attractive pictures or clever messages. Windows are great for letting in light, but they are even better for promoting daydreaming or distracting visually. A chalkboard without writing or a plain colored wall makes a dull but good backdrop for a speaker who wants to help the listener attend.

Figure 3-1 Suggested Seating Arrangement

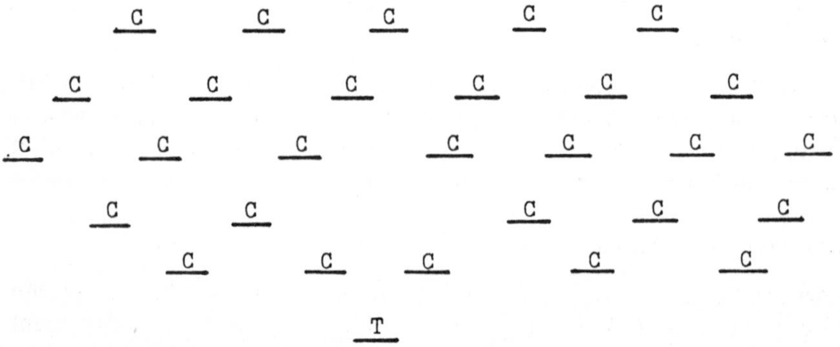

This arrangement of staggered seating can help children's visual and auditory contact in classroom communication.

People are conditioned not to interrupt a speaker; this includes even very young children. Therefore, pupils will sit through rather long periods of verbal instruction with little or no comprehension and never ask a question. If the speaker watches the listeners, very often the level of auditory awareness and comprehension can be discerned by their facial expressions.

When a face indicates a reaction such as "Huh? I don't understand," reword the statement or stop and ask the child or children to restate in their own words what you have been saying. If the child's face takes on an air of contentment that was not there at the beginning of the lesson, it might mean a case of daydreaming. Walk over and gently touch the pupil, look down, and smile. This simple gesture will pull the child back to the classroom and the lesson, at least temporarily.

Auditory Awareness

The preceding chapter suggested that auditory awareness is reflexive: an individual's initial reaction to sound was a reflex occurring as a function of the brainstem. However, awareness can be a more complex process of *tuning in* to sounds. In fact, it sometimes is helpful to consider awareness as a two-process function: tuning in and tuning out sound.

The most obvious reason for lack of auditory awareness is inadequate sensitivity to sound, as in the case of the deaf or hearing impaired. This discussion considers only individuals who have adequate sensitivity but who do not respond in a normal fashion to their acoustical environment.

Behavior that suggests lack of auditory awareness may be caused by, or be the product of, such conditions as: intelligence, emotionality, sensory modality preference, memory, and environmental factors.

Intellectual Capacity

In rare cases of profound mental retardation the individual may not have the necessary brainstem functioning to react to auditory stimuli. The application of behavior training techniques (conditioning) may affect positive auditory awareness.

Emotional Disturbance

An emotionally involved person may appear not to hear sounds within the environment. Individuals demonstrating this degree of involvement tend to be nonverbal. They either have not acquired oral expressive language or have withdrawn and stopped speaking. Autistic and autistic-like children may exhibit this type of behavior.

Educators of the psychotherapeutic school believe that the emotional problem must be cared for before language therapy should be initiated. On the other hand, behaviorists feel that the establishment of a good modification program that will elicit a language response will facilitate psychotherapy as well. They contend that a child who is not aware of sounds will not develop speech and that without speech, psychotherapy cannot occur.

Sensory Modality Preference

Most people have a preferred learning modality. They perceive information with greater ease and clarity through one avenue of sensory input than through another. Some individuals who learn through the visual or visuotactile sense elect to avoid auditory input. This is not a conscious effort; it is an acquired behavior in an attempt to turn off the modality that confuses them or interferes with learning. This may be especially true of those who have a specific learning disability related to auditory imperception.

Memory

Children who appear to be unaware of sound may never reach the point in an auditory evaluation where testing of memory occurs. Memory is considered a higher level function that, at least in part, depends on awareness. However, there are children who tune out sound; they appear to have an auditory awareness problem but really are manifesting auditory memory dysfunction (Heasley, 1974). These children lack the ability to recall auditory information. Their memory ability is sufficiently impaired that every auditory experience appears to be new. Auditory matching cannot, or does not, occur and matching is necessary for comprehension.

When auditory comprehension is lacking, the individual's acoustical environment is meaningless and confusing. To avoid living in a constant state of sound confusion, the child turns off sound.

Within the group of individuals who tune out sound because of auditory memory dysfunction, there may be subgroups of individuals who can recall nonlanguage sounds but not speech sounds. The author has seen children who listen and react to music or animal sounds but who walk away from speech sounds as though they do not hear them. These children appear to have selective auditory awareness and may be mislabeled emotionally disturbed or mentally retarded.

Environmental Factors

Children from sound-confusing or overstimulating homes occasionally turn off sound. For acoustic appreciation to develop, an individual must have the opportunity to select or differentiate sound components. In the case of children who are exposed to too many sounds or varieties of sound experiences at one time, this ability may be retarded. In an effort to understand what is going on, or to find a peaceful means of existing, they turn off sound or ignore it. Initially, this is selective audition; however, in severe cases that persist over extended periods, the manifestation can be a pseudo hearing loss or lack of auditory awareness.

Developing Sound Awareness

The following suggestions for developing auditory awareness are general procedures. In some cases the very nature of the method will dictate the type of learner for whom it is most appropriate. The other suggestions are applicable to several types of learners or learning problems.

Setting

If at all possible, remove the child from the usual instructional setting. If the pupil exhibits sound avoidance behavior in the classroom or therapy room, then the pattern has been established and can be changed best if the setting also is altered.

The room should be devoid of distractors such as pictures, windows, and brightly colored objects. The attire of the teacher should be as plain as possible. A colorless outer garment such as a smock that covers ties, bows, jewelry, etc., is helpful. The setting should be visually sterile.

The room should be sound treated and as free from sound distractions as possible. The space should not have heating pipes that rattle, air conditioning that hisses, or a clock that ticks audibly. It is essential that the only sound be the stimulus to which the child is to respond.

DO NOT SPEAK TO THE CHILD ONCE YOU ARE IN THE TREATMENT ROOM. Remember, if the child could understand and react to speech sounds, awareness training would not be necessary. Your voice also may add to the pupil's confusion and withdrawal behavior.

Stimulus

The selection of the stimulus (sound) may be one of the most important aspects of the remedial or training program. The objective is to have the child react to sound; therefore, the presenting sound must be one to which the pupil can respond.

Initially the sound should be one that the child has not experienced. The probability of success will increase if the stimulus is one that the child has not rejected already. Common sounds—bells, horns, animal noises, and speech—should be avoided until a consistent response is established. Sounds that are considered unpleasant or dull often yield positive results. Sounds at frequency extremes also have been found to be effective—for example, feedback from an amplifying system, screeching chalk, or unusual sounding noise maker.

Techniques

Place the child near a tape recorder or phonograph (earphones may be used). Turn the volume on, using an intensity level above normal. Turn the volume off. The ON time should not exceed one or two seconds. The only sign of response may be a change in facial expression or a slight movement of the body. If the child is known to be a tactile learner (a child who touches everything), it may be helpful to place the child's hand on the sound mechanism so that the child can receive the vibratory sensations.

When you are certain that the child is aware of the sound, demonstrate a response. For example, when the sound is emitted, raise your hand or drop an object into a bottle. If the child does not follow your example (does not understand), guide behavior by standing behind the child and lifting the hand when the sound is made. You usually will be aware of a muscle reaction in the child's arm that will clue you that your assistance in responding no longer is needed. Some further suggested steps:

1. Determine the child's favorite reward, such as food, a color, or being touched.
2. Pair the stimulus with the child's reward, that is, produce the sound and place the food in the pupil's mouth simultaneously. By pairing the reward with the sound, you can teach the child to associate the sound with a pleasant experience.
3. Issue the sound and reward the child if he indicates awareness. In most cases, if the first two steps have been successful, the child will indicate by facial expression or bodily gesture that he expects the reward because of the sound. When this occurs, the educator has elicited an awareness to sound response.

From this point on, the procedure is that of a typical behavior modification program. Initially a continuous reinforcement schedule should be used, decreasing the tangible reward until a state of constant reaction to sound is established without reinforcement.

Auditory Attention

It would seem that the word *attention* sufficiently describes a behavior, and no further discussion is needed; however, if the educator accepts that assumption, half the battle may be lost. Specialists working with children who have attention problems also must consider other mental and physical behaviors that accompany attention.

The instructional procedures for working with a child who is trying to attend but cannot are different from those used with a child who can attend but will not. For the former, the teaching strategies include attending tasks of short duration, leading to gradually increasing periods of attention. For the latter, the first step is to find the cause of the *will not* behavior.

In addition, the discrepancy factor—indicated differences in the child's ability to attend in relation to modality, media, and content—should be considered when planning an instructional program to improve attention. To ascertain this factor the following questions should be posed:

1. Does the child attend adequately if the information is presented through a different sensory modality (looking at pictures vs. listening to records)?
2. Is there a difference in ability to attend in relation to media (sounds on a tape vs. direct contact with speaker)?
3. Does the child have less difficulty attending if the material is light and pleasurable rather than of a more serious nature (storytelling vs. factual instruction)?

If the child can and does attend visually but not auditorially, it can be assumed that the dysfunction is auditory and not a general attention problem. However, if there is an intrafunction difference in relation to the form of presentation, the problem may not be that of the auditory process. In such cases it may be a learned behavior such as developing a preference for people rather than machines, or the reverse preference related to the fact that watching a speaker may be distracting.

When the inability to attend is related to content, it may be either a psychological problem or one of intellectual dysfunction. The degree of difficulty of material being presented affects attentiveness even in the normal learner. However, when the individual can and does attend auditorially to easy content and tunes out subject matter that is too difficult, it may be a problem of intellectual functioning or motivation and not necessarily auditory attention. Occasionally a child will be unable to attend because he believes the material to be too difficult or the task too unpleasant, thereby creating a psychological state that prohibits concentration and attention.

In these situations the child may be using an auditory function as an escape mechanism. The teacher must recognize this possibility and adjust the instructional procedures to accommodate for the underlying cause of the inattention.

Developing Auditory Attention

The first step in planning a remedial program for an auditory or visual attention span problem is to determine the child's average attending time. To do this, it may be necessary to observe the child's attending behavior for several days and under various conditions. Information gained from the observation should include (a) the average length of time the child attends, (b) the longest period of time the child attends, and (c) what type of auditory material holds the child's attention best or longest.

The first lesson should be planned to be about as long as the child's average attending time. The objective is to increase the child's average attending time to that of the observed longest attending time. For example, J.W. attends to an auditory situation for an average of three minutes. Under the most favorable conditions, using sounds the child enjoys, he attended for twelve minutes. The first lesson should be planned for a period of three minutes, or the average attending time. When J.W. is able to attend auditorially in a consistent manner for three minutes or longer, the length of the lesson is increased, with an average attention period of 12 minutes as the long-range goal.

The following ideas have been found to be helpful in working with auditory attention span problems. Additional materials are listed under commercial programs at the end of this chapter.

1. Play a record or a tape allowing the child to move to the music (free movement). Do not attempt to instruct. Play a record or a tape with instructions on it; that is, music plays and voice sings or says *skip*. Play a record or tape and instruct the child to perform a specific movement to a specific sound—the child skips to violin music, trots to drums, etc. This activity also improves auditory memory as the child is asked to remember activity and sound association.
2. Place pictures of objects or animals on a rack or holder in random order. Play a record or tape or tell a story that mentions the pictured objects. When the child hears the name, he points to the appropriate picture or puts it in a holder in correct sequence. This material can be used for auditory memory and sequencing as well as attention.
3. Sing the words to any nursery rhyme or Mother Goose story. The change from saying to singing usually fascinates children. The songs may be taped, using sound effects or the voices of the children in the class.

4. Give the children pencil or crayons and paper. As you read a story, the pupils are to draw a picture of the items mentioned. This can be taped and used as an independent activity or learning station task.
5. Use material such as is used commonly in oral directions, for example, putting the circle around a hat, drawing a letter in a box, etc. Set a timing device to the length of time it should take to complete the tasks or to achieve the lesson objective. Explain to the children that you are timing them, and that they are to listen to the tape and do all of the things mentioned. They can stop when the timer goes off. The length of time and the number of tasks are increased as improvement occurs. This procedure not only helps increase attention time but also tends to help children in overcoming distractions such as the ticking of the clock (figureground) and the artificial pressures created by timing.

Auditory Discrimination

Auditory discrimination is the ability to recognize differences among sounds. Sound response behavior is affected or regulated by this ability. Auditory discrimination also is a prerequisite for accurate auditory memory and an essential element of auditory comprehension. For example, people must be able to hear the difference between the sound of a fire siren and an air raid siren before they can store and retrieve the value of the two sounds and react appropriately. Imagine the possible consequences of school children reacting to a fire signal as though it were an air raid signal.

Many tests and most materials available for the development of auditory discrimination are designed for speech sound discrimination. A definition of discrimination may be limited to the ability to differentiate between the fine distinctions of speech sounds. However, auditory discrimination is a far broader task involving the four dimensions of sound: frequency, intensity, duration, and phase (Heasley, 1974).

An instructional program to develop auditory discrimination should include these four dimensions. A total program should begin with nonlanguage sounds and move through the process, concluding with the ability to hear tonal differences applied to the same word, such as the verbal *no,* meaning you may not, and the interrogatory *no?*

In writing a remedial program or an Individualized Education Program (IEP), the teacher should place the child in the developmental program at whatever point the child's measured ability fell below expectancy level (note the section in Chapter 1 on auditory discrimination tests). If, however, an applicable test is not available, the following instructional suggestions may be used also as an informal measure of the child's ability. The instructional program then should begin at the highest level at which the child is able to function adequately.

Developing Auditory Discrimination

Intensity

In most children the ability to recognize loud and soft develops normally as an outgrowth of reflexive or startle behavior and generally is the easiest level of discrimination with which to work.

Activity 1. Prepare a tape of loud and soft sounds. Using a musical instrument or a sound that does not convey meaning, play a series of sounds: three loud, pause, three soft, pause. This portion of the tape is used for training and awareness of the sound intensity. All sounds should be from the same source or instrument. The intensity levels should be of equal value and the difference between loud and soft should be extreme (gross difference). Continue to tape pairs such as: loud-soft, pause; soft-loud, pause; soft-soft, pause; loud-loud, pause; etc.

Cut geometric forms of colored construction paper in shapes such as circles and triangles. Make a large form in a dark or bright color and a small form in a white or light color. Place the forms on sticks in fan-like fashion or on a pendant.

Play the first three sounds, then hold up a large form to indicate loud sound.

Give each child a large form and play the first three sounds again. Hold up the form and encourage the children to do the same. Repeat this until the children respond each time a loud sound is completed.

Play the second three (soft) sounds. Use the small light forms as before. Give each child a small form and teach the appropriate response. The purpose of this is to teach the children to associate loud sounds with the large form and soft sounds with the small form.

Holding a form in each hand, have the children listen to the remaining sound pairs. If the pair is one loud and one soft, hold up both forms. If the pair is the same, both soft, hold up just the small form. For both loud sounds, use just the large form.

Continue through the tape. Repeat any or all portions until the children are able to respond correctly and spontaneously.

Activity 2. Prepare a tape as in the preceding activity but use various sounds (such as a horn, a whistle, and a siren). The first comparison is of similar sounds of dissimilar intensity; the second pair, dissimilar sounds of equal intensity, etc.

The purpose of this activity is to teach the children that the intensity of dissimilar sounds can be compared. Obviously children who need such knowledge do not comprehend an explanation so the procedure is intended as a training activity to develop automatic awareness of sound intensity.

Activity 3. Prepare a tape as in the previous activity, this time decreasing the difference in intensity levels. The purpose is to develop awareness of fine as well as gross differences.

Activity 4. Many variations of the above activities are possible, depending upon the functioning level of the children. Have them place their hands over their ears if both sounds are loud, over their mouths if both are soft, and fold their hands in their laps if they are different. If children are verbal, teach them to say loud, soft, and different. Use verbal response in place of motor response.

Activity 5. Prepare a tape as in preceding activities but instead of tones use environmental sounds such as a vacuum sweeper, doorbell, telephone bell, etc.

Activity 6. If the children are successful in the preceding activity, they can indicate an understanding of the sound by pointing to a picture of the object. In this way, you are working on total discrimination.

Pitch

The ability to differentiate differences in pitch is extremely important in understanding and using oral language. It is easiest to develop through nonlanguage sounds because the element of comprehension is not present. When asking a child to indicate if the end of a word is higher than the beginning (intonation or vocal inflection), you are requiring the highest degree of pitch discrimination and are dealing with a specific signaling device that facilitates comprehension.

Activity 1. Using a musical instrument such as a piano or xylophone, play four or five notes going up the scale. Play the instrument in full sight of the children so they can see your movement up the keys. Do the same thing going down the keys. Initially use your right hand for going up and left for going down.

Start with the children seated. If the sound goes up the scale, have them stand; for down the scale, have them squat. The object of this lesson is to show that some notes go up and are high and some go down and are low.

Play the highest note of the previous scale, then the lowest note. This indicates gross tone discrimination. Again have the children stand for high and squat for low. Continue the process but add two notes of the same pitch. To respond to sounds with the same pitch, children remain seated.

Activity 2. Remove all visual clues. Use a tape recorder. Play pairs of sounds, gradually decreasing the degree of pitch difference, such as going from a two-octave difference down to half a step (black key then a white key). Children respond as before.

Activity 3. Play a record or tape of sounds other than musical instruments such as pairs of bells, car horns, and even motors. Directions are as before.

Activity 4. Prepare a tape of sounds of similar and dissimilar pitch. Make a worksheet containing as many squares as there are sound pairs. Within each square place four circles (Figure 3-2).

Instruct the children to listen to the sounds. If they hear a pair of sounds that are the same and also are high sounds, color the top two circles. If the first sound is high and the second low, color the first circle on the top and the last circle on the bottom, etc. This activity can be used in a group situation or individually as in a learning station.

Speech Sound Discrimination

A total speech sound discrimination program should begin with phonemes produced in isolation, generally long vowel sounds. There are several reasons for beginning with long vowels: (1) because the difference in the sound of $\bar{a}$ when compared to $\bar{e}$ is marked or greatly different, (2) because it is impossible to produce a consonant sound beyond the point of articulation without adding a vowel sound, and (3) because long vowel sounds relate to letter names.

The following order is suggested for the development of a sequential program involving elements in isolation and in context:

Level 1: isolation—long vowels
Level 2: isolation—short vowels
Level 3: isolation—long and short vowel comparison
Level 4: isolation—consonants with schwa
Level 5: isolation—consonant blends with schwa
Level 6: context—open syllable, consonant with long and short vowels
Level 7: context—closed syllable, long vowels
Level 8: context—closed syllable, short vowels
Level 9: context—closed and open syllables, initial position consonant blends with long and short vowels

Figure 3-2 Sample Sound Discrimination Worksheet

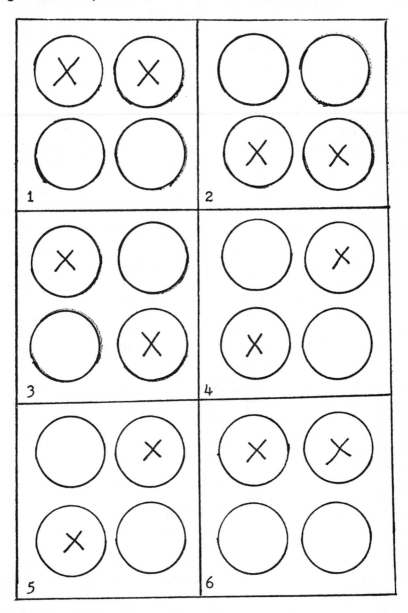

1. high - high
3. high - low
5. low - high

2. low - low
4. low - high
6. high - high

Level 10: context—open and closed syllables, consonants and consonant blends with vowel diagraphs
Level 11: context of two or more syllables—all sounds
Level 12: sentences—all sounds
Level 13: words—stress or intonation change
Level 14: sentences—word stress or intonation changes

It is not necessary to have every child do every level of the sequence. Children should be placed in the program at their needs level.

In addition to this developmental sequence, speech sound discrimination should be performed under both quiet and noisy conditions. That is, initially the instruction should take place in a sound-treated room or an area that is free of auditory distractions. The ultimate goal, of course, is to develop auditory discrimination under normal sound conditions or in a noisy room. The following ideas may be helpful in achieving this goal.

Activity 1. Prepare a list of sounds, words, and sentences using identical and different phonemes. It is best to order sounds beginning with different and using same after three or four items have been completed (Figure 3-3).

The number of comparisons or individual discrimination tasks per lesson should be based on the developmental level of the children and their ability to attend. For very young or hyperactive children, ten pairs usually is the maximum for one lesson. Forty pairs or 20 sentences are not unreasonable for older or more attentive children.

Activity 2. If the children are intellectually or linguistically able to comprehend oral directions, say, "I am going to make some sounds. Tell me if they are the same two sounds or two different sounds."

The words *same* and *different* may need explanation or instruction. Objects such as two red crayons to explain same and one red and one blue for different are helpful.

Any response that adequately indicates that the children are hearing and comprehending the sound differences can be accepted. Typical responses include "yes" for same and "no" for different, same, and not the same, as well as head nodding for yes and no, with yes being same and no being different.

Initially allow the children to see you produce the sound. When responses are consistently correct, change the directions. Say, "Now I am going to make some sounds but to make it more fun, I'm going to cover my mouth (or have you turn your back to me). Use your ears and listen to find out if the sounds are the same or different."

Change the instructions for the last several levels in the developmental sequence: "I am going to say two words. Listen and tell me if

Figure 3-3 Sample Lesson Lists

Level 1	Level 3	Level 4
ā-ū	ā-a	b-f
ū-ē	i-e	d-p
ā-ī	ū-ō	m-n
ē-ē	ē-e	v-v

Level 7
pat-pot
mid-mad
not-nat
lak-lak

Level 9
blak-bluk
trud-trad
flem-flom
slin-slin

Level 11
breder-brader
floten-fluten
grakeling-grukeling
sliket-sliket

Level 12
The butter is bitter.   The batter is bitter.
The milk is swimming.   The milk is slimming.
I see Val.   I see thou.
The ladle is little.   The ladle is little.

Level 14
The green house burned down.   The greenhouse burned down.
She is a bookkeeper.   She is a book keeper.

they both sound the same or if they sound different. Also, tell me which part of the word sounds different and what that difference is," and, "I am going to say two sentences. Listen and tell me if both sentences are the same. If they are different, tell me how they are different, or what you heard that was different."

Auditory Memory

Auditory memory is the ability to store and to retrieve information through the auditory modality. There are many reasons why individuals do not remember what they have heard. It is possible to appear to have a memory dysfunction when in reality the problem is inattention. People must attend sufficiently to process information properly for a lasting imprint that can be used later. Superficial attention does not facilitate recall.

Another common cause of poor auditory memory (or a less than desirable level) is modality preference. Many gifted persons are frustrated because their ability to recall verbal input is less than their recall of visual information. This usually is not a true auditory memory problem, it is a matter of using auditory information at a normal or average level while processing visual material at a superior level. It is a problem only when auditory recall falls below the expectancy level of the average individual.

When the ability to use auditory experiences is impaired, it may be because of (1) insufficient auditory exposure for level of intellectual capacity, or (2) improper reception or imperception. Some individuals lack brain cell function or capacity in the temporal lobe. They have difficulty storing and retrieving auditory information. The dysfunction may manifest itself as an immediate or a delayed recall problem or a combination of the two. With young children who have adequate short-term recall but poor delayed memory, it can be a case of insufficient exposure or practice.

Poor auditory memory that is associated with the aging process is due to brain cell chemistry. In these cases, past auditory experiences stored during a period of healthy cell condition are retrievable (youthful experiences), while more recent auditory exposure cannot be used because storage occurred after cell deterioration or chemical imbalance. For memory (a process of storage and retrieval) to take place there must be sufficient healthy cells and proper chemical balance to perceive and act upon the new input. Unfortunately, brain cell deterioration and chemical imbalance are not limited to the aged and can be found in very young children who have specific types of central nervous system diseases, malnutrition, or suffer from drug abuse.

The possible effects of auditory imperception on memory also must be considered. When an individual receives information in a distorted form, and particularly in varying degrees of distortion, it may be impossible to relate a current auditory experience to past experiences. For example, a child with an auditory reversal problem hears the word *pat* and learns the meaning through a tactile experience. During the processing, he stores *tap,* a sound order reversal. At a later date, the child hears the word *pat* again and attempts to match the word with a past experience, but obviously the match cannot occur; therefore the child cannot remember the word. If the child experiences the tactile sensation and attempts to label it, he may well retrieve the word *tap.* It then would appear that the child has an oral expressive problem.

For the most part, remediation of memory problems is limited to sessions of drill and repeated exposure to the material to be learned. There are times when it is wise to find a circuitous method such as mnemonics for remembering. The following suggestions have been helpful in the past, and a creative teacher will find that these basic ideas have many possible variations.

Developing Auditory Memory

Related Words

Activity 1. Tell a one-line story. Use a visual aid to promote attention and retention: "The boy is playing." Show a picture of a boy playing with a ball. Ask the child to repeat the story.

Tell the same story, adding the words "with a ball."

Repeat the story, adding an adjective such as "with a red ball," etc.

Begin the exercise with a sentence that contains the number of words the child usually can recall. If the child achieves 100 percent accuracy on the first attempt, move to the next level.

When the child omits, substitutes, or adds a word, stop. Go back to the last level where the pupil scored 100 percent and try for three consecutive correct responses. Should the child be unable to restate the stimulus material correctly, continue backward until he is successful. Remember that failure causes frustration, and frustration can cause temporary memory blocks. When the child reaches the failure level, it may be advisable to adjust the teaching plan to meet the learner's emotional needs. Don't press beyond a reasonable level.

Remove visuals when the child reaches expectancy level. Repeat the process without pictures, using short sentences and building to the short-story level.

Activity 2. Say to the children, "I am going to read a poem. The first time I am going to read all of the words. The second time I will leave out some of the words. Try to remember the correct word (or words). Help me make the poem complete."

Initially the missing word or words should be easy to remember, and context clues should be used to aid recall. Develop this procedure until the children can complete phrases and complete lines.

Activity 3. Begin the instructional day with a word or sentence for the children to remember. At various times throughout the day, ask the children the *memory word* or *memory sentence*. For more advanced or gifted children, plan a daily sentence, poem, or joke to be remembered the following day.

Activity 4. Tell the children you are going to play a record that tells a story. Assign the various characters to specific children and ask them to listen and try to remember their parts. After you have played the record, the children enact the story, using the language of the record as much as possible.

Unrelated Words

Activity 1. Place several objects in a row. Use items with which the children are unfamiliar or whose labels they have not committed to memory. Say the name of each object. Tell the children to close their eyes and name the object. Gradually increase the number of items to remember. Accept disarranged order at first, and work for sequence after the children have improved and gained confidence.

Continue as above, but do not include the objects or visuals. For example, say "I am going to say some words. After I finish, you say the same words—plant, book, up." As before, sequence follows development of nonserial recall.

Activity 2. The following are examples of variations of the technique in Activity 1. Each step is slightly more difficult than the preceding. Sequence must be correct.

"I am going to say some words. They are all the names of colors. When I stop, you say the colors I have said. Be sure you say them in the order I said them": red, blue, green, orange, black, etc.

"I am going to say some rhyming words. . . .": noon, June; rig, big, jig, etc.

"I am going to say some numbers. . . .": 2, 4; 4, 7, 8, etc.

Activity 3. Make a list of the telephone numbers of all the children in the class. Each day have the pupils work on learning the number of one child. After several numbers have been learned, have the children number a page and write the name and phone number of each one studied (learned). If the children are not yet writing, a toy phone can be used. Allow each child the opportunity to demonstrate his ability to recall the numbers by saying the number while dialing.

AIDS FOR CHILDREN WITH SENSITIVITY DEFICITS

Diminished sensitivity to sound unfortunately is a common occurrence. The incidence of hearing impaired (HI) children appears to have increased over the last several decades. This may be attributable to the population increase, improved medical care to infants and young children with serious illnesses, and improved methods for identifying hearing impaired children.

The practice of institutionalizing children with hearing loss is on a decline. This increases the probability that teachers and parents will be expected to teach language to the deaf or hard-of-hearing child. While a book of this nature cannot prepare the reader to deal with the many problems encountered in teaching language to hearing impaired children, it can present information that may be helpful.

Previously described auditory teaching techniques are applicable in most cases of minor hearing loss. For the severely impaired, two main avenues of help are employed: (1) nonverbal or manual communication, (2) the hearing aid.

Manual Communication

Hearing impaired children for the most part are more normal than exceptional. They need language as much as anyone. It is true that many of these children develop keen visual awareness. However, while this does not replace language, it can and should be used to improve language. Language learning should begin at birth for all children, the hearing impaired as well as those with normal auditory abilities.

Language does not have to be heard to be effective. There are several nonverbal methods that are helpful and can be taught by parents and teachers who have not had a great deal of specialized training. The most common method is that of manual communication (signing).

Teaching children manual communication as early as possible will give them the means by which they can express themselves in an acceptable manner and comprehend the language of others. However, manual communication always should be accompanied by speech. Intelligible speech should be the ultimate goal for the hearing impaired child, and it is learned best in a verbal language environment.

Signing may appear complicated when observing deaf individuals who are engrossed in conversation. In truth, it is not difficult. Most adults can master the manual alphabet in 15 to 20 minutes. Finger spelling—spelling words letter by letter—then becomes a matter of practice. As can be imagined, spelling each word is not practical. This is done only when an appropriate sign is unknown or when the user reaches a point of confusion as to meaning.

Manual communication, like oral language, has its dialect differences. Obviously, the difference is not in the way the word sounds but in how it is made. There are those who contend that this difference limits the applicability of signing. This is not true; it is as universal as oral speech, which uses various words to mean the same thing, such as bucket and pail.

Signs are practical gestures that relate to the object, action, or concept. Ice cream, for instance, appears as the motor action of eating an ice cream cone. Hold your hand in a loose vertical fist as if holding a cone; now, lick. Congratulations! You have just learned to sign.

As stated, speech and signing should be used at the earliest possible age in the development of the hearing impaired child. When feeding the infant, the parent or guardian should sign and say the word bottle as they would with a normal hearing child.

When hearing impaired children who use manual communication are integrated into a regular class, their success or failure can depend on the attitude of the teacher. There should be no hesitation. The teacher should learn to sign. Sources for learning manual communication are many, several of which are included in the materials and references at the end of this chapter. If the teacher learns a few signs in advance and teaches them to the other students, it can be a most rewarding experience for everyone.

The hearing impaired child also should be given every opportunity to learn to speech-read (lipreading). That is one of the reasons for encouraging adults in the child's life to speak while signing. This requires no added effort on the part of the speaker because speech should be normal, never exaggerated. As the child matures and learns to attend visually to the speaker's face, the need for signing should decrease. Visual attention to lip movement improves communication and aids the hearing impaired child in learning to form sounds that he cannot hear.

Hearing Aids

Manual communication and speech reading are aids in language development and communication, but they are not the end-all; they are starting points. Another helpful device, and a very important one, is the electronic acoustic amplifier, the hearing aid. The following information on the selection and use of hearing aids should be helpful in case referrals or when working with children who wear acoustical aids.

The selection of the hearing aid for the hearing impaired child is of no small matter and should be the responsibility of a professional, preferably an audiologist. It is not inexpensive, and bargain shopping is not recommended. This does not mean to imply that the most expensive is the best. The best can be measured only in effectiveness as it relates to improved auditory acuity.

The selection of a hearing aid should involve many persons, depending on the severity of loss and the age of the child. In the case of a school-age child, those involved might include the otolaryngologist, pediatrician, audiologist, speech therapist, classroom teacher, hearing aid dealer, parents or guardian, and, of course, the child. The audiologist should head this team because that specialist can identify the type and degree of loss, can make the earmold, and usually is willing to work with the hearing aid dealer over the years as adjustments and changes are required.

Two of the major considerations in selecting a hearing aid should be the appropriateness for the child's needs and the acceptability to the child. First, consider the acceptability to the child. An appropriately fitting, correctly amplifying, and electronically functioning aid that is not worn or turned on is of no use to the hearing impaired child. Unfortunately, this often is the case with school-aged children, especially teenagers. The child must see the need for the instrument and accept the responsibility for its operation and for wearing it. Obviously, this does not refer to the behavior of a 2-year-old, but the establishment of positive behavior may begin at that age or younger.

It is the responsibility of the adults in the child's environment to teach a positive attitude toward accepting the handicap and the hearing aid. Helping the child discover the benefits of using the hearing aid far surpasses the ineffective screaming of "Turn on your hearing aid."

There usually are two main reasons why children reject hearing aids. Older children tend to find the physical device offensive. They simply do not want to wear a gadget. They say it makes them different, it gets in their way, or it spoils their appearance. Therefore, it is most important that these children help in the selection of their own hearing aids.

The second, and perhaps most frequent, reason for rejecting the hearing aid is that it causes discomfort and confusion if it is not fitted or operated properly. Fitting and operation affect output or effectiveness. For example, an earmold that does not fit properly causes feedback that can be removed only by decreased volume and, in some cases, no volume. Loose or cracked wires that produce on-and-off sound can be annoying and confusing. No sound may be far more acceptable than noises that confuse or annoy.

To maintain proper operation, both the child and the adults involved should understand the aid and how it functions. Hearing aids are as individualized as eyeglasses, but there are some common aspects that can be considered here.

The Earmold

The earmold, as the name suggests, is a small device that is molded to fit within the outer ear canal. Its function is to give support for the aid, direct and amplify sound, and prevent acoustic feedback. Therefore, the fit is extremely important. If the earmold does not fit properly, it will cause feedback that sounds like whistles and squeals. Poor fit can cause irritation and extreme discomfort.

The material from which the earmold is made is of less importance than is the fit. It can be made with open vents, tubing, filters, etc. Although it is possible to purchase ready-made or stock earmolds, this is often unadvisable. Because the ear grows as the child grows, it usually is necessary to replace earmolds. A new earmold may be required every three to six months up to age 5. Thereafter until age 9, a yearly replacement is generally sufficient.

Components of the Hearing Aid

The components of a hearing aid are a microphone, amplifier, receiver, power source (battery), and volume control. The microphone picks up sound wave vibrations from the air and converts them to electrical signals. The signals travel through an amplifier (transistors) that can increase their strength. The amplification can be regulated by the volume control. The electrical signals then are picked up by the receiver and converted back to sound vibrations that are directed through the earmold to the eardrum.

Types of Hearing Aids

Hearing aids are classified by where they are worn—on the body or at ear level. On-the-body aids have a microphone, amplifier, and power supply in a case that is attached to the clothing or worn in a harness around the chest area. A thin wire is connected to the case and to an external receiver that is attached to the earmold.

There are both advantages and disadvantages to on-the-body hearing aids. They are larger than the ear-level models and can produce greater amplification. Because the microphone and receiver are not in such close proximity, feedback from a poorly fitted earmold is decreased somewhat. The disadvantages of body aids include appearance and bulk, the wires can be broken or disconnected easily, they pick up clothing sounds, and the volume can be changed accidentally.

In spite of the many disadvantages, some of which are not indicated here, the on-the-body model is recommended most often for children. However, some parents feel that having the aid so readily accessible may allow the child to toy with it. To avoid this, the aid can be worn in a harness on the back. This usually decreases child play and food spilled on the aid.

Ear-level hearing aids can be worn behind the ear, in eyeglasses, or all-in-the-ear. The behind-the-ear type consists of a curved case that rests on the mastoid surface and is connected to the earmold by a short plastic tube. The microphone and receiver are in the same case and very close to the earmold. The closeness increases the opportunity for acoustic feedback.

The eyeglass model is much the same except that the case is part of the eyeglass frame extending behind the ear. Again, there are advantages and disadvantages. The eyeglass model is less conspicuous and is more convenient to the wearer. However, when either the glasses or the aid needs repair, the wearer loses both appliances.

Ear-level hearing aids generally deliver less amplification than on-the-body models. In most cases the delivered gain is 55 to 60dB and the maximum power output is from 125 to 130dB.

The all-in-the-ear model fits directly into the ear canal. It is very fragile and even less effective than either of the other models. It is used primarily for adults with mild hearing loss.

Hearing aids also are classified as monaural and binaural. A monaural unit provides amplification for one ear; a binaural system consists of two complete hearing aids, one for each ear. In some binaural models, both systems are housed in one case with two separate cords and receivers.

There has been much controversy over the benefits of one system vs. two systems. It would appear logical to use binaural aids if there is loss of sensitivity in both ears. Research indicates that binaural units are of particular benefit to children with bilateral, symmetrical hearing loss—an equal loss in both ears (Ross, 1969; Fisher, 1964).

In addition to the standard monaural system there is a Y-cord hearing aid. The Y-cord provides a signal to two receivers, one in each ear, but uses a single monaural, on-the-body aid. Although it is less expensive, it may have limitations that need serious consideration before making a selection. For example, under some conditions it is not advisable to aid both ears. When one ear has significantly poor discrimination ability, the inferior ability may interfere with the better discrimination in the contralateral ear.

This section has barely touched on the topic. For additional information, contact the National Bureau of Standards, U.S. Department of Commerce, Washington, D.C. 20234.

COMMERCIAL MATERIALS FOR DEVELOPING AUDITORY SKILLS

The following materials are suggestions based on the writer's experience and that of this book's materials adviser. Any exclusions do not in any way imply rejection or lack of recommendation of other materials. It simply is impossible to include all sources. We therefore selected a few with which we are familiar and gladly would have included others if space allowed.

One of the criteria for selection was portability. All of the materials mentioned can be transported easily and require a minimum of space and equipment for use. This may appear to be a strange reason for suggesting a program. However, we have learned that with resource rooms, itinerant teachers, mainstreaming, etc., space and mobility are essential factors in educational materials.

Auditory Learning Materials for Special Education—Catalog (1974)
  Marsha C. Smith and Phyllis O'Connor
  Great Lakes Region Special Education Instructional Materials Center
  Michigan State University
  East Lansing, Michigan 48823

Purpose: Materials resource.

Population: All levels.

Description: This catalog is included because of its applicability to the subject here and because it is an example of material that is available through the Educational Resource Centers (a federal project) throughout the United States. The catalog was prepared in conjunction with The Consortium on Auditory Learning Materials for the Handicapped. The volume contains lists and descriptions of materials for the development of auditory skills as well as objectives, content, procedures, equipment needed for instruction, cost of materials, and summary comments based on teachers' responses to the material.

Basic Training in Auditory Perception (1970)
  Edward Scagliotta
  Concept Records
  Constructive Playthings
  Charles W. Clark Co.
  564 Smith Street
  Farmingdale, New York 11735

Purpose: Development of auditory discrimination.

Population: Four to nine years and intermediate EMR.

Description: This program is presented on three records. Volume 1 deals with sound discrimination; Volume 2 with figureground discrimination; and, Volume 3 with speech elements. The author suggests it be used with children from 4 to 9 years of age, as well as with the educable mentally retarded (EMR) and learning disabled (LD) who have specific problems with auditory perception and comprehension. It has been found helpful as an extra program for those children who have not developed in these areas when exposed to usual readiness material. Speech therapists and resource room teachers may find this program useful for working with children who have not made the language connection or who have not "tuned in" completely.

Early Years Language Program, "Listen Skills" (1971)
   A. Elaine Mikalson
   Weber Costello
   Mafex Associates, Inc.
   111 Barron Avenue
   Johnstown, Pennsylvania 15906

Purpose: Develop listening comprehension.

Population: Kindergarten—grade 1.

Description: The complete program of five units includes all aspects of language development. The "Listen Skills" unit is prepared specifically to develop listening and story comprehension and to stimulate creativity. The material includes records, sequential picture cards, and a teacher's guide. The program is geared for K-1 with normal children and has been used successfully with slightly older EMR and LD children.

Listening Skills Program (1970)
   Dorothy K. Bracken and Jimmye D. Hayes
   International Teaching Tapes, Inc.
   c/o Edw. Everstine
   Box 308
   Zelienople, Pennsylvania 16063

Purpose: Develop auditory readiness.

Population: Primary level.

Description: The tape cassette for this primary level program begins with auditory discrimination and continues through sense perception, the link between language and perception, meanings of sound symbols, recognition of intonation and rhythm in speech sounds, auditory sequence, comprehension and appreciation. It is an outstanding readiness and beginning language development program. The teacher's manual is easy to follow with clearly stated purposes. References and suggested extended activities are helpful to the teacher who wishes to understand or plan more auditory activities.

Manual Communication (1976)
  Dean A. Christopher, Ph.D.
  University Park Press
  233 East Readwood Street
  Baltimore, Maryland 21202

Purpose: Introduction to signing.

Population: Educators, parents, hearing impaired.

Description: This is a basic text with accompanying workbook. It can be used by the exceptional learner or the learning teacher. The 48 lessons cover many of the very necessary language concepts.

Outline of Language for Deaf Children (1970)
  Edith M. Buell
  The Volta Bureau
  1537 35th Street, N.W.
  Washington, D.C. 20007

Purpose: Educator's resource.

Population: Primary level hearing impaired.

Description: This book is an outline of sequential language tasks designed for use with deaf children of normal intelligence beginning with an entrance age of 5. Suggestions for teaching vocabulary, parts of speech, and language comprehension are useful to the beginning teacher and veteran.

Puppet Enrichment Program (1973)
  George B. Adams, M.Ed., and Arnold B. Cheyney, Ph.D.
  Ideal School Supply Company
  11000 South Lavergne Avenue
  Oak Lawn, Illinois 60453

Purpose: Development of understanding and use of oral language.

Population: Primary through age 10.

Description: This program is presented in two major sections, "The Listening Unit" and "The Oral Language Unit." Through the use of puppets and prepared scripts (included in the teacher's manual and records), aspects of both cognitive and affective abilities are developed. Spirit masters are included. The auditory abilities covered are: auditory perception through identifying, discriminating, and matching sounds; understanding stories; listening for specific purposes; following directions; building receptive vocabulary; and classifying and sequencing. The material is interesting and the vocabulary definitely is current, with appeal to today's children. Although it is most helpful as a beginning program, it has been used successfully with children up to age 10 and with intermediate EMRs.

Seeing Essential English: Codebraker (Revised Edition) (1978)
David A. Anthony, Wilmina G. Dekkers, and C. Bradley Erickson
Pruett Publishing Company
3235 Prairie Avenue
Boulder, Colorado 80301

Purpose: Beginning manual communication.

Population: Educators and parents.

Description: This is a picture textbook that presents signs, how to make them, and when to use them as they apply to total communication. It is designed for use by parents and teachers. It is far more than just signs, however, and incorporates facial expressions and body English with hand signs that communicate. A companion book is titled *Seeing Essential English Elementary Dictionary*. The two make a complete program for the beginner.

The Hand-Book (1976)
Sandra J. Lake
Communication Skill Builders, Inc.
817 East Broadway
P.O. Box 6081
Tucson, Arizona 85733

Purpose: Development of basic nonverbal language.

Population: Teachers and parents of nonverbal, low receptive skill children.

Description: This material is designed to develop total communication in the nonverbal child, specifically the deaf or hard of hearing who have little or no receptive language skills and who lack oral expressive, oral imitative, motor imitative, or attending skills. The instructions for presentation or teaching the signs are clear and step by step. Actual signs are presented in pictures of children and adolescents. The facial expressions clearly are part of the sign. The bibliography lists additional sources that teacher and parents will find extremely valuable.

Visco Developmental Training Program in Auditory Perception (1975)
Susan J. Visco, Ph.D.
Educational Activities, Inc.
P.O. Box 392
Freeport, New York

An in-depth program that is applicable for normal learners from readiness through grade 3, and exceptional learners of all ages (4–18), this is built on the hierarchy of auditory process tasks. The levels developed include attention to auditory stimuli, sound vs. no sound, sound localization, discrimination between sounds, sound sequences, auditory figureground, and associating sound sources. Instructional materials include a teacher's guide, spirit masters, and tapes. The program is best when used in its entirety over several years. It can be used as a plug-in system for children with specific auditory processing dysfunction if the diagnostician has determined the pupil's abilities and disabilities correctly and if the teacher is familiar with the whole program.

REFERENCES

Adams, G. B., & Cheyney, A. B. *Puppet enrichment program.* Oak Lawn, Ill.: Ideal School Supply Company, 1973.

Anthony, D. A., Dekkers, W. G., & Erickson, C. B. *Seeing essential English: Codebraker* (Rev. ed.). Boulder, Colo.: Pruett Publishing Co., 1978.

Bracken, D. K., & Hayes, J. D. *Listening skills program.* Zelienople, Pa.: International Tapes, Inc., 1970.

Buell, E. M. *Outline of language for deaf children.* Washington, D.C.: The Volta Bureau, 1970.

Christopher, D. A. *Manual communication.* Baltimore: University Park Press, 1976.

Fisher, B. An investigation of binaural hearing aids. *Journal of Laryngology,* 1964, *78,* 658–668.

Heasley, B. E. *Auditory perceptual disorders and remediation.* Springfield, Ill.: Charles C. Thomas, Publisher, 1974.

Lake, S. J. *The hand-book.* Tucson, Ariz.: Communication Skill Builders, Inc., 1976.

Mikalson, A. E. *Early years language program, "Listen skills."* Chicago: Weber Costello, 1971.

National Bureau of Standards, U.S. Department of Commerce, Washington, D.C., 20234.

Ross, Mark. Loop auditory training systems for preschool hearing-impaired children. *Volta Review,* 1969, *78,* 289–295.

Scagliotta, E. *Basic training in auditory perception.* North Bellmore, N.Y.: Concept Records, 1970.

Smith, M. C., & O'Connor, P. *Auditory learning materials for special education.* East Lansing, Mich.: Great Lakes Region Special Education Instructional Materials Center, 1974.

Visco, S. J. *Visco developmental training program in auditory perception.* Freeport, N.Y.: Educational Activities, Inc., 1975.

Wilt, M. E. A study of teacher awareness of listening as a factor in elementary education. *Journal of Educational Research,* April, 1950, *43,* 626–636.

Chapter 4

Speech Sound Production

THE DEVELOPMENT OF SPEECH

Throughout the ages of articulate humans there has been much discussion and many theories proposed on how and why speech—oral expressive language—developed. It has been concluded that speech and thought developed as the intellectual being had need to communicate and thereby gain greater control over the environment. This theory is based on the recognizable fact that today we use language to control the people around us, to foster growth, and for our general well-being.

It would seem that speech as an audible sound system may have been an afterthought in the original plan of humans' evolutionary development. This assumption is related to the fact that we do not have organs specifically designed for sound production. Speech organs, the parts of the body involved in speech sound production, were not intended for such a purpose initially; speech is a secondary function. For this reason the development of speech can be affected temporarily or permanently by health problems such as a head cold that blocks the nasal passages and can make speech sound odd or difficult to understand.

This chapter considers both the primary and secondary functions of the organs of speech sound production and the relationship between biological and communication functions. Normal speech development, articulation, fluency, and methods of identifying speech problems also are analyzed.

THE VOCAL ORGANS

If it is understood that the production of intelligible speech is dependent upon organs that primarily perform basic life functions, it is easier to realize the many possible conditions that can and do affect oral language.

The body parts, or vocal organs, are the lungs, the trachea, the larynx, the pharynx, the mouth, and the nose. How do each of these organs function in the speech sound production process?

Sound is energy, and as such has an energy source. In speech sound production, the original force is the exhaled stream of air emanating from the lungs. The primary purpose of the lungs is to supply oxygen to the blood and to carry off waste products produced through the metabolic process. Normally in exhaling, the escaping air is not heard and is simply part of the biological function. However, in speaking, the airstream is set in rapid vibration through vocal cord action.

The air moves out of the lungs through the trachea (windpipe) to the larynx, which contains the vocal cords. The larynx can open and close; in fact, its primary purpose is related to that specific ability to open and close. In the closed position it prevents food or other objects from entering the windpipe and lungs.

The effectiveness of the larynx as a speech organ depends largely upon the action of the vocal cords. They actually are two folds of ligament, one on either side of the larynx. They are attached to the thyroid (Adam's apple) in the front and to cartilage in the back. When the vocal cords are pressed together, the air passage is closed and the laryngeal valve is shut.

During normal breathing the vocal cords remain in a more or less fixed or at rest position. The area between the cords (the glottis) is sufficient to facilitate airflow for breathing. When a person intends to speak, a neural command (message from the brain) initiates movement of the vocal cords. The cords approximate, decreasing the glottal area and obstructing the airflow. As the pressure from the lungs builds up in the subglottal area, the air blows the cords apart, which produces a vacuum and causes the vocal cords to move together or close again. Vibratory movement of the vocal cords also is aided by the action of ligaments and muscles.

When humans speak, they attempt to control air pressure from the lungs and the tension and length of the vocal cords, producing the desired frequency. The vocal cord range of vibrations is from 60 cycles per second (cps) to 359 cps. This movement, along with various other acoustical factors, gives the average voice a range of about two octaves.

Next up the vocal passage is the pharynx. It is a tubelike structure that connects the larynx with the nose and mouth. The size and shape of the pharynx change during swallowing and speech.

Extending from the pharynx to the nostrils is the nasal cavity. The entire length of the cavity, approximately four inches, is separated by a partition called the septum. The nasal passage is a direct air intake to the trachea and lungs. The nasal cavity can be closed off from the pharynx and mouth by raising the soft palate.

As a part of the vocal tract, the nasal cavity is involved in producing the speech sounds associated with the letters *m, n,* and *ng.* Misdirection of the airstream through the nose affects sound production, giving speech a nasal quality (talking through the nose). Conversely, when air cannot pass through the cavity, it is impossible to produce nasal sounds.

The mouth is the last part of the vocal tract. Its primary function is to receive, chew, and taste food as part of the digestive system. As a speech organ it is the most flexible because the size and shape can be changed by movement of the palate, tongue, teeth, and lips.

The palate has three parts: the soft palate, the hard palate (roof of the mouth), and the alveolar (gum-covered teeth ridge). The soft palate is located at the back of the mouth and can be raised up and down. In the raised position the opening between the pharynx and the nasal cavity is closed and the airstream is directed into the mouth. Malformation of the soft palate (too small, too large, or misshapen) can affect the airflow direction. When the soft palate is malformed, misarticulations may occur.

The teeth, which were intended for the grinding of food as an aid to digestion, also play an active role in speech sound production. By placing the tip of the tongue on the teeth (producing /*th*/) or moving the teeth close to the lip (producing /*v*/), the airflow is stopped or redirected.

The tongue aids in the movement of food and contains the nerve endings associated with the sense of taste. In speech, the tongue is the single most flexible part of the vocal tract. The normally developed tongue can move up, down, forward, and back. The rapidity with which it can move facilitates the even flow of speech sounds. When the tongue cannot, or does not, move rapidly from position to position, speech is slurred and often unintelligible. Most persons have come to recognize how difficult speech is when the tongue is slowed down even partially, as it sometimes is after dental treatment.

The lips are the external closure of the oral cavity and serve many purposes. Their primary function is to prevent unwanted material from entering the mouth (and to keep food or liquid from spilling out during eating). Their function in speech production is to change the length and shape of the mouth and to direct or stop the airflow. When the lips are opened and closed rapidly, sounds are produced on puffs of air as in the phoneme /*p*/. Rounded lips aid in the production of sounds such as the long sound of *o*. A third lip position, separated, varies from nearly closed to very wide depending on the sound being produced and the individual's speech habits and characteristics. A person who smiles most of the time will speak with a widely separated position, while others never appear to move their lips and speak with a nearly closed position.

SPEECH SOUNDS—VOWELS AND CONSONANTS

In American English, and especially in language education, speech sounds are considered in two groups, vowels and consonants. The speech pathologist and the reading teacher may use the same words to describe sounds but may not be referring to exactly the same graphemes (letters). The speech pathologist groups sounds based on how and where they are produced.

To produce a vowel sound, the vocal cords must vibrate. Consonants may be produced with or without vocal cord movement. When the vocal cord moves, the consonant is said to be voiced, as with the *z* in zoo. When vocal vibration is not used, the sound is unvoiced as in the *s* sound in the word say.

Vowel sounds in American English are considered either pure vowels, diphthongs (pronounced dif-thongs), or semivowels. When speech pathologists refer to a diphthong, they usually mean any vowel sound that necessitates tongue movement from one position to another. The sound may be represented by one or more graphemes. The *i* in night is an example of a single-letter diphthong. This concept may appear confusing to individuals who have learned to associate a diphthong with a two-vowel letter combination.

In speech sound production, examples of pure vowels are the following: long *e* (eat), short *e* (fed), short *i* (it), short *a* (add) *ah* (father), *uh* (the), schwa *r* (bird), *aw* (thaw), and short *u* (put). Sounds considered to be diphthongs are: *oi* (toil), *au* (out), long *i* (night), long *a* (take), and long *o* (phone).

There are two semivowels in American English—*w* and *y*. To produce these sounds, the vocal mechanism is held in a partial vowel position and moves rapidly to the full vowel position that follows. The action is described best as a very fast vowel position followed by a normal vowel production. Semivowels always are followed by a vowel.

Consonant sound production, in addition to being voiced and unvoiced, is described in relation to how and where the sound is produced or articulated. Where a sound is produced refers to lips (labial), combination of lips and teeth (labiodental), teeth (dental), gums (alveolar), hard palate (palatal), soft palate (velar), and glottal.

How a sound is produced, or manner of articulation, is categorized as being plosive, fricative, nasal, liquid, and semivowel. Plosives are made by blocking the airflow and suddenly releasing it. Fricatives are made by constricting the airflow, producing a hissing quality. Nasal sounds are produced by blocking airflow from the mouth and directing it through the nose. Exhibit 4-1 indicates position and category of consonant sound production.

Development of Articulation

In the development of articulation, the age at which a child will produce a specific speech sound depends on many factors. It is relatively safe to say that vowel sounds are produced first in the normally developing child. The reason is that very little manipulation of the articulators is required to make a vowel sound. Observation of very young children (under age 1) will disclose that they produce many, if not all, consonant sounds. The production is accidental, however. In fact, during infancy many more sounds are produced than are used in our 44-phoneme American English language system.

Exhibit 4-2 indicates the order in which consonant sounds develop in most children. This does not mean that all children follow a set pattern. A child may produce eight to ten phonemes correctly by age 2 and complete the process by 7; however, the same child may say garage at 3 and continue to say yight for light until 6. The list is presented as a guide and an aid for those involved with speech sound production who wish to use a developmental order schedule.

The Central Nervous System and Speech Sounds

The ability to produce meaningful speech sounds depends on a highly complex nervous system process or processes. Sound production in the earliest stages is unintentional, undifferentiated, and reflexive. As the central nervous system (CNS) matures, the child tunes in to sound. At the point in auditory awareness that the child hears his own sound produc-

---

Exhibit 4-1 Consonant Sound Production Chart: Manner and Place of Articulation

	Plosive		Fricative		Nasal	Semivowel	Liquid	
Alveolar	t	d	s	z	n	y	l	r
Dental			th					
Glottal			h					
Labial	p	b			m	w		
Labiodental			f	v				
Palatal			sh	zh				
Velar	k	g			ng			

Exhibit 4-2 Developmental Order of Consonant Sound Production

Chronological Ages 2 through 8				
*h*e	*g*o	*r*un	*v*ain	*garage*
*m*e	sin*g*	*ch*op	*the*	*th*in
*n*ot	*f*eet	*sh*ip		
*w*in	un*i*on	*j*oy		
*b*ag	*s*ent	*z*oo		
*p*at	*l*et			
*t*ip				
*k*eep				
*d*ig				

The sound being produced is indicated by the italicized letter(s) within the sample word. The words are vehicles for the sounds and not necessarily words within the speaking vocabulary of the indicated age group.

tion, the process begins to be intentional but continues to lack meaning or representational intent.

Initially the child produces a sound that for some reason appeals to him and he attempts to replicate the production. It is not known whether the desire to reproduce a given sound stems from kinesthetic pleasure derived through movement of the articulators or whether the motivation is the sound itself. It may well be a combination of the two. Observation of deaf infants tends to suggest that without internal auditory feedback, the desire to produce most sounds disappears. The young deaf child's repertoire of sounds often is limited to noises associated with bodily functions.

During the early stages of experimentation with sound reproduction, the normal child attempts to develop the ability to control the tongue, lips, and cheeks. As the child matures, he develops the ability of the CNS to control motor movement consciously.

If the child receives environmental reward for the attempts to produce sounds, the process then becomes selective. The child tries to make an auditory match that requires movement of specific vocal organ parts through conscious motor control. The sound produced is intentional but not representational. For example, the child accidentally produces *da da*. The experience is pleasant, and the child attempts to reproduce the sound. A happy adult hears the sound and reinforces the child by repeating the syllables. The child again makes the sound and the pattern is repeated many times. The child's central nervous system is maturing; he is learning to use short-term memory and to control motor movement.

However, the child has not attached any significance to the sound. *Da da* represents father to the adult but not to the child.

Continuing reinforcement by the adult in the form of repetition, smiles, and touches helps the child in attaching meaning to the utterance. When *da da* becomes a male figure, the sound becomes a word, and the child has begun to use language.

When the point is reached in language acquisition that an utterance has symbolic meaning, the child is retrieving stored auditory, visual, and motor information. The integration of this information by the central nervous system allows the child to think *da da* and to produce the sounds without conscious control. That is, the child *thinks* what he is going to say, not how he is going to move his articulators to produce the desired sounds.

The normally developing language user consciously selects the sound or sounds to be produced; once the intent has been determined, the motor process becomes automatic or reflexive. If the integration of thought and corresponding correct movement does not occur automatically, the child may be said to have central nervous system dysfunction or a specific language disability.

ARTICULATION ERRORS

More than two-thirds of the children in the caseload of the public school speech pathologist identified as having a speech or language problem have articulatory disorders. Common cases can be grouped as (1) those who demonstrate omissions, substitutions, and distortions of specific sounds, and (2) those with dialects or nonstandard productions.

There are two major reasons why parents and educators should be concerned about a child's ability to articulate correctly:

1. When a child misarticulates, especially if the number of instances is excessive, it is difficult to understand the speech and to determine the intent of the communication. This condition may inhibit the child's desire to speak, cause withdrawal, or give rise to antisocial behavior.
2. Misarticulations are often indicative of physiological and psychological problems that may affect later academic achievement seriously.

Within the group of children who omit, substitute, or distort sounds are subgroups or categories—those with (1) normal developmental misarticulations, (2) immature articulation, or (3) organically caused misarticulations. The normal developmental and the immature groups at some point may be one and the same. The difference, if one exists, occurs when the problem persists beyond the age of 7 or 8.

In most cases in the first group, normal developmental misarticulations, the child will outgrow the problem. If, for instance, the original cause was poorly developed auditory skills, when the ability improves and the child hears the fine differences in speech sounds and recognizes errors, he corrects them without therapy. Those whose problem continues often are demonstrating a habit. They hear the difference and may be able to produce the sound correctly but because they learned to make it incorrectly, they continue to do so.

Although there are many possible causes, assume that children in the second group—the immature articulators—have poorly defined auditory discrimination and improper movement of the articulators. As they mature, they develop the ability to hear the differences in speech sounds, at least those sounds produced by other speakers. They can control their articulators. However, the immature pattern has been reinforced or is acceptable to the user. In some cases the parents think it sounds cute, or the children learn that people notice them, and even negative attention can be rewarding.

The third group, those whose problem is organic, fortunately are few in number. These children often are physically handicapped in other ways as well.

Parents and educators, if they are to help and to understand the child's problem, should be aware of the type and cause of the articulatory deficit. The following material explains the types of errors mentioned previously as being most common. The explanations are brief—intentionally. The discussion of all types and of all causes fills many volumes to which speech pathologists have directed much time. A teacher or parent with basic knowledge can communicate better with the specialists in their efforts to carry out recommended programs.

Omissions, Substitutions, Distortions

An omission error is one in which the speaker fails to produce a sound (says elicopter for helicopter). A substitution is the production of a sound in place of another (yelicopter) for (helicopter). Distortions are more difficult to exemplify because they vary from speaker to speaker. Partial production occurs, but the sound takes on characteristics not generally included, such as a lisp.

Dialects and Nonstandard Production

Dialects and nonstandard production are grouped together here because in some çases the labels are interchangeable, or the production belongs in both categories. There actually are two categories of dialects, social and regional. According to Marcus (1977), a social dialect reflects the language habits of a speech community; a regional dialect is used by people of a specific geographic region.

Many regions of this country have developed sound patterns that reflect a cultural heritage. The correct structures of American English have been incorporated in the dialect. A person using the dialect has no difficulty being understood by the general public, and the speech sounds would be acceptable to an employer in that region. A dialect becomes a problem when the difference in utterances prevents or limits the speaker's ability to communicate with the general public, find employment, or pursue an acceptable life in society.

Nonstandard production is pronouncing words with missing elements, substituting sounds for words, and running words together. Examples include the following: *wit* for *with, runnin* for *running, yeh* for *yes,* and *tiznt* for *this is not.* Nonstandard production is related more closely to a speech community than to a total geographic region. The same criteria for judging a dialect problem apply to nonstandard production.

Causes of Articulation Disorders

There are many causes and causal combinations of articulation problems, several of which have been indicated in the discussion of types of articulation deficits. However, the prevention or correction of misproduced sounds often depends on the parent's and the teacher's understanding the etiology of the problem. The most frequently encountered causes are poorly developed auditory discrimination, mental retardation, structural defects, sensory impairment, and environmental factors.

Poorly developed auditory discrimination has been cited as the probable cause of several types of articulation problems. In fact, it cannot be overstressed. Poole (1934, p. 160), is quite clear: "In order to produce a sound intelligently, a child must be able to hear that sound." At the outset the child simply does not listen to hear. The final result may be far more important than the misarticulations. The relationship between auditory discrimination and speech has been well established (Travis & Rasmus, 1931; Templin, 1957). In addition, slowness in developing adequate auditory discrimination and correct articulation has been shown to be related to retardation or disorders in other language areas such as reading and writing (Monroe, 1932; Betts, 1943; Wepman & Morency, 1971; Webber, 1971).

Mental retardation alone does not cause a child to misarticulate. There are many mentally retarded (MR) children who speak quite clearly. However, with lowered intellectual capacity, the child's ability to acquire correct articulation may diminish proportionately to the degree of retardation. In most MR cases, speech and language should be considered in relation to the child's mental age, not chronological age. In addition, there are specific causes for mental retardation that affect the physiological development of the individual. The Down's syndrome child is a case in point. These children often have structural abnormalities that are characteristic of the syndrome (shape, length, and mass of the tongue); therefore, the misarticulation may result from the structure and not the lowered intellectual capacity, or it may be a combination of the two.

One of the least common causes of articulation problems is that of a physiological deficit. However, from the point of view of many parents, this is the logical cause: "There is something physically wrong with my child." They would like to believe that with the aid of modern medicine and technology, the problem can be corrected with a single procedure. Unfortunately, this seldom is the case, and even with corrective measures to repair the physical malformity, a prolonged period of speech therapy may be required.

Teeth and bite are probably the most common of the structural defects. Bite refers to the closing of the teeth. A malocclusion or bite problem may be an overbite, underbite, or openbite.

An overbite occurs when the top teeth protrude. When the upper and lower jaws are brought together, there is improper alignment with a space above and in front of the lower teeth. In such cases a sound distortion may occur, usually some type of lisp. The underbite is the reverse of that condition. The lower jaw protrudes and, when closed, may cover all of the upper front teeth. This condition may affect many sounds; fortunately, it is very rare.

Openbite refers to the existence of a space between the upper and lower front teeth when the back teeth are together. While the individual with an overbite usually can move the lower jaw to bring upper and lower teeth into closer proximity, the openbite cannot be corrected this way. The *s* and *z* sounds usually are affected; in severe cases, the front-of-the-tongue sounds also may be distorted.

The tongue, the hard palate, the soft palate, and the lips also may have structural defects. It almost can be said, "The poor tongue." It often is the first thing parents think about when the child does not "sound right." Even adults who persist in misarticulating like to attribute their errors to the size or shape of the tongue. Except where the tongue formation or growth is defective because of genetic programming, cases of a structurally defective tongue are rare. There are, of course, instances in which the frenum of the tongue is shortened (tongue-tied). This condition can be corrected surgically with little or no permanent effect on the developing speech.

The hard palate is the roof of the mouth. The most serious malformation is the cleft palate, which is an opening along the central line or ridge of the hard palate. Individuals with this condition cannot block the airflow from moving into the nose. Sounds that are produced in the mouth are affected, giving their speech a nasal quality. The physical condition can sometimes be corrected by closing the opening surgically or by using an appliance, or artificial palate, known as an obturator. Even after repair, extensive speech therapy usually is needed.

The soft palate (velum) is the fleshy structure that is visible at the upper rear of the mouth. As described under speech organs, the velum moves up and down during swallowing and speech. Occasionally the soft palate does not rise sufficiently to complete closure. This may be because of paralysis or structural inadequacy. Signs of soft palate malfunction may resemble those of the cleft palate in that air leakage from the improper closure affects speech production, giving a nasal quality to specific sounds, particularly vowels.

The lips need not be described structurally; however, there are labial conditions that should be known. The size, shape, and flexibility of the lips can affect all labial sounds. The lips are used to extend the vocal tract and to stop and/or direct airflow. Paralysis or restricted lip movement impedes clarity of sound and may make speech unintelligible. The cleft lip, often referred to as harelip, is a genetically caused malformation of the upper lip. It may accompany the cleft palate or may occur without other structural defects. The condition can be surgically corrected but the degree to which it is repairable depends on the severity of the malformation. Several operations may be required before the lip approximates normal proportions and is flexible enough for correct sound production.

As noted previously, misarticulations may be the manifestation of a more serious underlying problem. This may be true in the case of sensory impairments. The most obvious condition is the lack of auditory sensitivity, or deafness. In most cases, this condition is identifiable readily. Other sensory deficits may be less recognizable, with resulting subtle signs that, if not discovered, eventually may have a marked effect on the child's development and learning capacity.

This reference is to tactile and kinesthetic sensory data. Children who have lowered levels of tactile sensitivity may not feel where their tongue is placed in relation to the contacting structures. When kinesthetic sensitivity is impaired, tongue movement information may be lacking. In either case, the lack of sensory awareness can affect articulation; more importantly, the condition may be indicative of more serious central nervous system dysfunction.

Most authorities agree that speech is an imitative process: children learn to produce what they hear. Therefore, the immediate speech environment affects what the child says and how it is said. In relation to misproduction of speech sounds, there are three general groups of environmental factors that are common. The first, and probably the most frequent, is poor speech habits. This type of misarticulation is nonstandard production and is discussed in the earlier section on social dialects.

The second group includes children who misarticulate because someone in their environment has an articulation problem. For example, a mother with a cleft palate is the child's primary speech model. The child hears the mother's nasal speech and learns to produce sounds that match those of the model. The child has normal closure, but learns to misdirect his airflow in an effort to imitate the mother. To correct the sound, the child often needs the same type of therapy that would be employed with a true cleft palate case after corrective surgery. A more common situation involves familial misarticulations: the oldest child in a family develops a lisp, and each child thereafter also lisps. In this group, the first person, or model, may have had an organic cause for misarticulating; the imitators do not.

In the case of misarticulation because of family influence, it often is necessary to remediate the entire family. It is of little use to attempt to correct a sound if the learner will continue to have an incorrect model at home. Obviously, the problem is extremely complicated when the model is a mature adult, especially if the adult has an organic disability.

The last group, and least common, involves those with accented speech. That is, someone in the child's environment learned American English as a second language and produces specific sounds in a fashion not common in this country. It is not a dialect; it is sound distortion. The misarticulation often is limited to a single sound and usually can be corrected without too much difficulty. As above, family therapy may be required.

FLUENCY

The term fluency refers to the melody and rhythm of spoken language. In the developing child, fluency is learned, or at least practiced, during the stage of speech use called jargon. This usually begins at about 18 months and continues until age 3. Jargon is make-believe language. The child makes sounds that have word tones, uses these nonsense words with real words, and strings them together in groups resembling sentences. To the casual observer the child is speaking a foreign language. Close attention to the utterances will show that the child is practicing rhythm and tone. The make-believe speech will rise in pitch and volume if the child becomes angry with a toy and be lowered and slowed if the child is putting a stuffed animal to bed. Practice with fluency at this stage is extremely important for later language development.

Fluency as an integral part of language does not enter into the expressive aspect of the communication system until the child begins to put real words together to form phrases and sentences. As most children have very little connected speech until about age 3, fluency does not usually become a problem until that age.

At approximately age 3, most children are capable of holding relatively long conversations. Most parents are pleased and even anxious to reach the stage in the parent-child relationship where conversation is possible. The child wants to talk, and the parents want to understand. It is this mutual desire to communicate that can cause difficulty with the child's fluency development.

The young child has limited vocabulary and immature motor development. When he attempts to speak, he may have difficulty finding the word or in controlling the articulators in producing the desired sound. The result of these conditions may cause nonfluent language or stuttering.

Stuttering is, among other things, the repetition of a single sound (*M,M,M,M*other), a syllable (*non,non,non*sense), a complete word (*give,give,give* it to me), or a phrase (*I said,I said, I said* not now). In addition to repetition, the nonfluent speech may be characterized by prolongations (*mmmmmm*ay) or inappropriate hesitations (Give me. . . the book).

Nonfluent speech is normal. Every child at some point in his development has found himself unable to produce an even flow of words for expression. In fact, most adults, if honest, will admit to periods of nonfluency. Nonfluency or stuttering does not become a language problem until the user views it as such. Because of this, stuttering sometimes is classified as to the stage of recognition—primary, transitional, and secondary.

Primary stutterers are those who have occasional periods of nonfluency but are not concerned with the situation. The individuals will speak freely, apparently not bothered by repetitions. When nonfluent speakers begin to correct the condition, show stress, or use circuitous methods to avoid the situation, they may be classified as transitional. At this stage they may begin to think of their nonfluent speech as a problem and may begin to avoid specific sounds. They still are willing to converse and have not reached the point where speech is a major concern. They know they stutter sometimes and wish they didn't, especially because their parents or someone else will call attention to their speech.

Secondary stutterers are stutterers. They are aware that their speech is characterized by nonfluencies and use many tactics to cure, avoid, and overcome the problem.

Stuttering is an insidious language problem that generally need not have occurred. Rarely is the condition related to an organic cause. Occasionally it begins as a psychological problem: the child is overly critical of himself, is overly concerned with perfection, or believes himself inadequate and manifests nonfluency to justify that self-appraisal, and so on. The most frequent cause is environmental. Well-meaning adults try to help the normally developing child by saying "slow down" or "say it again." This type of help calls attention to the nonfluent speech and eventually may produce a secondary stutterer.

The diagnosing of stuttering usually is very difficult, and labeling as such should be avoided as much as possible. Assessment and remediation of the condition should be undertaken by a competent speech therapist. This does not mean that parents and teachers should not be able to recognize symptoms or use appropriate intervention which has been suggested by the speech specialist.

The previous description of classes should be helpful in recognizing a stutterer. A primary stutterer does not have a language problem and can be thought of as a normal speaker who cannot get words out fast enough. It does not bother the child and it does not stop him from trying. The best intervention for these children really is no intervention. Allow them to try to speak; accept whatever they say. Do not tell them to stop, slow down, or say it again. Do not allow other people to call attention to the stuttering. Help the children enjoy life by sharing many moments of conversation with you, no matter how annoying it may be to you. If you accept them and their speech, they will, too.

Recognizing transitional stutterers is very important. It is at this stage that intervention may save a life of agony. The usual, or common, signs are self-initiated attempts to control or correct speech and a decrease in desire or attempts at verbal communication. When the child shows signs of recognizing the situation, he probably is on the way to having a problem. The first step is to have an honest discussion indicating that you are aware that occasionally the child has difficulty. Explain that most people including yourself, have similar moments. Make it quite clear that you accept the child and his speech. The second step is to seek the help of a trained professional.

Secondary stutterers are difficult to describe because the possible characteristics are so numerous. They may retreat into the world of written words, avoid speech, appear antisocial, or try to be a clown so that people will laugh with them and not at them. Their speech may be cluttered and have blockage or prolongations that appear to be strange nonlanguage sounds. Facial expressions may indicate tension. The list of physical, linguistic, and psychological behaviors is nearly endless. In such cases, acceptance and professional help are the only answers.

Remediation for secondary stutterers may require the services of a psychologist as well as a speech therapist but, except in rare cases, the situation can be improved. The stutterers can be helped to find the path to a normal well-adjusted life.

Speech errors, regardless of type or cause, are deserving of serious consideration by educators and parents alike. The most frequent types and causes of speech problems have been discussed in an effort to aid the reader in recognizing and understanding the most typical of atypical speech.

EVALUATING ARTICULATION

Teacher-Prepared Informal Measures

Classroom teacher assessment of speech sound production identifies children for referral to the speech pathologist. For informal screening it is not necessary to use standardized measures or to test all phonemes. The most frequently misarticulated sounds usually will be sufficient for initial identification. Exhibit 4-3 indicates the phonetic symbol. The italicized letters within the words represent common error phonemes.

The educator's steps in a planned program to identify speech errors are: (1) listen to the child's speech, (2) note sound errors, and (3) determine error position within words and regularity of misarticulations (Step 3 is optional). The following suggestions can be used to complete these steps.

1. Listening to the Child's Speech

Although errors can be noted as the child speaks, a tape recorder is recommended. Many distracting events can occur and some sounds require close study. Replaying the tape makes identification easier for the untrained ear. In addition, recording affords the evaluator an opportunity to work with several children during a single session.

Exhibit 4-3 Most Frequently Misarticulated Sounds in American English

Phonetic Symbol	Letter(s)	Phoneme in Context
k	k	*k*ic*k*
g	g	*g*a*g*
f	f	*f*an
v	v	*v*ow
θ	th	*th*in
s	s	*s*ay
z	z	*z*oo
∫	sh	*sh*e
t∫	ch	*ch*eap
l	l, le	app*l*e
r	r	*r*un
ʒ	ur	h*ur*t
α	er	und*er*

The children should have time to become comfortable with the tape recorder. When they have learned to speak so that their voices record with clarity (volume and pitch) and the rate is normal for the speakers, begin screening procedures. Any one of the following three activity methods can be used. Selection may depend on time restraints and the children being tested.

Activity 1. Select large pictures of objects with labels that contain the sounds to be tested. Pictures should indicate clearly the desired response, and the vocabulary should be appropriate for the children being tested. On the back of each picture write a short sentence or question that can be used to elicit the desired reponse when the child does not name the object spontaneously. The order of presentation is not important. However, when a sound is suspect, do not use it as the first sound tested.

Say, "I am going to show you some pictures. When I call your name, please tell me the name of the object."

When taping a group session, be certain to name the child before the response. Otherwise voice identification on the tape may be a problem.

Activity 2. Make a list of questions that will elicit responses that contain the target phonemes. If the children are young or mentally retarded, visuals may be helpful. The questions should be interesting and appropriate for the children's age and developmental level.

Say, "I'm going to ask a question. When I call on you, please answer the question in your own words and use a sentence if you can think of one."

The following are examples of questions intended to elicit /p/ in the initial position from three different age groups:

Primary: "What animal makes a sound like oink, oink?"
Intermediate: "When you tear your jeans, your mother might sew a piece of material over the hole. What do we call that?"
Secondary: "What is the name of the car made by General Motors that is also the name of a city in Michigan?"

Activity 3. This procedure is recommended for children who can read and who do not have a reading problem. This is a speech sound production measure, not a reading test.

Select or write paragraphs or short stories that contain words with target sounds. Give the children a copy of the material and allow them to read it silently before reading aloud.

Say, "Here are some short stories. Read them silently. If there are any words you don't recognize, I will gladly tell you what they are. When I call on you, try to read with expression, as though you were saying the words, not reading them."

The following paragraph contains all of the suggested phonemes. The italicized letters indicate the phoneme being tested but would not be in italics on the child's copy.

Have you *ev*er seen anyone *k*i*ck* a *f*ootball like *Th*ad? It wa*s* a *sh*ame he *g*ot h*ur*t jumping the h*u*r*dl*e in prac*t*ice. He can *r*eally *z*oom that ba*ll*. The *ch*eer leaders *s*ure *g*et e*x*cited when he score*s*.

2. *Noting Sound Errors*

Make a chart placing the letter or letters that represent the phonemes across the top. Under each phoneme write *I* for initial, *M* for medial, and *F* for final position. List the names of the children tested in a column to the left. As you listen to the tape, put a mark under the phoneme to indicate an error.

Exhibit 4-4 is a sample chart indicating errors of four children. The completed chart indicates which children are having problems and the sounds on which they erred. Its use facilitates grouping when several children make errors on the same sounds.

3. *Determining Regularity of Misarticulations*

This step is not necessary for screening. It is included for readers who do not have the services of a speech pathologist.

Exhibit 4-4 Sample Error Sounds Chart

Sound	k	g	f	v	s	z	sh	ch	l	r	ur	er
Position*	IMF	IMF	IMF	IMF	IMF	IMF	IMF	IMF	IMF	IMF	IMF	IMF
John					xxx		xxx					
Paul								xxx				
Mary										xxx	xxx	xxx
Pat					xx		xxx					
*I stands for initial, M for medial, and F for final position.												

In this step, the error phoneme is checked several times in each position to establish the fact that the child consistently misarticulates a specific sound.

When the screening has been completed, or at least Activities 1 and 2, there should be sufficient information on which to base referrals. Although there are situations when referral is questionable, cases that should be included involve (1) misarticulation of vowel sounds, (2) unintelligible speech, (3) errors in /s/ and /r/ sounds, and (4) misarticulations of three or more sounds.

When professional help is not available, it is advisable to continue the evaluation of any child who has an error on screening. In this event, any of the many good tests available may be used.

Formal Measures

The formal assessment of speech and language is the responsibility of the speech pathologist (pathologist, therapist, clinician, and language specialist are interchangeable terms; usage depends on personal preference of the professional). These professionals are generally certified specialists. Many of the diagnostic tools and corrective procedures they employ require extensive training before they can be utilized with speech handicapped individuals. However, an understanding of the tools and procedures most frequently used can be helpful to the classroom teacher and to parents of speech impaired children. To familiarize the reader with formal speech evaluation, two traditional tests that are commercially available and a procedure that is used less frequently have been selected.

Traditional assessment and therapy are sound oriented. However, there is another method of dealing with articulation. It is referred to as *distinctive feature*. The concept is not new; it was discussed more than a century ago by Jan Baudouin de Courtenay (Walsh, 1974). However, not until the last several decades has the idea received serious and continuous attention. Among the reasons for this lag is that, to date, proponents have not agreed on such points as terminology and number and type of features to be considered.

The basic premise of distinctive feature analysis is that language sounds have specific characteristics that can be systematized. These characteristics or features include how the sound is produced, where it is produced, airstream restriction, and so on. The list of possible critical distinctive features is quite long.

Recently several workable systems have been developed and are being used in articulation assessment and therapy. A brief discussion of the concept is included here because of its growing popularity and potential value in understanding articulation.

This discussion uses the system developed by Kamara, Kamara, and Singh (1975). They devised a Distinctive Feature Wheel listing nine critical features: frontness, labial, sonarant, nasal, continuant, sibilant, voice, lateral, and dental. A + indicates presence and a − indicates absence of a feature. Features of 25 phonemes are charted.

In using the wheel, the examiner finds the actual sound produced and the target sound. These sounds are compared for presence or absence of features. For example, a child says *b*atato for *p*otato, a /b/ for /p/ substitution. According to distinctive features, the phoneme /p/ is + frontness (articulation at or in front of alveolar ridge) and + labial (articulated by lips); all other features are −. Phoneme /b/ is + frontness, + labial, and + voice, other features − (Kamara et al., 1975). The two phonemes have eight of the nine features in common when produced correctly. In comparing the child's production with the target phoneme, one feature that is not characteristic of the sound is present. According to the authors of the wheel, the fewer the distinctive feature differences (error features), the less deviant the sound. In this example the sound was one feature off target.

The application of distinctive feature systems to articulation therapy is relatively new. Stated briefly, therapy is directed toward the production of absent features or the elimination of features not characteristic of a sound or group of sounds. For additional information on distinctive feature analysis and therapy, the reader is directed to Costello (1975), Emerick and Hatten (1979), and Faircloth (1974).

COMMERCIALLY AVAILABLE TESTS

The Goldman-Fristoe Test of Articulation (1972)
  Ronald Goldman, Ph.D., and Macalyne Fristoe, M.S.
  American Guidance Service, Inc.
  Publishers' Building
  Circle Pines, Minnesota 55014

Population: 2 years and up.

Purpose: Articulation.

Description: This measure has three subtests: Sounds-in-Words Subtest, Sounds-in-Sentences Subtest, and Stimulability Subtest. It is designed to assess all consonant sounds in initial, medial, and final positions, vowel sounds, and all but one diphthong. The subtests may be used separately.

The Sounds-in-Words Subtest requires the child to name items depicted in 35 pictures. The Sounds-in-Sentences Subtest uses a story format in which the examiner reads a story with accompanying pictures. Emphasis is placed on key words. The five pictures are turned back and the child is asked to retell the story, using the visual clues to aid recall. Scoring of this subtest requires close attention to the child's response. A trained evaluator can use this measure to screen syntax and vocabulary. The third subtest is used to determine stimulability: can the child imitate the sound?

The first two subtests enable a classroom teacher with little or no speech training to determine which sounds a child misarticulates; the position within words of the misarticulated sound; the type of error, such as omission, substitution, or distortion; and whether the error is one made frequently by children of the same sex and age. An individual with understanding of speech sound production also can determine whether the errors are related to articulator placement and type of consonant voicing (nasal, plosive, fricative).

The Arizona Articulation Proficiency Scale (Revised) AAPS (1972)
  Janet B. Fudala, M.A.
  Western Psychological Services
  12031 Wilshire Boulevard
  Los Angeles, Calif. 90025

Population: 3.5 years to adult

Purpose: Identification of articulatory deficiencies.

Description: The AAPS has two subtests, The Picture Test and The Sentence Test. The Picture Test uses 48 cards with black-and-white line drawings to elicit words containing the phonemes to be tested in initial or final position. Medial consonants are not tested. The author's rationale for omitting medial position is that consonants are initial or final sounds in syllables. Syllable patterns are C-V, C-V-C, or V-C. When a consonant occurs in the middle of a word, it is either in initial position of the syllable (la-*M*ent) or in final position (ro*B*-in). Therefore, if a sound is misarticulated in initial or final position, the same sound error doubtlessly will occur if the sound is produced in the middle of a word (Fudala, 1972).

The Sentence Test contains 25 sentences with a reading level of approximately third grade. The subject is asked to read the sentences in the order presented in the Protocol Booklet. The sentence language is appropriate for children and adults.

This test has standard normative data interpretation. In addition, there is a formula for determining the probable frequency of occurrence. This information is related to data on the number of times a sound appears in American English, and the effect the misarticulated sound or sounds will have on intelligible speech in connected discourse.

TEACHER-PREPARED ACTIVITIES TO IMPROVE ARTICULATION

Causes and types of speech sound errors have been discussed. Some of that information can be applied now in developing a program using an earlier example, the child who substitutes /b/ for /p/.

The error phoneme and the type, substitution, have been identified. Consider how the two sounds are made. Both are labial plosives. The lips are closed and the airstream is stopped, then allowed to burst out. Therefore, it can be assumed that the problem is not caused by lip movement or airstream control.

The difference in the two sounds is that /b/ is voiced and /p/ unvoiced. The child did not misarticulate other unvoiced sounds, so it also should be assumed that that is not the problem. Auditory discrimination testing indicates that the child has difficulty with several sound comparisons. Functioning otherwise is within normal limits.

To summarize the problem, the child has a sound substitution problem not related to the articulators, produces other unvoiced sounds correctly, and has some speech sound discrimination confusion. Based on this, the educator plans a program that includes the following: hearing speech sound differences, practice in producing the sound in syllables, production of the sound in words, and producing the sound in words contained in connected speech. The activities at each level may be planned for a period of several days or even weeks, depending on the child's developmental rate.

Hearing the Differences in Speech Sounds

Activity 1. Make a file of pictures showing objects, actions, or classes of items that begin with /b/ and /p/. Say to the child, "Here are some pictures. I am going to name some objects in one of the pictures. Point to the object whenever the name begins with /p/, the beginning and ending sound in pop." Produce the /p/ unvoiced; do not add a vowel sound.

The first object named should have /p/ in the initial position. If the child responds correctly, give praise and say another word that does not begin with the target sound. Do not use /b/ at this time.

If the child has no difficulty to this point, continue on, mix the sounds, and add /b/ words to the activity. Make the task more difficult as the practice progresses. Use rhyming words such as, "Show me the bale," "Show me the pail."

Lessons should be of sufficient length to hold the child's attention, and no more. Progress at the child's rate and do not expect to cover gross and fine differences in a single lesson.

Activity 2. Read, tell, or use a tape of a story that contains many /p/ and /b/ sounds. Give the child a *P* card. Ask the child to listen to the story, and when a /p/ word is said, hold up the card. Again progress from gross to fine differences. (For additional activities to develop auditory discrimination, see Chapter 2.)

Producing the Sound in Syllables

Activity 1. Begin this stage with a tactile and auditory awareness of the difference between /p/ and /b/. Ask the child if he ever has felt sound. Briefly discuss how sounds are produced and allow the child to feel your voice box move. Make the /b/ sound, then the /p/. Have the child describe the tactile difference. Have the child try to produce the sounds. By repeating this several times, the child should begin to feel and hear the difference in the two sounds. Following this activity the sounds in syllables should be easier to master.

Activity 2. Sing a Sound. Explain to the children that sometimes when we sing, we don't sing words, we sing sounds, usually *la, la, la*. Using a tune the children know, have them substitute *pa* for the words. *Yankee Doodle* is a good tune for this sound.

Activity 3. Make a list of sounds that can be imitated. The list should begin with the /p/ sound. For example, *Ping-Pong* like a plastic ball, *peep peep* like a chick, *put, put* like an engine, and *purr* like a kitten.

Say to the children, "Today we are going to pretend we are things. We are going to make sounds like things, not people. Let's pretend we are _____ ." Let the children suggest things to be.

This same activity can be used in working with the final position as well. *Pop pop* like popcorn, *cheep cheep* like a bird, and *zzzzip* like a zipper are examples of final position thing sounds.

Activity 4. Children like funny-sounding words. For this activity, nonsense type syllables or words are used to stimulate interest and as stimulus syllables.

Say to the children, "Today I am going to read you a story that has words that aren't words; they are silly syllables. When I finish the story, I am going to ask you some questions. All the answers will be silly syllables."

The following story is an example of a silly syllable story.

> There once was a pok. Not a bad pok, just a mad pok.
> The reason he was mad was because he had lost his pum.
> Now a pum is important, without it a pok can't pip.
> "Gosh darn," said the pok, "I'm not a bad pok, I'm a mad pok.
> I've lost my pum, and a pok without a pum can't pip."

Ask the children such questions as: "Who or what was the story about?" "What had it lost?" "Why was it important?"

To continue this activity, have the children draw a picture of a pok. Allow them to be as imaginative as possible. Ask them to think of other things a pok might lose that also begin with the /p/ sound. In this way the children create their own silly syllables and stories.

The following example is a final position story:

> I have a fip. His name is Wip. He is a flip. He likes to zip, skip, and rip. One day he hit his plip. Boy, did that make him yip. In fact, it made him _____ (children can complete idea with final position /p/ silly syllables).

Producing the Sound in Meaningful Words

At this level the child should be able to produce the sound correctly in words. Practice need be nothing more than asking the child to repeat words or to name objects for spontaneous production. However, making practice seem like fun often helps activate the less interested child and tends to improve production. In the example activity, both imitation and spontaneous speech can be planned. The activity is a game and a learning experience called "Treasure Hunt for the Sound of _____ ."

Collect objects that have labels that begin with /p/. Hide some of them around the room. Place the remaining items in a large box (treasure chest).

Take the objects out of the chest one at a time and say, "This is a *(name the object); what is it?"* Have the children repeat the name of the object (imitate). If they have no difficulty producing the sound in imitation, change the procedures. Say, "What is this?" When the objects have been named, explain that the box really is a treasure chest and that hidden in the room are other treasures that begin with the /p/ sound. Tell them they are to go on a treasure hunt. As they find the objects, they are to bring them back to their seats. When all objects have been found, the children return the treasures to the chest, naming each item as it is put away.

Words in Sentences

Spontaneously producing the sound correctly is the goal at this level. The suggested activities begin at the imitation level and progress to the spontaneous level.

Activity 1. Write or use prepared rhymes, jingles, or poems with words that contain the /p/ phoneme. Say to the children, "I am going to read a rhyme. When I finish, we will learn the rhyme together."

The following material uses /p/ in the initial position:

> There once were two pigs, Pat and Paul.
> One was short, and one was tall.
> Paul had a pail, but no tail.
> Pat had a shaw, but no paw.
> Poor pigs,
> A pail but no tail.
> A shaw but no paw.

Activity 2. This is a variation of the old standard, "I'm thinking of something . . ." The directions are, "Today we are going to play a game that is called 'Where Is It?' I will describe an object, and you are to tell me where it can be found. All of the places will begin with the /p/ sound. Please answer in sentences, not just the place."

Use things that are real and imaginary. The following list includes something real and something imaginary for where, what, and who.

I'm thinking of:

- a small red eraser, where is it? (It is on the pink pencil.)
- a king is at home, where is he? (He is in his palace.)
- something we buy in a box and eat at the movies, what is it? (It is popcorn.)
- an animal that looks a little like Tony the Tiger but is a funny color for an animal, what is it? (It is a pink panther.)
- a group of people who came to this country and settled in Massachusetts, who were they? (They were the Pilgrims.)
- a puppet that told lies, and his nose grew longer, who was he? (He was Pinocchio.)

Activity 3. This story activity is used to elicit spontaneous connected speech. To aid the child in creating a story, cut out small pictures and paste them on a strip of paper as in a comic strip. The pictures should feature people, animals, and objects that have the target sound in their names or labels. If prompting is necessary, make it in the form of a question. Do not say the word with the lesson sound.

Say to the children, "Here are some pictures. They tell a story. Look at them and make up your own story about what you see."

COMMERCIAL MATERIALS FOR THE DEVELOPMENT OF SPEECH SOUNDS

For additional ideas and sources for developing correct articulation and standard speech sounds, several programs have been selected with which the author is familiar. Unfortunately, space does not allow the inclusion of all the many excellent materials available in this field. The author therefore has attempted to select what might be considered one of each, or a sample of hardware and software programs for developing articulation, and material for working with nonstandard speech.

Speech Therapy with Beginning Sounds (1970)
ESP, Inc.
P.O. Box 5037
1201 East Johnson
Jonesboro, Arkansas 72401

Population: Primary and intermediate grades.

Purpose: Correcting articulation.

Description: This program is designed to teach sounds associated with 22 consonant letters or letter combinations. There are 12 audio tapes in each program. Each side of the tape has a 15-minute lesson, or 24 lessons per program. A workbook of spirit masters accompanies the tapes. Sounds are taught in developmental sequence from sounds in isolation to contextual use in stories. The material can be used for developing reading readiness, correcting articulation, and improving nonstandard sound production. It is applicable to all ability levels and can be used independently by the student as it is self-instructional. The program can be helpful to the regular class teacher who has a large group and very little time for individual instruction.

Speech Improvement (1969)
  Merritt Jones and Mary Petlas
  Wadsworth Publishing Co., Inc.
  Belmont, California 94002

Population: Preschool–intermediate.

Purpose: Resource for teachers.

Description: This is not a typical program. It is material for the development of speech sounds presented in a book format. It covers the ideas presented in this chapter, but in more depth. The entire book is devoted to speech sound production and presents specifics on each phoneme plus practices or lessons for developing correct articulation. This is a good source for classroom teachers who do not have the services of a speech pathologist and who need a practical program.

The St. Louis Program (1969)
  Ruth Dray
  Imperial International Learning Corp.
  P.O. Box 548
  Kankakee, Illinois 60901

Population: Intermediate.

Purpose: Correcting nonstandard speech sounds.

Description: This is an audiovisual program specifically designed to instruct children who use nonstandard speech sounds. The sounds are produced on the tapes; the child is asked to respond by repeating the sound, then the sound is produced again on the tape. There are illustrated pupil booklets with each lesson. The teacher's manual is clearly written, and the directions are easy to follow. This program is directed toward specific speech characteristics of the St. Louis area; however, with slight modification it can be used in other regions where nonstandard speech has the same or similar characteristics.

BCP Method Cards, Communication Skills (1977)
Office of the Santa Cruz Superintendent of Schools
Santa Cruz, California 95000

Population: All levels.

Purpose: Language lesson guides.

Description: This is not a commercial program. It is a compilation of lessons or strands for teaching various language skills. It was developed by the Santa Cruz County School District with the aid of a Federal grant and is included in this section as an example of the type of material that is available upon request.

The volume on communication skills could be included as applicable material in several chapters in this manual. The content includes lessons for the development of auditory perception, language comprehension, sign language, and articulation. Each page, or card, contains information as to necessary prerequisites, ability level, interest level, time requirements, suggestions for grouping, and the number of instructors needed to conduct the lesson. The lesson portion also indicates materials and step-by-step procedures. The strands were suggested by contributing teachers and are teacher-tested practical ideas.

Other school districts also have compiled computerized educational programs. The reader should contact the nearest Special Education Resource Center for additional information on similar programs.

Voxcom (1975)
Tapecon, Inc.
10 Latta Road
Rochester, New York 14612

Population: All levels.

Purpose: Individualizing language instruction.

Description: Voxcom is a tape recorder in the traditional sense but also is a card recorder-player. Sounds, words, sentences, and stories can be recorded on talk/tape, a special tape which is affixed to a card. Visuals such as printed words and pictures also can be placed on the card. The card is inserted in the machine and as it passes through, the learner can see and hear the lesson. The cards can be programmed so that the child's response can be recorded on the same tape. Complete lessons can be individualized in minutes. As an oral and written audiovisual aid in language learning, this device, or one like it, has endless possibilities.

REFERENCES

BCP method cards, Communication skills. Santa Cruz, Calif.: Office of Santa Cruz County Superintendent of Schools, 1977.

Betts, E. Factors in readiness for reading. *Educational Administration and Supervision,* 1943, *22,* 199–231.

Costello, J. Articulation instruction based on distinctive features theories. *Language, Speech and Hearing Services in Schools,* 1975, *6,* 61–71.

Dray, R. *The St. Louis program.* Kankakee, Ill.: Imperial International Learning Corp., 1969.

Emerick, L. L., & Hatten, J. T. *Diagnosis and evaluation in speech pathology* (2nd ed.). Englewood Cliffs, N.J.: Prentice-Hall, Inc., 1979.

Faircloth, M. A. Comparison of linguistic feature systems. *Journal of Speech and Hearing Disorders,* 1979, *6,* 376.

Fudala, J. B. *The Arizona articulation proficiency scale* (Rev. ed.). Los Angeles: Western Psychological Services, 1972. (Originally published, 1970).

Goldman, R., & Fristoe, M. *Goldman-Fristoe test of articulation.* Circle Pines, Minn.: American Guidance Service, Inc., 1972.

Jones, M., & Petlas, M. *Speech improvement.* Belmont, Calif.: Wadsworth Publishing Co., Inc., 1969.

Kamara, C., Kamara, A., & Singh, S. *Manual of instruction for distinctive feature wheel.* Athens, Ohio: Speech and Hearing Systems, Inc., 1975.

Marcus, M. *Diagnostic teaching of the language arts.* New York: John Wiley & Sons, Inc., 1977.

Monroe, M. *Children who cannot read.* Chicago: University of Chicago Press, 1932.

Poole, I. Genetic development of articulation of consonant sounds in speech. *Elementary English Review,* 1934, *11,* 159–161.

Speech therapy with beginning sounds. Jonesboro, Ark.: Educational Sensory Programming, Inc., 1970.

Templin, M. C. *Certain language skills in children.* Minneapolis: University of Minnesota Press, 1957.

Travis, L. W., & Rasmus, B. The speech sound discrimination ability of cases with functional disorders of articulation. *Quarterly Journal of Speech,* 1931, *17,* 217–226.

Walsh, H. On certain practical inadequacies of distinctive feature systems. *Journal of Speech and Hearing Disorders,* 1974, *39,* 32–43.

Webber, M. S., *Prediction of word recognition deficits from articulation and auditory discrimination ability at time of first grade entrance.* Unpublished dissertation, Temple University, 1971.

Wepman, J. M., & Morency, A. S. *School achievement as related to speech and perceptual handicaps.* Washington, D.C.: U.S. Department of Health, Education, and Welfare, Bureau of Research, Project #70461, Contract #OEG-2-7-070461-4543, 1971.

Chapter 5

Oral Language

STAGES OF ORAL LANGUAGE DEVELOPMENT

Language is a system of abstract symbols with meaning common to a specific group of users. The language may be composed of sounds as in speaking, recorded marks as in writing, or manual gestures as in signing. Oral language—speaking—is the most convenient form of immediate communication. It is primarily through oral language that individuals act and react within the social environment.

The use of verbal symbols affords the speaker opportunity to seek and gain information, respond instantly to others, and express emotions and needs. Without adequate oral language that is comprehensible to the listener, the speaker literally is handicapped.

Teaching children to communicate through the use of the spoken word may well be the most important educational responsibility of parents and teachers. To assist persons involved with developing oral language skills in children, this chapter deals with stages of language development, the effect of related processes on language, ways of identifying oral language problems, and methods for developing or remediating oral expressive language.

In the normal acquisition of oral language, the learner progresses through stages or periods of development that more or less resemble the development of all other children of the same culture. Stages are interrelated; they are not clearcut, with one ending and another beginning. Each stage may be considered a step toward total language development; the learner may, and usually does, carry over lower level skills while developing the next level or ability.

Stages of language development generally appear within an age range. That is, specific language behaviors can be expected from a child of a given age. However, for many reasons, a child may deviate from the expected age performance and still be developmentally normal.

Vocalization begins at birth with crying and other physiological sounds. During the first and second months, cooing sounds appear. Babbling occurs at about three months and is the main sound behavior until the sixth month, or later. Lallation, which is the stringing together of sounds that resemble speech but have no recognized meaning, may continue well into the real language stage.

With stimulation and reward for efforts, the normal child begins saying recognizable words between nine and fourteen months. At about 1½ to 2 years of age, children begin to put together two-word and three-word sentences. Between the third and fourth years, all basic syntactic structures are evident in connected speech.

First words usually are nouns. *Da Da* and *Ma Ma* tend to lead the way because these sounds are encouraged and rewarded by the proud parents. Nouns such as bottle, water, milk, and names of other environmental objects appear at about 12 months. Receptive language develops rapidly at this period. Many children can respond correctly to complex utterances by others.

Early sentences may consist of a complex word such as "Play," which means "I want to play." By eighteen months the noun-verb sentence pattern usually is established, although elements may be implied as in the example above.

Many children use common prepositions correctly by the age of two. Naming objects is a favorite entertainment. Although authorities differ on vocabulary count, it is not unusual to find children of that age with 300 or more words at their command.

Correct use of pronouns occurs at about age 3. These children begin to comprehend comparisons and apply opposites (big–little) to objects, actions, and people. Recognition of colors and use of color words is not uncommon. Vocabulary usually triples over the two-year level.

The four-year-old may use rather complex sentence structures. Among the language accomplishments of this group are understanding of verb tenses, although endings of irregular verbs may be incorrect; understanding of concepts such as when or where; and changing noun forms correctly. Counting is fun, and the four-year-old knows number names, but order may be confused and digits omitted when counting to ten.

Expressive vocabulary doubles by the five-year level with as many as 1,500 to 1,800 words in correct use. By the time children are five, they have fully intelligible speech, although some misarticulations still may be present.

With the maturation of the central nervous system, which also is complete at about this age, the child develops hemisphere dominance. Left and right are understood and used in describing or giving directions. Concepts such as same and different are comprehended; however, the child's verbalization of the comparison may be in lower terms such as like and not alike.

Linguists do not agree on what constitutes a word. For instance, some feel that a word form change should be considered another word, that is, run, runs, running are three words. Because of the lack of agreement, reports of vocabulary count of five-year-olds and six-year-olds vary greatly. More than two decades ago, Templin (1957) found that the average six-year-old had an expressive vocabulary of approximately 2,500 words and a receptive vocabulary of 15,000 words. It would seem reasonable to assume that with the expanded communication media (radio and television), today's children may exceed these figures.

Sound and Structures

As previously discussed, the stages of language development pertain to sound production and vocabulary. Other aspects of oral language development are equally important but often are overlooked. They are the use of sound and structures to convey meaning. Initially, the application of these linguistic principles is developed informally through unplanned conditioning. This type of primary learning is the base from which comprehensible language develops in the normal native speaker.

Native speakers are those who have learned the system as a first language. They are easy to recognize because they automatically and correctly use the unique linguistic characteristics of the system. They *sound* right when they speak.

Normal children learn to use the sounds and structures of the language to communicate their needs at a very early age. The first to develop is intonation, which includes patterns of pitch, stress or accent, and sound interruptions. When infants produce differentiated cries, they are demonstrating primary usage of intonation.

In communicating through sound, people use intonation to convey meaning. In nonverbal communication, such as whistling, people know if an individual is giving approval or disbelief by the tone or changing pitch and volume. The word "no" uttered by a speaker can mean "you can not" or "you don't really mean it?" The change in meaning is conveyed by altering the sound pattern. A drop in voice indicates a negative; variations with rising inflection suggest inquiry or disbelief. Similarly, the word "produce" can mean vegetables (PRO-duce) or accomplishment (pro-

DUCE). The alteration of meaning is accomplished through tonal inflection.

In connected discourse, the meaning of a larger linguistic unit may depend on intonation as much as on the words. Intonation is the oral counterpart of punctuation. Say the words, "I did that." Say them as a statement indicating the completion of a task. Now say them as a question indicating lack of awareness of what you had done.

Written language uses commas, periods, exclamation marks, and question marks. Oral language uses the difference in tone to change ɑr convey the meaning.

Ordinarily, intonation is not taught; it is learned or acquired without formal instruction. However, children who cannot discriminate differences in pitch and stress may have difficulty in comprehending and in expressing ideas conveyed through intonation. When this occurs, remediation or intervention is required.

As the normal child matures linguistically, the next step is combining words into sentences. Initially, sentences may be single intoned words that imply entire units. From auditory experiences, the child informally learns how to order words into sentences.

American English has basic patterns called sentences. In the early stages of development, the most commonly employed is the noun-verb pattern (Mary works.). This pattern, as do the others, has variations such as noun-verb-adjective and noun-verb-adverb. Other sentence patterns include the following: noun-verb-noun (Mary likes milk); noun-verb-noun-noun (Mary gave her son milk); noun-linking verb-noun (Mary is a mother). By adding other parts of speech, expanding, transforming, and inverting, variations of these patterns are nearly endless.

Incorrect Word Order

Learning the basic patterns and at least common variations is part of normal development and usually is complete by the time the child enters kindergarten. Many of the more sophisticated variations are learned after formal language instruction has begun.

Occasionally a child will use incorrect word order. There are several reasons for this type of language behavior. A child from a bilingual home may apply correct structures for the model's native language but not correct syntactical function order in American English. When this situation is noted, intervention should be initiated. The problem can be corrected easily, but the effectiveness or permanency may be affected if incorrect order is used consistently in the home.

The second generic reason for incorrect word order is central nervous system dysfunction. Problems of this type are referred to as specific language disabilities. The dysfunction may affect receptive, expressive, or both processes and is discussed under neurological dysfunction later in this chapter.

Structure Words

As stated earlier, the development of the ability to combine words, or to form sentences, occurs in an unstructured fashion. The child who uses a noun and a verb has formed a simple sentence. The expansion of the sentence depends on the learner's ability to acquire and use structure words.

Structure words are noun markers, verb markers, phrase markers, question markers, and sentence connectors. They include such words as *and, the, because, when,* and *up.*

Structure words have little meaning or content except in language. They do not refer to concrete objects or specific places and events. Of the many words available to the user of American English, the smallest linguistic group includes structure words; however, they are among the most frequently used.

Structure words allow the communicator to convey meaning clearly and to express ideas with fluency. Complex and compound sentences are dependent upon correct use of structure words.

Oral language difficulty with structure words is relatively rare. The exclusion of structure words in a conversation is a sign of immature speech. The problem is associated primarily with mental retardation or experience deprivation. Remediation can be tedious and requires much repetition or drill.

Word-Form Changes

Correct usage of word-form changes is probably the last structural function to be learned or used correctly. Word-form changes include plurals, possessives, adjective comparisons, affixes, and verb parts. The ability to form simple plurals such as *s* to *toy* occurs at about the same time as the child acquires the word for expression. Even normal children attempt to generalize and apply basic rules to all words. For example, "Here are two sheeps," is not uncommon. Similarly, the addition of *ed* to signify past tense often is applied incorrectly (sing*ed*).

The application of word-form changes that are consistent occur developmentally until about the time the child enters school. Many of the exceptions are not learned or used correctly until age nine or ten.

The correct use of word-form changes is perhaps the most difficult linguistic task for the language learner. In American English this may be attributed to the inconsistency and variations of the language.

Many normal children have difficulty using plurals and verb forms correctly. The mentally retarded often have extremely limited knowledge in this area. Speech characterized by incorrect word forms also is common to the culturally different. In most cases this is not a language disability; it is a matter of experience and learning.

RELATED PROCESSES

Oral language is a form of expression that is the end product of many processes. A step-by-step consideration of processes affecting oral language should include intellectual, neurological, visual, auditory, and motor functions as well as the effect of experience and motivation on these interrelated processes and abilities.

Intelligence and Oral Language

The relationship of intelligence and the development of language is a well-established fact. Measurement of intelligence is based on level of language development. Oral language, particularly vocabulary, is generally considered the most reliable indicator of intelligence. However, the premise that language development is dependent upon intelligence contains a dichotomy.

If intelligence is accepted as the mental ability to learn and to reason, it also must be recognized that without language, learning and reasoning cannot, or probably will not, occur beyond an instinctive or reflexive level. There must be a system of symbols with which to think (reason), otherwise thinking (reasoning) is extremely limited. And, if intelligence is mental ability without which people cannot learn, it would seem reasonable to assume that without mental ability they cannot learn a language system.

The dilemma appears to resemble the old question, "Which came first, the chicken or the egg?" The answer may never be known to the question, "Does language develop because of the level of intelligence or does intelligence develop because of language?" What is known is that decreased mental capacity affects language learning, and that without language a person with potentially high-level intelligence is limited in reasoning and learning ability. The relevance of this understanding becomes clear when establishing realistic language goals for the mentally retarded and when attempting to determine the intelligence of a language-handicapped individual using a traditional language-based IQ test.

Auditory Abilities and Oral Language

It is reasonably safe to say that in normal development of oral expressive language, an individual first must acquire auditory receptive language. For this to occur, the language learner must have auditory sensitivity within the speech range (without or with amplification); that is, the learner must have the ability to hear others speak. Secondly, the learner must have the ability to perceive speech correctly in relation to order or sequence and intonation or pitch, and with clarity or fine difference discrimination. The learner must have repeated experiences hearing others speak because it is through repetition that the individual builds lasting impressions that are stored as memories that are retrievable when needed. And lastly, the learner must have the necessary neurological integration or intelligence to retrieve or remember the sound combinations called words, their varied meanings, and their order in connected discourse.

In addition to these abilities, which are basically external or receptive abilities, the learner must have the ability to reauditorize or hear himself. In the development of correct speech and language, the individual experiments with sound matching. Sound matching may occur when repeating, as in echolalic speech. For example, a mother says, "Pretty baby," and the child attempts to repeat or match the sounds. At a higher level of development, a speaker may recall the sound and meaning of a word and attempt to match a verbalization with the memory.

In individuals with highly developed oral language skills, sound matching (or hearing themselves) often is so automatic that it is not at a conscious level. In fact, it is not until an obvious or unintentional sound error occurs that they become aware of this particular auditory ability, yet it is an internal monitor for speech sound production.

SPEECH SOUNDS AND LANGUAGE

Oral language is a system of speech sounds that are intended to convey meaning. If sounds are distorted, omitted, or substituted, the message may be unclear. Similarly, if rate is too slow, too rapid, or uneven, communication is affected. In American English a simple change of stress or syllabication can change the meaning of a word or make it unrecognizable.

Read the following sentence aloud. Say the words as spelled and stressed:

"Də yəgitəmācy of də ishū́ iz kear."

Now decode the message. What does it mean? Does it make sense?

Substitute *th* for *d, l* for *y, j* for *g,* and add an *l* after the *k* in kear. The spelling is not correct American English but you can identify the words. Your knowledge of American English will guide you to the pronunciation.

The sentence is: "The legitímacy of the issúe is clear." The message now has meaning because you read the sentence with the correct sounds and with the stress used in your native tongue, standard American English.

The relationship and importance of speech sound production to the intent of language should be clear. Oral language facilitates communication when the speaker and the listener use the same sound system.

LANGUAGE EXPERIENCE

With a few exceptions, all children have language experiences. It is the quality and quantity of the experiences during critical periods that affect development. Causes for language delay or faulty development attributed to the environment include nonstandard speech, bilingualism, impoverished language environment, overstimulating environment, and emotional instability.

The effect of nonstandard speech and language in the home goes beyond that discussed in Chapter 4 under sound production. Nonstandard language may include errors such as pronominal speech, incorrect noun and verb forms, and lack of tense and number agreement. In standard American English a speaker says, "My aunt has a car." Using a nonstandard form, the speaker might say, "My aunt she gots a car." Such cases do not lack understanding of linguistic structures and vocabulary is not lacking. They simply are different from the standard form used in most academic settings and by the general population of the country.

Bilingualism as a possible cause of language delay needs clarification. A home in which two or more languages are spoken does not necessarily mean that developing language learners will have difficulty in acquiring American English. The fact is, many children have the capacity to learn several languages simultaneously. However, when the primary language model does not speak American English, or does so only partially and incorrectly, the burden of acquiring two languages may be too difficult for the young child. Occasionally when this occurs, neither language develops fully, and remediation is required. The more common situation is one in which the child correctly learns the model language; American English becomes the second language and may be limited in both receptive and expressive forms. As in the nonstandard situation, the child does not have delayed language, just delayed American English. The condition is quite dissimilar from that of a specific language disability.

In Chapter 4, the need for language stimulation is explained as it pertains to developing speech sounds. However, the importance of environmental language stimulation cannot be overstressed. In a home where language is viewed primarily as a tool for meeting basic needs, the child has relatively little modeling from which to learn. When communication is restricted to short verbalizations, such as commands and admonishments, the child is not motivated and may be afraid to respond verbally. Environmental situations of this sort lead to negative conditioning and underdeveloped language.

On the other hand, overstimulation may be as detrimental to language development as the above situation. Picture a home where several adults and many children of varying ages reside. Radio and television sets are blaring away. Half a dozen conversations are occurring simultaneously. For the child who has not developed auditory discrimination, these sounds may become an impenetrable wall, a totality without differentiation. Individual phonemes and words are not heard; they are perceived as a whole.

Under these conditions, several things may occur. The child may learn and develop acute discriminatory abilities; the child may produce numerous misarticulations and use limited vocabulary; or the child may withdraw, tuning out sound because the barrier is incomprehensible and even frightening.

In the first of these conditions, the child undoubtedly is a superior auditory learner. In either of the two other situations, the child has immature or delayed language development that will require remediation.

The last of the suggested causes, emotional instability, may well be the most difficult to identify and remediate correctly. When a parent is unstable and displays erratic behavior, the effect can be far reaching.

The emotionally disturbed often present as normal, interested parents. Their language may be average to superior. When giving case history information, they speak fluently and indicate that they talk with and encourage conversation with the child. In fact, they do on occasion talk and participate in language play with the child. It is the other times that foster language problems.

It is the inconsistent adult behavior, first talking and playing, and then screaming, crying, and being abusive that confuses, frustrates, and frightens the child. Under such conditions the child does not know when or how to respond verbally. Saying nothing may not be the right behavior, but may be viewed as safer than speaking.

Part of the far-reaching effect of learning in an emotionally unstable environment is that the child may generalize and expect this type of behavior from all adults. When this occurs, language is delayed and the child may be labeled incorrectly.

Children who do not speak freely and do not use language at an expectancy level may be diagnosed as mentally retarded, learning disabled, or emotionally disturbed. Such children may not have learning problems, simply parent problems. They have learned quite well; they understand that if they don't talk to an adult, they might be safe. Appropriate remediation for these children may well begin with the troubled parent. Remediation through building confidence and language modeling usually is required as well.

LANGUAGE LEARNING DEFICITS

There are many types and causes of oral language deficits. The most common are maturational in nature. Most learners will outgrow these deficits and are the most easily remediated when conditions are favorable for therapy.

Unfortunately there also are children who do not develop oral language, or who have language deficits because of central nervous system dysfunction. Among these groups are the mentally retarded, the specific language disabled, and the cerebral palsied.

Delayed Language Development

The term "delayed language" can be misleading. It is intended to imply that the language learner has not developed speech at an average rate. This text attempts to distinguish various types of delayed language.

A child may be slower in developing language than a sister or a brother, yet this may be normal for that individual. Comparing a child's language development to that of siblings is more than unfair. Similarly, comparing language development to chronological peers also may be using incorrect norms. Language development should be considered in relation to mental capacity, experience, motivation, and other factors relevant to a specific child.

There is no hard-and-fast rule for when language will or should reach a developmental landmark. If an average child raised in a reasonably stimulating language environment begins saying words at about one year, it can be expected that, all things being equal, a truly mentally retarded child will begin speaking proportionately later. At least this is true for most educable mentally retarded. This does not necessarily apply to the trainable nor to the severely and profoundly retarded.

In addition to lowered mental capacity, or rate of development, the effect of any concomitant debilitating condition must be considered in determining language delays. In the case of a mentally retarded child with cerebral palsy, the inability to communicate may be the result of the lack of motor control. While speech is delayed or not present, it is not necessarily delayed language development.

In children with delayed speech who will develop to a normal or acceptable level, the cause of the delay must be taken into account. The most common causes are maturational lag, environment, and personality.

Maturational lag in this context refers to delayed, or slower, central nervous system development. Chapter 1 describes the central nervous system in relation to auditory processes. These same process dysfunctions, which may inhibit receptive abilities, can and do affect expressive skills. The child who cannot process auditorily at a developmental rate will be unable to express similar types of information.

When maturational lag results from delayed central nervous system development, the cause may not be readily identifiable. An electroencephalogram will show aberrant brain patterns related to seizure and other disorders but may not indicate retarded neurodevelopment. Identification may be based on clusters of behaviors that are common to children with developmental delays. For example, many children with delayed language also are slower in developing motor skills.

The delayed neuromuscular development and the delayed language may result from retarded myelin growth. As noted in Chapter 2, the myelin sheath is not complete at birth and continues to develop during the early years of life. The myelin sheath acts as a protective cover for the nerves and facilitates transmission of impulses. Retarded and incomplete myelin formation may impede language development.

Maturational lag also may be attributed to emotional maladjustment. A child may not develop language at an expected rate because of internal conflict. The child may be quite able intellectually and motorically, but because of external pressures becomes disturbed or confused. For example, a parent may demand sophisticated language from a child. When the learner cannot meet the language standards, the child becomes confused and frightened. As a result, the child may retain immature speech and language patterns or stop speaking altogether.

The opposite behavior by parents also can cause emotional instability, with resulting delayed language. Parents who need a dependent child also exert pressure. This type of parent does too much, is too helpful, and is not demanding enough. If a child wants something, it can get the parents' attention with a grunt, a point, or a cry and a guessing game begins, "Do you want_____?" This behavior continues until the child is satisfied. Oral language is not needed; the parent speaks for the child, and consequently speech does not grow or develops far below the average rate.

Central Nervous System Impairment

The term aphasia often is used to describe a language disability associated with central nervous system dysfunction. In fact, the term is used too often. Aphasia is a disruption of language function. Childhood aphasia, while not uncommon, is extremely difficult to diagnose correctly. The term is often applied inappropriately to language deficits that do not have organic causes.

Aphasia is caused by injury or improper development of the brain. The impairment is in the critical speech area. While both hemispheres have the capacity to receive, store, integrate, and send language, the critical language area in most people is in the left half of the brain.

The most frequent cause of aphasia in children is anoxia—the lack of oxygen to the brain. During prenatal development, it can cause improper fetal development. At or after birth, a lack of oxygen or an insult or injury to the head can cause deterioration of brain cell tissues. Brain damage can occur as a result of extremely high temperature. Aphasia may be the result of fevers that accompany diseases such as encephalitis and meningitis.

If the brain damage occurs at birth, it may cause delayed language development. If the affected area is impaired sufficiently, language may not develop. These children often are misdiagnosed as being mentally retarded or emotionally disturbed.

When damage occurs after the onset of language, the loss may be partial or complete. In such cases, it is somewhat easier to recognize because the cause usually is known and the behavior is more readily distinguishable from other conditions.

Aphasia may be receptive, which is a lack of ability to understand oral language while intellectual capacity is adequate. It may be a dysfunction at the level of integration where symbols are used for thinking, or it may be expressive—the level where symbols are used as a means of communicating. If the dysfunction is receptive or integrative, it may appear to be expressive because these abilities are necessary for formulating thoughts with words.

The individual with oral expressive aphasia is unable to use verbal symbols (words). The condition at its extreme renders the person unable to speak; in its mildest form, the impaired language user may have difficulty in finding or saying a specific word at the appropriate time.

METHODS FOR EVALUATING LANGUAGE

The diagnosis and labeling of specific language problems should be done by highly skilled, trained professionals. However, there are informal methods and commercial tests that classroom teachers and paraprofessionals can use for screening or initial identification. The material in this section is indicative of the numerous available materials.

Informal Techniques, Teacher Prepared

The first and foremost means of identifying a possible language problem is quite simple: *Listen to the child.* Give the child opportunity to speak. Observe language in various settings such as during an instructional period, in structured and unstructured play or recreation, and in an informal social time.

Compare the child's language to that of his peers. Remember, peers are not just other children of the same chronological age; they are from the same cultural background and have similar intelligence.

A somewhat more structured form of observation may be achieved with a language sample, which is simply a timed period of conversation. The purpose may be to establish level of vocabulary, articulation, or syntax.

The first step in taking a language sample is to get a good tape recorder. Allow the child to use the device several times before taping the sample. When the child feels comfortable speaking into the recorder, the sample will be more accurate.

Consider your objective. Then prepare material that will aid you in eliciting the language response that will provide the information you seek. Prepare questions on topics that will be of interest to the child. Ask the child to respond to your questions. The language should be spontaneous for the most part. The following suggestions can be used to engage the child in conversation. The type of problem suspected governs the approach.

Vocabulary

Select pictures that depict scenes, objects, or actions of interest to the child. Ask the child to describe what is happening or how you use the objects.

Use an object or a picture. Say to the child, "Here is a _____ ; think about it for a few seconds. Then I want you to tell me three stories about it." The number of stories required would depend on the child's age, etc.

Show the child an object such as a car. Say, "This is a toy car. Tell me as many words as you can think of that describe this car or a real car."

Use a picture of food, people, animals, or an athletic event. Ask the child to name as many other things like this as he can. For example, "Here is a picture of a hot dog. Tell me what we do with this and then name as many other things that we use the same way as you can."

Syntax

Use the first two ideas under vocabulary.

Show a series of cartoon pictures. Ask the child to look at the pictures and then tell you the story. For some children you can remove the cartoon strip and ask the child to recall the story (sequential memory).

Use a series of pictures that show comparison, tense, or number. Ask the child to give you a sentence for each. For example, the first picture might depict a little child, the second two larger children, and the third three adolescents. The desired response might be, "Here is a little child; here are two bigger children; and these three are the biggest."

Show the child two pictures depicting action such as a child about to eat a piece of cake and one after the cake is nearly consumed. Ask the child what is happening in each picture. The desired response might be, "He is going to eat. He has eaten." This procedure can be used for several language elements.

Tell a short story. Ask the child to retell the story. Repeating a story is not as desirable as spontaneous samples because auditory memory can affect results, and the language may be a repetition of the model's language and not an accurate sample.

Commercial Language Assessment Instruments

The criteria for selecting material for evaluation vary with the user. The classroom teacher generally considers validity, ease and time of administration, applicability of the data to a specific group of children, and the cost of the material. The same criteria are used here in selecting a small sample of instruments from the large number that are commercially available.

A Spoken Word Count (1969)
Joseph M. Wepman, Ph.D., and Wilbur Haas, Ph.D.
Language Research Associates, Inc.
P.O. Box 2085
Palm Springs, California 92262

Population: Applicable at all levels.

Purpose: Identify word use deficiency.

Description: This test determines the use and frequency of words and parts of speech in a child's vocabulary. Information related to a child's speech can be compared to three normative, chronological lists.

Bankson Language Screening Test (1977)
Nicholas W. Bankson, Ph.D.
University Park Press
Chamber of Commerce Building
Baltimore, Maryland 21202

Population: Primary and intermediate.

Purpose: Quick screening of general usage.

Description: Although numerous language screening devices exist, this measure is selected because it includes several items that are not oral expressive language but may well affect language development. The test takes a language specialist approximately 25 minutes to administer. It helps to identify children who need in-depth diagnostic work and to select a caseload. The test covers morphological rules, semantic knowledge, syntactic rules, and visual and auditory perception. Standardization population includes children age 4.1 to 8.0 years.

Inventory of Language Abilities (1972)
Esther H. Minskoff, Ph.D., Douglas E. Wiesman, Ed.D., and J. Gerald Minskoff, Ed.D.
Educational Performance Associates
563 Westview Avenue
Ridgefield, New Jersey 07657

Population: Primary levels.

Purpose: Identify possible language disabilities.

Description: The inventory helps teachers and clinicians in identifying children who may have a specific language disability. As in the Illinois

Test of Psycholinguistic Abilities, 12 Linguistic areas tapped include: auditory reception, visual reception, auditory association, verbal expression, manual expression, auditory memory, visual memory, grammatic closure, auditory closure, and sound blending. The information from the checklist questions can be used to determine need for diagnostic testing and remediation. One of the values of the instrument is that the teacher is directed to observe specific language behaviors.

James Language Dominance Test (1974)
Peter James
Learning Concepts
2501 North Lamar
Austin, Texas 78705

Purpose: Identify first language.

Population: Primary and intermediate levels.

Description: This test determines which language, Spanish or American English, the child comprehends and speaks better. The teacher can ascertain if the child uses both equally well or is superior in one. Designed to be used with Mexican-Americans, this test needs vocabulary changes when other Spanish-speaking children are assessed. Testing takes about seven to ten minutes. It can be used for determining class placement, need for additional testing, grouping, and program planning. Evaluators should be bilingual.

Picture Articulation and Language Screening Test (1976)
William C. Rodgers
Word Making Productions
P.O. Box 15038
Salt Lake City, Utah 84115

Purpose: Articulation and language quick screen.

Population: Primary levels.

Description: This screening device can be administered in a classroom setting. It takes about two minutes per child to screen articulation and language. Since the administrator needs a minimum of instruction, aides and volunteers can give it. It is recommended for use at the primary level or in remedial settings.

Preschool Language Scale (1969)
Irla Lee Zimmerman, Violette G. Steiner, and Roberta L. Evatt
The Charles E. Merrill Publishing Company
Box 508
Columbus, Ohio 43216

Purpose: To determine age placement of language development.

Population: One-and-one-half to seven years.

Description: This scale attempts to determine receptive, expressive, and phonetic skills. It is an easy-to-use scale that produces an age placement. The manual is written clearly and each measurement item is explained as to rationale, with research references included. The age range is 1½ to 7 years. Administration time is approximately half an hour. The scale is particularly good for use with young handicapped children such as those with cerebral palsy. The material is part of the *Slow Learner Series* edited by Kephart.

Verbal Language Development Scale (1971)
Merlin J. Mecham
American Guidance Service, Inc.
Publishers' Building
Circle Pines, Minnesota 55014

Purpose: Determine life activity vocabulary.

Population: Mentally retarded.

Description: This is an extension of the communication portion of the Vineland Social Maturity Scale. It gives a picture of the language used by the mentally retarded in daily life activities.

The Test of Language Development (TOLD) (1977)
Phyllis L. Newcomer, Ph.D., and Donald D. Hammill, Ph.D.
PRO-ED
33 Perry Brooks Building
Austin, Texas 78701

Purpose: Language comparison to norms.

Population: Four to eight years.

Description: TOLD measures semantics, syntax, and phonology of children from ages 4 to 8 years, 11 months. The test consists of five principal and two supplemental subtests. The authors created this test by incorporating and revising some of the best ideas of older measures. They eliminated the need for using subtests from three or four tests to compare strengths and weaknesses of a child's language. Test scores are given as language age equivalencies. A raw score converted to a Language Age Score means that the child is performing at a level comparable to children of a specific age group.

METHODS AND MATERIALS FOR DEVELOPING ORAL LANGUAGE

The total responsibility of teaching oral language formerly rested on the family unit. Undoubtedly, that period of human history was a sad time for many exceptional individuals. Language learning was not structured, and structure is necessary for the atypical language learner.

Fortunately, today's special child has improved language learning opportunities, both in the home and in formal educational settings. The teacher need not be a trained professional because many of the available commercial materials are well-thought-out programs with easy-to-follow directions. The following suggestions, commercial materials, and programs can be used by classroom teachers, language specialists, paraprofessionals, and parents.

Teacher-Prepared Methods and Materials

Vocabulary Development

Activity 1. Select an object with which the child is familiar but does not use the label in expression. It is helpful to begin with a toy or an item of food. Once the procedure is learned, any noun or part of speech can be taught.

For this example, the word *ball* is the noun to be learned. Show the child the ball. Say, "ball." Help the child form the sound if necessary. Indicate verbally or by gesture that the word is to be repeated. Praise any attempted production that resembles the sound of the word.

Continue this procedure until the child says ball. In succeeding lessons the procedure is repeated until the child is saying the word with relative ease and without prompting. Allow the child to play with the ball as a reward.

Show the child the ball again. Ask verbally or with gestures, "What is this?" When the child responds correctly without hesitation, it can be assumed that the word has been learned. However, regular reinforcement through repeated experiences is suggested.

After several names of toys have been learned, place two or more known objects in a box. Have children close their eyes and select an object. If a child names the item correctly, it becomes that pupil's toy for the day.

To add other parts of speech to the child's vocabulary, use the procedure described above. For verbs, say, "bounce ball." Have the child perform the movement. To teach adjectives say, "red ball," and for an adverb, "throw quickly!" Always begin with a known word. Do not attempt to pair two unfamiliar words.

Activity 2. To develop vocabulary in more advanced language users or the gifted, it is sometimes necessary to tap a human weakness. In this case it is the power or urge to persuade others.

Select a word that is not in the children's listening vocabulary. The word should have several meanings and synonyms. Place the various definitions and the synonyms on individual tapes, using one definition per tape. Make a tape for each child in the group. In addition, make a tape that lists all of the definitions as they appear in the dictionary and then the synonyms, but not their obvious meanings.

Give each child a tape. Tell the group that they are going to learn a new word, and that you have put the definitions and synonyms on the tapes. They are to listen to their tape and learn the meaning of the new word. They are not to discuss the word before they meet later as a group.

When the group meets, explain that some of the definitions are correct for the new word, others are not. It is their job to persuade the other members of the group that the definition they have is the correct one. They can use their knowledge of the root words, derivation, affixes, and so on.

Each member of the group gets an opportunity to guess the correct meaning. They then list what they believe to be correct and in the order in which they believe the definitions appear in the dictionary.

Play the tape with the correct definitions. Children who have identified the meanings correctly get points. A record of successes can be kept. This builds interest in learning new vocabulary so that they might know a word should you select it. It also fosters listening and thinking abilities.

Additional points can be earned every time a child can and does use the word correctly in the course of the educational day. Use may be verified by at least one listener.

Syntactical Development

Activity 1. To develop the correct use of plurals, the materials may resemble those used for evaluating. In fact, procedures for determining skills can be very helpful in teaching, as in the following suggested method.

Collect pictures of items or objects that have irregular plural forms. Group them in categories, that is, unchanged spellings as in fish and sheep; spellings where the final consonant is changed before adding an affix, as in leaf to leaves; and spelling changes, as man to men.

Make a list of sentences in which the singular and plural forms are used. Show the child a picture of the noun in question. Demonstrate correct usage by reading the sentence. Read the sentence again. When you come to the noun, pause and indicate that the child is to fill in the blank. Continue this through the group until the child gets the idea.

In the lessons that follow, begin the session by reviewing the sentences learned the day before. After reviewing, ask the child to make up a sentence like yours. Show the picture or objects. Attempt to get spontaneous production. Help the child when necessary.

When the child is developing sentences using correct plural forms of known words that have been practiced, add a picture of an object that follows the pattern but has not been used previously. If the child is able to generalize and make the change, it is indicative of internalized learning.

After completion of two or more sets, mix the objects or pictures. This will require the child to move from form to form and will help you in further determining the level of understanding.

Activity 2. To teach tense, use the cartoon strip idea. In the first picture, show someone or something about to perform an action. A silly picture helps to hold interest. For example: A peanut that has human characteristics that include eyes and mouth is looking at an elephant. In the second picture the peanut is beginning to eat the elephant. In the last picture the elephant is gone, and the peanut has a bulge in the middle and a smile on its face. The desired response includes the following: is going to eat, is eating, and has eaten, or ate.

This idea can be used in the comparison of adjectives. Have a set of cards. Each card depicts a different size, shape, or color or other comparable concept. An example of adjective comparison might be three trees of various sizes. The desired response would be: the tree is big, this tree is bigger, and this tree is the biggest.

COMMERCIAL MATERIALS

From the wealth of excellent materials and programs available, some of the samples selected are traditional, others are unique. For the most part, these programs are relatively inexpensive and generally within the average materials budget.

ANCHOR: A Handbook of Vocabulary Discovery Techniques for the Classroom Teacher (1970)
Mary E. Platts
Educational Services, Inc.
P.O. Box 219
Stevensville, Michigan 49127

Purpose: Vocabulary enrichment.

Population: Intermediate levels.

Description: *ANCHOR* is one of a series designed to provide enrichment activities. (*SPICE* may be the best known of the series.) This volume is designed to aid in vocabulary development of children functioning at the fourth-grade to eighth-grade levels. Although most average students will enjoy these lessons, they are particularly good for stretching the minds of the gifted and talented. Titles begin with "Chinese English" and end with "Notable Quotes." Activities include word puzzles, brain teasers, word meanings, and many more. The material is very good for planning lessons when you don't feel like creating your own ideas.

Developing Oral Language in Young Children (1974)
John F. Murphy, M.Ed., and Charles A. O'Donnell, M.Ed.
Educators Publishing Services, Inc.
75 Moulton Street
Cambridge, Massachusetts 02138

Purpose: Language development and enrichment.

Population: Primary levels.

Description: This material is designed to develop language through listening, self-image, vocabulary and perception, number concepts, motor activities, and fun games. It can be used by parents and professionals equally well. The authors suggest instructional periods of fifteen minutes. They include a brief guide of what can be expected in normal development and a charting procedure for a period of one year for checking the child's development. The vocabulary in this program is extremely interesting, as are some of the assigned tasks.

Developmental Language Lessons (1977)
Charlene W. Mowery
Teaching Resources Corporation
100 Boylston Street
Boston, Massachusetts 02116

Purpose: CRT, placement and instruction.

Population: Primary—intermediate levels.

Description: This material is an all-in-one diagnostic and developmental program that uses criteria reference testing techniques. It can be used by classroom teachers and speech clinicians. The first step is diagnostic. When the child's level has been established and strengths and weaknesses determined, the pupil is placed in a developmental or remedial program. Lessons are printed clearly on cards neatly packaged in a compact box. The lessons last from three to twenty minutes. Criteria reference testing is planned to monitor the child's progress. Instructional areas include noun modifiers, personal pronouns, main and secondary verbs, negatives, conjunctions, interrogative reversals, and Wh- questions. This program can be very helpful in writing Individualized Education Programs (IEPs) for children with language delay or culturally different speech.

GOAL: Level I Language Development (1977)
    Merle B. Karnes, Ph.D.
    Milton Bradley Playschool
    Springfield, Massachusetts 01101

Purpose: Develop prereading skills.

Population: Preschool—primary.

Description: This program is designed specifically to help teachers working with prereading skills. Lesson plan cards for eleven language skills are easy to follow and implement. Areas covered are auditory reception, verbal expression, auditory association, auditory sequential memory, and grammatic closure. These materials can be used to remediate weaknesses noted on the Illinois Test of Psycholinguistic Abilities and as supplements to an oral expressive language problem.

Mainstreaming Language Arts and Social Studies: Special Ideas and Activities for the Whole Class (1977)
    Ann H. Adams, Charles R. Coble, and Paul B. Hounshell
    Goodyear Publishing Company, Inc.
    Santa Monica, California

Purpose: Total language reinforcement program.

Population: Primary grades through 7.

Description: The title of this material is self-explanatory: it does what it says. The material includes a wide variety of activities and lessons for regular teachers with mainstreamed children and for those who have special learners who have not yet been labeled as such. This could have been included in the section on written language because some of the activities seek to develop reading and writing. There are suggestions or themes for 36 weeks. The ideas are planned for elementary students, but some lessons are appropriate for junior high.

Newby Visual Language (1976)
    Robert Newby, M.A.
    Newby Visualanguage, Inc.
    P.O. Box 121
    Eagleville, Pennsylvania 19408

Purpose: Total language understanding and enrichment.

Population: Hearing impaired and oral language disabilities.

Description: This material was developed for work with deaf and hearing impaired individuals but is applicable to those in the hearing population who have specific language disabilities or inadequate language development. The program is divided into separate series covering verbs, adjectives, pronouns, and prepositions. For example, Series 1-Verbs, Set A, deals with 83 commonly used idioms. The material consists of 249 cartoon-styled pictures that can be used for determining special needs and for a flexible instructional program. The drawings appeal to upper primary through secondary level learners. The lessons can be for receptive auditory language, oral expressive language, or written language. The pictures are black-and-white and can be reproduced for Dittos or transparencies but not for producing master sets. The wide variety of pictured content affords the creative teacher opportunities to use this material for many purposes other than those suggested by the author. Teachers of the gifted have found this material helpful for creative writing, story telling, and so on.

On Stage: Wally, Bertha, and You (1971)
    Alex Urlan
    Encyclopedia Britannica Educational Corporation
    425 North Michigan Avenue
    Chicago, Illinois 60611

Purpose: Language enrichment.

Population: Primary levels.

Description: Wally and Bertha, two lovable puppets, introduce young children to fun-filled and creative learning experiences. While the activities are focused on the affective domain, lessons involve language development and communication. Children with limited exposure to standard American English will benefit greatly from the language enrichment activities.

The *Teacher's Handbook* contains an Objective Chart—a quick cross-reference guide for selecting objectives and activities that will meet the identified needs of each student. This provides assistance for teachers who are using Individualized Education Programs. Areas in language and communication include oral language development, listening skills, classification skills, and story telling. Additional teaching activities are included in the Resource Paks for students needing further experiences. The activities are motivating to children, and Bertha and Wally add their dialogue to stimulate the discussions.

Opposite Talk (1972)
    Westinghouse Learning Press
    100 Park Avenue
    New York, New York 10017

Purpose: Improve vocabulary.

Population: Primary levels.

Description: This word-growth program of music, humor, songs, and narration is designed to help primary grade children develop a basic speaking vocabulary and word relationships. To provide a systematic approach, a pretest is included for determining the initial placement of each student. Filmstrips with accompanying cassettes or records along with preprinted masters provide activities in the auditory and visual modalities. The materials can be completed in teacher-directed lessons or in independent study. A posttest is included to determine the final mastery of the concepts. The *Teacher's Guide* provides a detailed description of each activity plus follow-up and extension activities. This program is especially useful for students with deficiencies in vocabulary because of cultural and/or educational difficulties.

Peabody Language Development Kits (1965)
    Lloyd M. Dunn, Ph.D., and James O. Smith, Ed.D.
    American Guidance Service, Inc.
    Publishers' Building
    Circle Pines, Minnesota 55014

Purpose: Develop listening and speaking.

Population: Preschool—primary levels.

Description: This material has become a standard in language develop-ment. The instructor need not be a trained professional to use the kit effectively. Included are a variety of audiovisual materials as well as manipulative objects, puppets, and so forth. The directions are clear and the lesson plans are easy to follow. One of the advantages of this kit is that the user is free to modify lessons to meet the needs of the child being instructed.

Speaking Over Barriers (1971)
  Bell System
  The Pacific Telephone and Telegraph Company

Purpose: Develop telephone skills.

Population: Mentally retarded primary levels.

Description: This is an interesting guide to developing telephone skills with the mentally retarded. However, its use is far broader in scope. The suggested lessons include such learning concepts as auditory discrimina-tion, vocabulary, number concepts, speech and articulation, manners, dexterity, and safety. It can be used with mentally retarded children for whom it was developed, others with specific language disabilities, and/or those who are lacking in experience. It is an excellent additional source for teachers who want variety and practicability in their curriculum.

The MWM Program for Developing Language Abilities (1972)
  Esther H. Minskoff, Ph.D.; Douglas E. Wiesman, Ed.D.; and J. Gerald
    Minskoff, Ed.D.
  Educational Performance Associates
  563 Westview Avenue
  Ridgefield, New Jersey 07657

Purpose: Remediate specific language disabilities.

Population: Primary and intermediate levels.

Description: The MWM Program is designed to improve basic psycholin-guistic skills necessary for total communication. The kit includes an easy-to-follow *Teacher's Guide,* an *Inventory of Language Abilities,* and manuals for developing receptive and expressive language abilities. The inventory is a checklist for observing specific behaviors. The categories on language behaviors are auditory reception, visual reception, auditory association, visual association, verbal expression, manual expression, auditory memory, visual memory, grammatic closure, visual closure, and the combination of auditory closure and sound blending. The program includes material and methods for developing ability in each of the inventory categories. This is especially helpful for remediating specific language disabilities as noted on the Illinois Test of Psycholinguistic Abilities.

What's Goin' On? (1974)
    Keith D. Vogt
    Learning Stuff
    P.O. Box 4123
    Modesto, California 95352

Purpose: Develop vocabulary, sentences and sequential memory.

Population: Primary—intermediate levels.

Description: *What's Goin' On?* is a set of 24 cards (6½″ by 14″). Each card has three pictures depicting sequential action in a situation. The pictures are story starters intended to encourage children to speak and write in sentences or create entire stories. The pictures depict a variety of experiences from buying ice cream to a frog race. The drawings are appropriate for upper level primary and beginning intermediate or older mentally retarded students. The cards can be used for developing vocabulary, tense, sentence structure, and sequential memory.

REFERENCES

Adams, A. H., Coble, C. R., & Hounshell, P. B. *Mainstreaming language arts and social studies: Special ideas and activities for the whole class.* Santa Monica, Calif.: Goodyear Publishing Co., Inc., 1977.

Bankson, N. W. *Bankson language screening test.* Baltimore: University Park Press, 1977.

Dunn, L. M., & Smith, J. O. *Peabody language development kits.* Circle Pines, Minn.: American Guidance Service, Inc., 1965.

James, P. *James language dominance test.* Austin, Tex.: Learning Concepts, 1974.

Karnes, M. B. *Goal: Level I language development.* Springfield, Mass.: Milton Bradley, 1977.

Mecham, M. J. *Verbal language development scale.* Circle Pines, Minn.: American Guidance Service, Inc., 1971.

Minskoff, E. H., Wiesman, D. E., & Minskoff, J. E. *Inventory of language abilities.* Ridgefield, N.J.: Educational Performance Associates, 1972.

_____ . *The MWM program for developing language abilities.* Ridgefield, N.J.: Educational Performance Associates, 1972.

Mowery, C. W. *Developmental language lessons.* Boston: Teaching Resources Corp., 1977.

Murphy, J. F., & O'Donnell, C. A. *Developing oral language in young children.* Cambridge, Mass.: Educators Publishing Services, Inc., 1974.

Newby, R. *Newby visualanguage.* Eagleville, Pa.: Newby Visualanguage, Inc., 1976.

Newcomer, P. L., & Hammill, D. D. *The test of language development.* Austin, Tex.: Pro-Ed, 1977.

Opposite talk, New York: Westinghouse Learning Press, 1972.

Platts, M. E. *Anchor: A handbook of vocabulary discovery techniques for the classroom teacher.* Stevensville, Mich.: Educational Services, Inc., 1970.

Rodgers, W. C. *Picture articulation and language screening test.* Salt Lake City, Utah: Word Making Productions, 1976.

Speaking Over barriers. The Pacific Telephone and Telegraph Company, 1971.

Urlan, A. *On stage: Wally, Bertha, and you.* Chicago: Encyclopedia Britannica Educational Corp., 1971.

Vogt, K. D. *What's goin' on?* Modesto, Calif.: Learning Stuff, 1974.

Wepman, J. M., & Haas, W. *A spoken word count.* Palm Springs, Calif.: Language Research Associates, Inc., 1969.

Zimmerman, I. L., Steiner, V. G., & Evatt, R. L. *Preschool language scale.* Columbus, Ohio: The Charles E. Merrill Publishing Co., 1969.

Chapter 6

Reading Readiness

DEVELOPING READINESS SKILLS

Reading ability, from readiness through the comprehension of complex written material, is developed sequentially, skill upon skill. The initial reading experience may determine the path of the child's academic future. An inadequate foundation for instruction can cause reading difficulty throughout the child's school years. A negative encounter can turn off a learner for life. The beginning reading experience is a crucial event, and readiness is the key to success.

Traditionally, children have been deemed ready for school and subsequent reading instruction on the basis of a chronological age established by law. Unfortunately, age is perhaps the least valuable indicator of readiness.

According to Ilg and Ames (1965), even if it were possible to determine the average age at which children are ready for school, it would not solve the problem. An average age would mean that about 50 percent of the children would be ready by age *X*, the other children at a younger age or at an undetermined age beyond the average.

The questionable validity of age criteria for school entrance has been considered seriously. The outcome of readiness studies has led to the development of programs such as Head Start and the establishment of preschool screening procedures.

These measures are commendable but are not sufficient to stem completely the tide of school failures that are attributable to readiness level. The term *lack of readiness* is avoided here because it implies that only the immature encounter difficulty. This is not the case. The *overready* also may experience problems with school adjustment.

It is the educator's responsibility to understand the reading process and to teach the child skills that are appropriate for the individual's development. This understanding includes the relationship of visual, auditory, and language skills as well as the effect of motivation on reading.

Vision

In the normally developing child, vision is the first of the sensory modes to add significantly to the learning process. Visual experiences can be stored and retrieved for appropriate application without language. Initially, visual learning is meaningful on a concrete level.

A child sees a person. The person touches, cuddles, feeds, and in general makes the child comfortable by creating a feeling of well-being. Similarly, objects within the child's visual range are experienced as pleasurable in that they meet basic needs. A bottle means satisfaction and the elimination of immediate discomfort. The child does not need to manipulate abstract symbols (use language) to experience the meaning or the purpose of people and things.

Nonlanguage experiences involve large objects and can be viewed at a distance. In a human infant, this is quite important. In fact, physiologically it is a necessity. The shape and structure of the eye in a newborn or young child does not facilitate near point vision. The slightly overelongated shape of the eye makes seeing difficult within a short distance. The incoming picture does not focus properly on the retina. The condition is referred to as hyperopia or farsightedness.

Farsightedness, the inability to see comfortably at near point, is normal developmentally. As a child matures and strengthens muscles and tissue, the shape of the eye modifies. This change permits focus at the proper point.

The rate at which the normal eye matures depends in part on experience. Children who have repeated near point experiences develop the ability to focus and hold on small objects and print within a short range. A lack of close-up exposure may retard visual development.

The difference in type of visual experience may account for some readiness level discrepancies encountered by American children. In this country it has been suggested that female children usually are ready for school before their chronological and mental age male counterparts. One of the specific differences noted has been visual readiness. It would appear that the type of little girls' experiences helps their visual development, while culturally expected male behaviors do not include similar opportunities.

Several years ago a group of early childhood educators visited the Soviet Union. The American teachers were appalled when they saw three-year-old boys copying bead designs. They were heard to say, "What are these people thinking about? Don't they know that little boys do not have the necessary visual-motor development to string tiny bead patterns?''

Obviously the little boys in that nation had developed the necessary abilities; they were stringing beads every bit as well as the little girls, and apparently enjoying the experience.

A teacher should not generalize and assume that all little boys are farsighted when they enter school. Nor should the assumption be made that all little girls are ready visually. Recognition of individual differences in children can help avoid boredom for the visually mature and prevent frustration and possible physical discomfort for the visually immature.

Auditory

The normal developmental language sequence for children who do not have severe sensory impairments is listening, speaking, reading, and writing. Although reading is a visual decoding process, beginning reading instruction for the most part is an equal mixture of auditory and visual learning. The teacher speaks; the child looks and listens.

The acquisition of a reading vocabulary depends on the child's ability to see the word, to match the visual image with a previously stored imprint, and to retrieve the word when appropriate. The ability to complete the process is made easier if the word has been encountered first as an auditory experience. Using the word in speaking helps visual retention and comprehension even further.

Readiness for reading includes adequate development of auditory skills. Specific auditory skills or abilities that are developed as part of a readiness program are vocabulary, perception (discrimination), attention, and memory.

Oral Language

Although it is quite possible to have an adequate auditory vocabulary and not use it in speaking, the condition is not typical. Expressive language is far more obvious than receptive language and is considered indicative of academic readiness. Adequate vocabulary development, articulation, and syntax are requisites for reading instruction.

Consider the effects of misarticulated sounds on phonic analysis. If for no other reason than the fact that the teacher may not be able to judge the accuracy of a response, the mispronounced phoneme could impede reading instruction. Before visual recognition occurs with any degree of regularity, the ability to hear and to reproduce the sound correctly is necessary.

Similarly, understanding and using syntactical structures in oral language facilitates reading comprehension. Ordinarily the child who is ready to read is one who has developmental language skills that are at least equal to the level of the language in basal readers.

Motivation

If it were necessary to identify the single most important criterion for reading readiness, in the opinion of the writer, it would be motivation. If at all possible, a child who wants to read will learn in spite of handicaps. The child who is motivated will learn without formal instruction.

It is not unusual for a parent to say, "But I never taught her to read, she just began on her own." Of course, that is not completely true. Someone helped. It may have happened as the child was being read to and followed along, turning the pages, or the child may have asked an adult, "What is this word?"

These examples not only are indicative of how some children learn to read, they also are the best possible examples of readiness. Developmental readiness occurs when the child learns to read naturally and not as a result of an educationally imposed requirement. This does not mean that parents and educators cannot plan or formally help the child to prepare to learn to read. The stage may need some setting; that is called *readiness activities*. However, when the child points to a word and says, "That word is 'look'," that is readiness, and it should be self-motivated as much as possible.

EVALUATING READING READINESS

A reading readiness evaluation can be as informal as an unstructured observation or as formal as the use of a battery of standardized tests. Informal measures often are teacher-prepared or commercially available checklists that rely on subjective appraisals. Formal procedures include intelligence testing, standardized reading readiness tests, speech and language testing, visual examinations, and audiological evaluations.

Informal Readiness Measures

The informal measure used most frequently is the reading readiness checklist. While helpful as a screening device, a checklist does have shortcomings.

It can be used as a prescreening and postscreening measure at the kindergarten level. It should be completed by the teacher during the first several weeks of school. Based on the indicated strengths and weaknesses, referrals for formal testing should be made at once.

Children with marked deficit areas should be identified and special intervention programs should be planned at the kindergarten level. Special programming at this point can prevent failure and possibly the need for special class placement in later years.

Skill testing is equally as important for children with high readiness indicators. Boredom for the gifted is as frustrating as failure is to the less capable. If accelerated programming is not available, horizontal enrichment should be initiated. Undereducated gifted children can be as disruptive in the classroom as the hyperactive brain-injured child.

Used as a posttest for average children and low special needs pupils, the checklist can be a valuable tool for early grouping in first grade. In addition, a comparison of pretest and posttest skill checks will indicate program and teaching effectiveness.

A modification of the checklist can be used in recording entire class progress toward readiness. The chart can be used as a continuing evaluation of readiness and as a motivational device. It is particularly valuable in primary educable mentally retarded and specific learning disability classrooms.

To prepare the chart, make a grid with space for the names of children down the left side and space for writing deficit areas across the top of a large sheet of oak tag. Make smaller squares within the category squares for recording progress steps.

Print the children's names in large letters for ease of recognition. Color code for children who cannot identify their names, or when two or more children have the same first names.

Skill areas should be listed across the top of the chart. They should include areas previously identified as deficit skills. Categories might include auditory discrimination, articulation, eye-hand coordination, letter recognition, and so on. Line drawings can be used in place of titles; that is, an ear might mean auditory discrimination, or an eye could be used for visual discrimination.

Some children will have mastered a specific skill. In that case the corresponding area should be colored in or starred, indicating successful accomplishment.

Explain the chart to the children. Tell them that they will be learning to do the things on the chart. Make it sound like fun. Turn learning problems into sources of pride for them. Explain that the boxes that are colored in are bonus steps because they can do them already. If the children are motivated properly and are rewarded for small realistic gains, they will work harder and help keep their own records.

When the child has mastered or acquired adequate ability in each of the areas, the chart is completed by placing a picture of a book in the last square. A small award ceremony should accompany the sticker. A special treat and a preview of the basal reader to be used for instruction makes it seem that they really have succeeded. It becomes a minigraduation day.

The chart also can be used as a visual aid for parent conferences, program planning, and administrative decision making in relation to grouping or class placement.

Commercial Readiness Tests

With increased emphasis being placed on early childhood education and the prevention of learning problems, many new measures of readiness have been developed recently. The commercially available assessment tools range from standardized, normative checklists to clever evaluation programs that are fun to take and use. The measures selected here have appeal for various reasons. They are a very small sample of some of the excellent commercial materials that are available.

Animal Crackers (1973)
Dorothy C. Adkins and Bonnie L. Ballif
CTB/McGraw-Hill Book Company
P.O. Box 404
Hightstown, New Jersey 08520

Purpose: Motivational assessment.

Population: Preschool–Grade 1.

Description: Although this is not a reading readiness test, it is a readiness factor assessment. It is intended to determine motivation to learn, an element which is an important part of reading achievement. It deals with achievement-oriented behaviors and not necessarily intellectual capacities or experience. It is easy to use, can be administered by paraprofessionals as well as teachers, and is helpful in determining attitudes toward learning.

Brigance Diagnostic Inventory of Basic Skills (1977)
Albert H. Brigance
Curriculum Associates, Inc.
Woburn, Massachusetts 01801

Purpose: Assessment of readiness and academic skills.

Population: Kindergarten–Grade 6.

Description: The inventory assesses readiness, reading, oral language, and spelling. In the readiness section, 24 areas are investigated. Some of the specific abilities associated with reading readiness include visual discrimination, visual motor, visual memory, directionality, verbal directions, articulation of sounds, alphabet, and letter recognition. The areas in reading include word recognition, reading rate and comprehension, word analysis, and vocabulary.

Administration directions are easy to follow, and the teacher may adapt the recommended procedures and uses to fit the program. Specialized training is not necessary for administration. Information from this measure is extremely helpful in writing instructional objectives. The student record book also can be used for instructional programs.

A companion book, *The Brigance Diagnostic Inventory of Early Development* (1978), also is useful in assessing readiness, particularly the sections on response to books, speech and language, general knowledge, discrimination, and alphabet.

Circus (1974)
  Scariva B. Anderson, Gerry Ann Bogatz, Thomas Draper, Ann
    Jungeblut, Grat Sidwell, William Ward, and Allen Yates
  Addison Wesley
  South Street
  Reading, Massachusetts 01867

Purpose: Comprehensive assessment of educational needs and abilities.

Population: Preschool–kindergarten.

Description: This was prepared to give a broad scope of assessment to young children. There are fourteen direct measures or tests and two inventories. Areas assessed are receptive vocabulary, quantitative concepts, visual discrimination, perceptual motor, letter and number recognition, auditory discrimination, letter discrimination, functional language, auditory comprehension, productional language, general information, visual memory, and problem solving.

Subtests are to be used when appropriate to a specific program or to the purpose of the assessment. Proposed uses of this material are presented clearly. Scoring and interpretation are not difficult, and arrangements can be made with the publisher to have the material scored. The tests were standardized on basic types of children and, because of the theme, are appealing to almost all young children.

Developmental Test of Visual-Motor Integration (1967)
  Keith E. Beery, Ph.D.
  Follett Publishing Company
  1010 West Washington Blvd.
  Chicago, Illinois 60607

Purpose: Assessment of visual-motor integration.

Population: Kindergarten–grade 8 (age norms 3–14).

Description: This test is a series of 24 geometric forms to be copied with a pencil on paper. Visual-motor integration is an essential task in reading and writing. The test is planned for use by preschool teachers and teachers of handicapped children. It is a tool for educational assessment. Results of the test can be used to identify children who need added maturational time or who have specific problems needing additional testing and special class placement. It can be group administered. Directions are clear and easy to follow for administration, scoring, and interpretation.

Preschool and Early Primary Skill Survey-PEPSS (1973)
  John A. Long, Ed.D., Morton Morris, Ed.D., and George A. W.
    Stouffer, Ed.D.
  Mafex Associates, Inc.
  111 Barron Avenue
  Johnstown, Pennsylvania 15906

Purpose: Identification of strengths and weaknesses associated with school success.

Population: Preschool–lower primary.

Description: PEPSS can be used with small groups or administered individually. There are four subtests that assess visual recognition, discrimination and association, cognition of story sequence, and perceptual motor skills. Each subtest takes 15 to 20 minutes. The tests are easy to administer and score. Results can be used for planning instruction, grouping according to needs, or referrals. The manual includes interpretation information. The test is relatively culture-free and can be used not only with children suspected of having learning difficulties but also with the normal. Special training for administration is not necessary; the test needs only paper and pencil, with no extra equipment.

Revised Pre-Reading Screening Procedures (1977)
Beth H. Slingerland
Educator's Publishing Service, Inc.
75 Moulton Street
Cambridge, Massachusetts 02138

Purpose: Identification of deficits in perception and language recall.

Population: Kindergarten–grade 1.

Description: This consists of twelve subtests that assess these areas: visual discrimination of letters and words for matching, visual discrimination for matching from recall, near point and far point copying, visual perception and memory requiring a motor response, auditory perception and memory, letter knowledge, auditory comprehension, auditory discrimination for initial consonants, and auditory association. The directions for administering and scoring are clear and easy to follow. The test is designed to be used with children with average to superior intelligence. It aids in determining readiness to learn to read, write, and spell through conventional methods. In addition, it helps to identify children with specific language disabilities and possible perceptual difficulties who need additional testing or who have delayed readiness.

It can be used with groups of up to twenty children. Testing time varies with the size of the group and maturity level. Most subtests take very little time, and best results are achieved if Test VII, Visual-Motor, is given separately. Materials include a teacher's manual, test booklets, and observation and summary sheets.

Sound-Start Murphy-Durrell Prereading Phonics Inventory (1976)
Helen A. Murphy, Ph.D., and Donald D. Durrell, Ph.D.
Borg-Warner Educational Systems
600 West University Drive
Arlington Heights, Illinois 60004

Purpose: Identification of children who need Sound Start Program.

Population: Kindergarten–grade 1 and other readiness level children.

Description: This was designed specifically to be used as a screening device to identify children who would profit from the Sound Start Program. There are four subtests. Lowercase letter names determine the number of letters a child recognizes visually. Letter name-sounds in spoken words measure the ability to match sounds in words with printed letters. Writing letters from dictation is self-explanatory. Syntax matching is matching the spoken word with a word in print. The test is easy to administer and to interpret. Program planning with this information can be quite easy. It can be group administered, and testing time varies with the children's developmental level and size of the group to be monitored.

READINESS ACTIVITIES

Teacher-Prepared Methods and Materials

Previous chapters suggested ideas for developing auditory and oral language. These abilities are prerequisites for reading and the activities should be considered reading readiness preparation. In addition, reading readiness includes eye-hand coordination, gross and fine motor development, and vision.

Language Development

Reading material is primarily written stories, at least during beginning instruction. To prepare children to identify the meaning of a story, to understand the sequential development of a plot, and to draw inferences and conclusions, storytelling and storybook reading are helpful and enjoyable instructional approaches.

Having the children follow the print while being read to can help develop left/right understanding. Listening and seeing a story unfold is exciting and good motivation for future reading.

The procedure for directing a child to listen with meaning is similar to that for directing a reading activity. The steps are: readiness, establishing a purpose, checking understanding, and developing vocabulary. To understand these steps, a teacher-prepared story and worksheets are used here. The pictures on the worksheets (Figure 6-1) are not in correct order.

Readiness: Begin with a discussion of animals. Include those mentioned in the story that follows. Make sure the children are familiar with the physical appearance of each; use pictures if necessary.

Setting a purpose for listening: Say, "This is the story of a little mouse who was very lucky. You see, he thought being himself was not good enough. He thought he wanted to be something else and he got his wish. But that wasn't why he was lucky. Listen to the story and see if you can find out why he was lucky. Also, try to remember the three things that happened to him in the story."

Figure 6-1 Sample Worksheet to Develop Left/Right

I'm A Mouse

Little Mouse was rather ordinary, to be sure. He had the usual two ears, two eyes, four legs, a tail, and so on. Here is a picture of him. He could run like other mice, squeak like other mice, and even eat cheese like other mice. But that wasn't enough for Little Mouse. He wanted to be different.

One day when he was playing on an old dump he saw something shiny. He looked closer. It was a very tiny little box, almost like a golden match box.

Little Mouse decided to open the box. As he did, he heard a lovely little voice tinkle, "Thank you, I've been closed and dark inside for so long. Seeing the sunlight is just marvelous."

Picture 1

Now Little Mouse was just a tiny bit scared. However, he squeaked "Hello, I'm a mouse." The little voice said, "Yes, I know. I also know that you are unhappy."

Little Mouse explained that he wished he could do things other mice couldn't. He wanted to be different. The little voice tinkled a laugh and told him that he was in luck. The box was magic and could give him three wishes. Each wish would have to be on a different sunny day. He could have his first wish that day.

Little Mouse thought and thought. Finally he said, "If I had legs like a frog I could leap up, snatch my food, and hop away. I'd be a better food gatherer than all the other mice."

Suddenly Little Mouse felt the earth shake. He trembled at the strange feeling. When it was all over, there he was with not just ordinary mouse legs, but legs like a frog, and with webbed feet, too.

Little Mouse said thank you, and promised to return on the next sunny day. He closed the box and leap-frogged away.

Picture 2

Now he was a funny sight, as you can see. But he was feeling very proud; no ordinary mouse was he.

Along the way he met some other mice. They stared. They couldn't believe their eyes. They said, "Hello, what are you?"

Suddenly Little Mouse realized what he must look like leaping along. He smiled and said politely. "I'm a frouse." That of course meant frog-mouse.

That night Little Mouse did in fact leap up and snatch some food. But he also learned that frog legs have their bad points. He couldn't run up and down the walls, and he couldn't play tag with the other little mice. He decided, oh, well, to leap was worth the loss of a silly game of tag.

Since he couldn't play with his friends he decided to watch television with the people in his house. Of course, they didn't know he was watching. The show was all about wild animals. Little Mouse was fascinated with the giraffe. As he watched the giraffe stretch its long neck to get the tender leaves on a tree he thought, "Yes, a long neck. That will make me an even better food getter."

On the next sunny day he returned to the dump. He opened the box and claimed his second wish. He asked for a long neck just like the giraffe.

As he leap-frogged away with his new long neck he met some mice. They said, "Hello, what are you?" Little Mouse was feeling very special so he smiled and said, "I'm a frouseraffe." As he leaped away from the mice he had his first understanding of what having a really long neck can mean. His head was now so much higher up than before that he hit it going under a fence that would have been no problem before.

All the way home he was very careful. When he got home he tried his new neck. Sure enough, he could reach around corners and steal snacks from the kids in the house and they didn't even catch on. Having a long neck was good for food getting, even if it did get in the way sometimes. Being a frouseraffe wasn't so bad if he could just remember to duck going under fences and into mouse holes.

It rained for the next few days and Little Mouse had plenty of time to think about what the next and last wish would be. The

Picture 3

first day he considered wings like a bird. He would be a frouseraffird. He imagined himself flying. But then he realized what a problem it would be with his long neck and webbed feet. Yes, he decided it would be a bit awkward.

Picture 4

The next day he thought that maybe bigger ears would help. Ears like the elephant certainly should be better to hear with. If he could hear better he could warn the other mice when people were coming; maybe he could even be a hero. Then of course he would be a frouseraffele, or would he be a frouseraffphant? As he pictured himself with giant floppy ears, he began to laugh at the sight of himself. Oh, well, since it is only make-believe, why not have wings and big ears, be a frouseraffirdphant.

Picture 5

Now, he thought, that really would be silly. In fact, maybe the whole idea was a little dumb. He hadn't been able to play with his friends since becoming a frouse. Being a frouseraffe had made it impossible to curl up in the family nest. Now big ears, what problems would they cause? Besides, what good is it being a good food getter or a hero if you didn't have friends and family. He decided to sleep on the idea. Tomorrow he would decide.

The following day was bright and sunny. Little Mouse awoke with a kink in his neck, and a kink in a long neck is no ordinary kink. That did it. He had made up his mind.

He washed, ate his breakfast, and leap-frogged out of the family's tiny hole, being very careful not to bang his head on the way.

When he got to the dump he had a minute or two of real fright. The rain had made a puddle and the tiny box had floated away.

Little Mouse almost cried. He wasn't going to get his last wish. (At this point ask the children what they think the wish will be.)

Suddenly, a tiny glimmer of bright shone from the other side of the puddle. Little Mouse, using his frog legs and webbed feet, leaped and swam across to the other side. Yes, it was the box.

Very carefully Little Mouse cleaned off the mud and opened the box. Again the voice tinkled "hello." It reminded Little Mouse that he had one more wish.

In a very grateful mouse squeaking voice he replied, "My third wish is very important. I have been a frouse and a frouseraffe. I've thought about being a frouseraffird, a frouseraffephant, and even a frouseraffephantird. But I've finally decided the best of all. Please little box, for my third and last wish, can I go back to being an ordinary little mouse?"

Picture 6

The little box tinkled happily and in a flash Little Mouse was once again an ordinary mouse, a very happy ordinary little mouse who believed himself to be very lucky to be an ordinary mouse.

Picture 7

Checking comprehension: Have the children answer questions related to why Little Mouse was lucky and what happened to him. Have them retell the story in their own words.

Developing vocabulary: Ask them questions about specific vocabulary in the story; that is, how did the little box sound? and how did Little Mouse move after he had new legs?

Follow-Up Activity to Teach Left/Right

Have a Ditto sheet containing six pictures of Little Mouse (Figure 6-1). Give each child a piece of newsprint paper about 11″ × 22″. Fold the paper in half. The children should cut the story pictures from the Ditto sheet and paste them on the left side of the newsprint, using two rows of pictures placed from left to right in story sequence. On the right hand side they can create their own mixed-up animal. Later, when time permits, have them tell a story about their animal. Encourage them to create a new plot. If their story is audiotaped, it can be typed or manuscripted later and attached to their drawing for a new listening and language development lesson.

This sample activity illustrates a lesson that can be used to develop the following: auditory attention, vocabulary, memory and comprehension, visual discrimination, sequential memory, oral language syntax, vocabulary, and eye-hand coordination. Variations of this approach are endless. The stories need not be teacher prepared.

Visual Development

Visual experiences are receptive and therefore must be accompanied by an expressive mode if they are to be observable by a teacher. Activities to develop visual skills include aural language and/or motor activities. The following suggestions, while visually oriented, include aspects of other modalities and are especially helpful if the additional modes are the child's strong learning avenues. This allows teaching underdeveloped or weak areas through stronger modalities.

Activity 1. Alphabet and color blocks are good readiness activities. Although they are available and convenient, it is not necessary to purchase blocks; homemade ones are just as effective. Lumber yards will usually save scraps if requested. These scrap blocks can be painted in solid colors and patterns.

A set of twelve 1-inch cubes or strips of 1″ by 2″ wood make excellent sequential memory materials. Paint two blocks or strips the same color. One set of six different colors is used for patterns, the other set is manipulated by the child.

To begin the development of visual sequential memory, give the child two blocks of different colors or designs. Explain that you are going to show him a block. When you cover it, the pupil is to select the same color block from his pile.

Place a divider between the child's blocks and the pattern blocks. Expose a block for approximately two seconds. Cover it and have the child push the correct matching block forward. Check for visual accuracy and reinforce the child; if the response is correct, praise or give some form of reward.

When the child is able to recall a single color with 100 percent accuracy, the number of distractions (child's blocks) is increased to three and pattern blocks to two. Increase the number until the child can handle four colors correctly. Exposure time is increased two seconds per object to be viewed.

When this is accomplished, the directions are changed. Say, "I'm going to show some blocks. Look at them carefully. When I cover them, you select the same blocks in the same color order." Begin with two and continue requiring 100 percent accuracy through correct sequencing of the six blocks. Variations of this can be done with geometric forms, designs, and letters. Materials can be wood, plastic, or heavy paper.

Activity 2. Another visual activity that is a favorite with many children is practice puzzle work. Variations of this approach are numerous. For the example here, alphabet puzzles are used.

For the complete alphabet (capitals and lower case) you will need 52 pieces of cardboard or other similar material and an equal number of pages of tissue or onionskin paper. With colored markers, draw a letter of the alphabet on each card. Place the paper over the completed figure and duplicate it. The forms should be the same in color, size, and shape. Outline or cover the pattern (paper figure) with glue and sprinkle sand or another granular substance on the sticky surface. With a sharp pair of shears cut the cardboard form into large irregularly-shaped pieces. The cardboard pieces are the puzzle, and the paper letters are the pattern.

Give the child the puzzle pieces and the pattern. Explain that the pupil can look at and feel the pattern while putting the pieces together. To check the accuracy of the work, the pupil can place the paper over the puzzle. This develops independent work habits. The pattern helps the child see the total form while the pieces of the puzzle help develop discrimination and visual closure.

For storage, place the puzzle pieces in an envelope marked with the appropriate letter and clip it to the onionskin paper. If onionskin typing paper has been used, the box it came in can be reused for filing the material.

Commercial Materials

Alpha Blocks (1977)
  Guidance Industries
  Box 247, 61 Camino Alto
  Mill Valley, California 94941

Purpose: Letter recognition.

Population: Prereading.

Description: This material is for the parent or teacher who prefers a commercial set to teach the alphabet. The instruction booklet that accompanies the set provides good ideas that are different from the usual.

Basic Colors (1976)
 Clearvue, Inc.
 6666 North Olephant Avenue
 Chicago, Illinois 60631

Purpose: Visual recognition and vocabulary.

Population: 4 to 8 years mental age.

Description: Materials in this program include six filmstrips, audiotapes, and duplicating masters. The colors green, yellow, blue, orange, and red are introduced through crayons. The accompanying stories build vocabulary through entertaining stories. All concepts are presented and reinforced aurally and visually. The follow-up activities suggested in the manual are easy to use and are added reinforcement for the slower child.

In addition to the colors program, a companion work, *Basic Relationships* (1976), is helpful in developing spatial, temporal, and quantitative relationships. The material includes filmstrips and audiotapes as with the preceding program. The stories in this program are clever and use the natural imagination of children to make learning fun.

Eye-Hand Integration Exercises (1976)
 Developmental Learning Materials
 7440 Natchez Avenue
 Niles, Illinois 60648

Purpose: Left-right concept.

Population: Kindergarten–grade 2 and special education.

Description: This inexpensive material helps teach left-right and up-down relationships and improves fine motor control. Many kindergarten and first-grade children, as well as exceptional children, have difficulty internalizing these concepts. Really understanding left-right may prevent reversals. The exercises take very little time and can be worked into most programs easily.

Flip-Chex (1975)
 Educational Concept Corporation
 308 West 16th Street
 Austin, Texas 78701

Purpose: Perceptual development.

Population: Kindergarten–grade 1 and special education.

Description: *Flip-Chex* is the title of five programs for reading and mathematics. Perceptual Development I and Perceptual Development II are good, independent, self-checking programs. After a child has been found to have a perceptual weakness, needs are recorded on a prescription sheet that actually is a personal chart with program titles. The teacher marks the sheet indicating the material a child should use. The child checks the sheet and gets the box with the corresponding number and title. After having completed the task, the child flips the box containing the material; if the task has been completed correctly, the child sees a picture. The flipped box checks the work, thus *Flip-Chex*. The material is easy to use and, besides developing visual perception skills, motivates the child to learn and fosters independent work skills.

MCP Reading Readiness Program (1972)
  Modern Curriculum Press
  13900 Prospect Road
  Cleveland, Ohio 44136

Purpose: Various readiness activities.

Population: Pre-reading–grade 1.

Description: Many formal readiness programs are costly and require special audiovisual equipment. This is an inexpensive book that has ideas for activities and games to develop auditory discrimination, visual recognition, and eye-hand coordination. It can be used by anyone working with children at the prereading and beginning reading level. Additional materials include lesson plans and a multimodal approach for teaching the alphabet.

Pre-Reading Skills for the Learning Disabled (1977)
  Society for Visual Education, Inc.
  1345 Diversey Parkway
  Chicago, Illinois 60614

Purpose: Development of perceptual skills and attention.

Population: Kindergarten–grade 3 and special education.

Description: This program includes sixteen sets of audiovisual materials. Although the title suggests its use with a specific group, its application for developmental readiness activities is very good. For example, "Developing Figure-Ground Skills" uses four standard Mother Goose stories to improve attention span and visual figureground. At intervals in the telling of the story, the child must find a hidden item on the worksheet. Time for interaction and discussion is built into each filmstrip. Because the material is based on good children's literature, far more than visual perception is developed. The young gifted learner enjoys this as much as does the remedial child.

REFERENCES

Adkins, D. C., & Ballif, B. L. *Animal crackers*. Hightstown, N.J.: McGraw-Hill Book Company, 1973.

Alpha blocks. Mill Valley, Calif.: Guidance Industries, 1977.

Anderson, S. B., Bogatz, G. A., Draper, T., Jungeblut, A., Sidwell, G., Ward, W., and Yates, A. *Circus*. Princeton, N.J.: Educational Testing Service, 1974.

Basic colors. Chicago: Clearvue, Inc., 1976.

Beery, K. E. *Developmental test of visual-motor integration*. Chicago: Follett Publishing Co., 1976.

Eye-hand integration exercises. Niles, Ill.: Developmental Learning Materials, 1976.

Flip-chex. Austin, Tex.: Educational Concept Corp., 1975.

Lang, J. A., Morris, M., & Stouffer, G. A. W. *Preschool and early primary skill survey* (PEPSS). Johnstown, Pa.: Mafex Associates, Inc., 1973.

MCP reading readiness program. Cleveland: Modern Curriculum Press, 1972.

Murphy, H. A., & Durrell, D. D. *Sound-start Murphy-Durrell phonics inventory*. Arlington Heights, Ill.: Borg-Warner Educational Systems, 1976.

Pre-reading skills for the learning disabled. Chicago: Society for Visual Education, Inc., 1977.

Slingerland, B. H. *Revised pre-reading screening procedures*, Cambridge, Mass.: Educator's Publishing Service, Inc., 1977.

Chapter 7

Reading

DEVELOPMENTAL READING

How do children learn to read? Do you remember how you learned? Probably not. In fact, most adults have forgotten how they analyze unfamiliar words, or why a word sounds the way it does. A mature reader analyzes unfamiliar words without specifically considering the linguistic principles necessary to identify the sound and meaning. If reading instruction has been successful, word recognition is an almost automatic process. Reading with ease and facility is developed through systematic sequential instruction.

The identification of a specific reading problem becomes meaningful when the evaluator knows and understands the sequence of skills necessary for reading achievement. A review of the reading process can be helpful for even the experienced teacher.

Reading is the ability to recognize the printed word and to determine the meaning of the words as they are used in larger linguistic units.

Reading is not word recognition or word naming. Word recognition is a part of reading. The intended meaning is not conveyed by a word but by words joined together in sentences and paragraphs.

The reading process includes word perception, understanding of words as they are used in sentences, reacting to the ideas conveyed by the words, and matching these ideas with previous experiences. Each of these components is necessary if reading is to occur.

Word Perception

Word perception is a way of saying word recognition with meaning. Word perception may be achieved through one of four procedures: memory, context clue, word analysis, and dictionary use.

Memory

A word that has been memorized can be recognized without analysis and is referred to as a *sight word*. Generally, sight words are recognized as a word form.

Word-form recognition that uses unit length, letter heights, and other shape characteristics is referred to as *configuration*. Although the use of configuration is limited by the frequency or commonality of word shapes, it is one of the first clues the reader applies.

Recognizing a sight word in relation to letter order requires visual sequential memory. Noting the variations in letter formation, direction, and fine differences in form requires visual discrimination.

In normal or rapid reading, recognition of a word or phrase is not completed letter by letter but by an educated guess based on past experience. Closure, or the *cloze procedure,* is the act of supplying missing elements, or filling in the blank. The reader sees a partial configuration and, relying on memory, completes the form to achieve word perception.

Recalling visual experiences with words is memory of word form and the most frequently applied word perception aid. Memory for word form is facilitated through close visual attention to detail, configuration, and letter order. The ability to associate or recall meanings of words further helps in the perception of written language.

Context Clues

Determining the meaning and/or sound of an unfamiliar word because it is appropriate in the sentence being read is word perception through context. It is a form of cloze procedure in that the reader attempts to fill in with a known word that appears to make sense as to meaning. For example: "The action was deleterious; it could have cost the person's life." The word deleterious may not be in most people's reading vocabulary. However, the meaning can be derived from other words in the sentence. The word action implies something occurred. Because the action might have caused the individual's death, it can be assumed that the unfamiliar word means harmful or injurious. Phonic analysis will help the reader in determining the sound, so word perception has occurred.

For another example, take these sentences: "Dr. Brown is a psychiatrist. His son calls him a shrink." The unfamiliar visual word to the beginning reader may be psychiatrist. Analyzing the word for sound could be difficult. However, most people know that in the vernacular, a shrink is a medical doctor who deals with mental conditions. The meaning and the sound can be determined from past experience, the remembrance being triggered by the word "shrink," or a context clue.

Word Analysis

The third procedure in determining word recognition is word analysis. A reader analyzes a word structurally or phonetically, or both.

Structural analysis is the identification of sound and meaning through the recognition of word parts. Word parts include root words, inflectional endings, prefixes, and suffixes. The word *run* is the root word in *runs*; the *s* is the inflectional ending. In the word *rerun* the root is *run* and *re* is the prefix. The meaning of the word becomes clear if the reader understands both the prefix and the root word.

Structural analysis also is applied to compound words. In unlocking the meaning of a word such as *baseball,* the reader must know the meaning of *ball,* the root word, and of *base,* the descriptor word. When the word is analyzed correctly, the reader forms a mental picture of a specific object, a small white ball, used for a specific game that requires bases and baserunning.

Phonetic analysis is the application of sounds to letters. The appropriate sound may be constant or may be determined according to a language law or linguistic principle.

Phonetic analysis is one of the more difficult processes used to arrive at sound and meaning. In American English, sounds associated with letters are inconsistent. A child acquiring phonic analysis skills learns the regular patterns. The irregular spelling patterns or letter sounds are learned after the child has developed a large sight vocabulary and can compare patterns with known words.

Standard American English uses 44 phonemes in speech. However, these 44 sounds are represented by 26 symbols in writing. In addition to the standard sounds, regional dialects add to sound-letter problems. For example, the letters *an* should be voiced constantly as *pan* in a consonant, vowel, consonant pattern. This is not always the case. In at least one part of the country the word *can* has two sounds. In the sentence, "I can can," the first vowel is the short sound, the second one is close to that of a long vowel. The sentence means, "I am able to process food."

Phonetic analysis requires the user to produce consistent sound patterns when speaking and be able to hear the differences in sound production. Because of the many possible sound-letter combinations in American English, phonic analysis often is learned after the child has acquired a large sight vocabulary and is able to rely on known sound-letter patterns to unlock the pronunciation of new words.

Dictionary Use

Usually the last method of achieving word perception is through the dictionary. A reader who encounters an unfamiliar word may use a dictionary to verify or determine either the sound or meaning of a word. If the new word defies the usual analytic steps, the dictionary may be the only possible way of decoding it.

Comprehending the Written Word

In reading, as in oral language, the meaning of a word is determined in part by its use in a sentence. Vocal clues that help in understanding spoken words are missing in written language. The reader depends on punctuation for pause and juncture clues. Inflection, or rise and fall of voice, is suggested by a period, exclamation point, or question mark. The degree to which the reader can and does use these visual clues helps or impedes understanding.

"Stop." "Stop!" "Stop?"

How did you read the preceding three single-word sentences? If you read them aloud, did they sound the same? If you comprehended the meaning as indicated by the punctuation, you voiced three different sentences.

Understanding of written material can be at several levels, depending upon the content and the intent of the writer. In beginning reading material, understanding is at a concrete level. Stories are written in basic statements. The reader is required to understand simple facts.

As the reader matures and the material becomes more complex, comprehension entails the ability to associate ideas and events with past experiences, infer meaning from implications, and interpret symbolism. It is at these more abstract levels that mental images are formed, and the reader goes beyond the immediate meaning of words. Comprehension becomes a personal experience. Word perception then is far more than a simple decoding process.

Word Analysis

The two phases of word analysis, phonic and structural, require careful visual attention. The purpose of applying analysis to an unfamiliar reading word is to determine the sound and, possibly, the meaning. The user must possess knowledge of letter sounds, word parts, and accent. To develop such knowledge requires an instructional program that is sequential. The teacher must know the sequence and be prepared to instruct the child when a prerequisite skill is weak or missing.

There are several principles that make teaching word analysis easier:

1. A child must be able to hear a sound and to differentiate it from among other sounds before being expected to associate the sound with a specific visual letter. A good instructional program does not require the learner to memorize rules, particularly those that have relatively little applicability beyond a cluster of spellings. For example, "When two vowels go a-walking, the first one does the talking, and the second one is silent." Many primary grade children have learned to recite that saying. Unfortunately, when they tried to apply it to words such as taught or language, it just didn't work. Rules should not be taught as verbalized statements. They should be applied as understandings of the language.
2. The learner should be taught at the child's needs level. Adhering strictly to a canned program can be disastrous. If a child has internalized an understanding, which is a natural process, it is not necessary to use every page in a workbook or every lesson in the teacher's manual. However, if a child has acquired splinter skills (learned something out of sequence), it may be appropriate to go back and teach the skills on which the higher level function depends.
3. Perhaps most important, the learner should have sufficient experience in seeing and hearing patterns of sound and letter groupings to form a generalization that is readily applicable. Word analysis takes a minimum of time if the user has ready mental access to the appropriate linguistic principle. It is when the reader tries to remember the rule that analysis becomes tedious.

When normal children have learned that reading is speech in written form, can discriminate among speech sounds, and have at least a minimal sight vocabulary, they are ready to analyze words. Knowing the alphabet sequentially is not an absolute prerequisite. Alphabetizing has little or no relationship to reading. The child who has mastered the alphabet is demonstrating learning potential or readiness for additional instruction.

Although formal instruction in phonic analysis generally is introduced before structural analysis, the processes are interrelated. Instruction in the two methods of analysis is taught best when appropriate to the child's reading needs and readiness level.

Phonic Analysis

American English is not a consistent letter-to-sound system. There is a greater correspondence of sound-to-letter with consonants than with vowels. Therefore, it is helpful to begin with consonant sounds.

The first consonant letters taught are those that have a single sound. The letters *b, d, f, k, l, m, n, p,* and *t* are heard as consistent phonemes. Although the sounds they represent may have variant spellings (*ph* for *f*), or the letters may not represent a sound (*k* as in know), the exceptions are infrequent. When children see *k* as in kitten or *f* as in fat, they can be relatively sure of the corresponding sound.

The letter *q* may be included in the first group if the children have learned words containing the sound. However, it is used infrequently and need not be considered an essential letter.

The letter *r* in initial position is included in the learning process. The schwa *r*, as in bird, is taught best with the vowels.

Consonants with more than one sound are taught when children have learned a sufficient number of sight words to note a spelling comparison. These letters are *c, g,* and *s*. Consonant blends or diagraphs (two letters representing a single sound) follow logically after the single consonant has been learned.

Learning vowel letter sounds relates to the child's ability to discriminate between long, short, and *r* controlled sounds. Hearing the differences facilitates attaching the correct sound to the vowel-consonant or consonant-vowel pattern. For example, in a one-syllable word, a single vowel followed by a consonant (closed syllable) is the short sound as in *at*. When the single vowel is in the final position (open syllable), the sound is usually long as in m*e*.

Vowel diagraphs (*oa* as in boat) are generalized early in vowel learning. The diphthong (*oi* as in oil) is among the last to be learned as an identified sound unit. Vowel-consonant combinations that are considered irregular spellings are learned as whole units (*ough* as in though).

The next stage in phonic analysis is hearing syllables and stress. When children have learned to attach vowel and consonant sounds to letters and to blend these sounds to form one-syllable words, they are ready to hear word parts and to note tonal differences. The ability to hear and understand that one syllable is accented or stressed slightly more than another is a necessary skill in determining vowel sounds.

The child must have the ability to hear and understand that in a polysyllabic word such as elephant, the medial vowel is neither long nor short, but a schwa sound (ə), and that that sound is used for vowels in unstressed syllables. This is a generalization that is confusing for both decoding and encoding in American English.

Structural Analysis

Structural analysis is not a separate entity in decoding written words. It is learned most effectively if it is based on known words and related to phonic analysis. Identifying the sounds of a letter is related to the reader's ability to syllabicate and to identify root words and suffixes correctly.

The first level of structural analysis is usually the recognition of *s* as an indicator of the plural form. When children learn that *hat* becomes *hats* by adding the *s,* they have had their first experience in understanding root words.

The introduction of common endings follows in logical order and as children encounter them in the reading vocabulary. Through reading words such as *jump* and *jumping,* the *ing* ending is learned. Doubling the final consonant is learned with words such as *running.*

The introduction of compound words at this point helps the children hear, see, and understand word parts. Using words from their sight vocabulary, the children hear and see the parts of two-syllable words such as baby and pony. With this knowledge, they form an understanding that in a two-syllable word that has a consonant-vowel, consonant-vowel pattern, the vowel is the last letter of the syllable and usually has the long sound.

Hearing two parts to words such as *absent* helps the learner recognize that words can be divided between two consonants. When this occurs, the first vowel usually is short because the syllable ends with a consonant. Additional generalizations with words such as *butter* and *happy* are learned easily because double letter consonants almost always are visual clues to syllabication and silent letters.

The division of multisyllabic words is taught initially through sound. When the child can hear the several word parts and can tap out the rhythm and stress of a word, long words become an enjoyable challenge.

The use and understanding of prefixes and suffixes are introduced next. Affixes with specific meaning changes are among the last structural skill to be acquired. Endings such as *ity* (familiarity) and *ious* (laborious) require a high-level experiential background. Affixes or word parts with non-English derivations (pedestrian) are learned as a final skill.

INSTRUCTIONAL CLASSIFICATIONS

Developmental Reader

There are three instructional classifications of readers: developmental, corrective, and remedial.

The developmental reader is one who is at grade expectancy. An expectancy level is an achievement level estimated by determining the difference between the mental age and the number of years of formal instruction, or age at school entrance. An average child with a chronological age of ten has a mental age of ten. Assuming that this child entered grade one at age six, the expectancy level would be grade four, the difference between the mental age and six. If this average ten-year-old was instructional at a beginning fourth reader level, the child would be a developmental reader.

Corrective Reader

A corrective reader is one who is reading below grade level or expectancy level. The degree of discrepancy between expectancy level and actual level of performance may be several months to many years. The label is not related to a specific language disability or to the degree of reading retardation but to the type or etiology of the problem.

The causes of corrective conditions include lack of motivation, poor or inadequate instruction, lack of readiness or experience, emotional problems, and sensory acuity. The reading problem may manifest itself as a word recognition deficit, poor comprehension, or a combination of the two.

A corrective reader has the intellectual potential to learn but, for one or more reasons, has not acquired the skills necessary to function adequately. The use of the word corrective implies that with instruction at the proper level, and in some cases correction of the cause, the child will learn to read without the use of specific remedial techniques.

Many children in this group lack motivation or readiness at the time of beginning instruction. A poor beginning probably is the number one cause of corrective problems. Many, if not most, of the children seen in public schools by the remedial reading teacher fall into this category.

An informal survey of a group of children being seen by a reading specialist indicated that 80 percent came from homes where reading seldom occurred. More than half of the families did not subscribe to a daily newspaper, nor did they read to their children. One nine-year-old who was enrolled in a reading laboratory school was heard telling the teacher, "My grandma thinks that I'm going to learn to read. But I ain't!" The reading problem was caused by environmental factors and total disinterest in academics.

In the case of the child who lacks readiness, the problem may be compounded by outside pressures and educational practices. The child is not ready to attend to instruction in grade 1, but is promoted to the next grade. The second-grade teacher introduces new skills. The child now has interest in learning but lacks the necessary prerequisite knowledge; thus, the new skills are meaningless. Reading is a process of sequential steps; a poor foundation or a missing step affects the total product.

Another condition that is not uncommon is the effect of outside pressures. Teachers and peers tend to chastise the poor reader. No one likes to be looked down upon or be the recipient of nasty remarks. When a child recognizes a disapproving glance by the teacher or is called dumb by peers, a negative reaction may occur. The child may become angry and display antisocial behaviors, swear, become physically abusive, or become passively aggressive and refuse to attempt to learn. The list of possible behaviors is nearly endless; however, the result usually is the same: the child does not learn to read, and the discrepancy between grade expectancy and performance increases.

Although the lack of readiness and motivation may be a crucial factor for the corrective reader, there is one positive aspect: many of these children do reach a point where they are ready to learn. When this occurs, taking them back to their instructional level can result in rapid gains.

The child with emotional problems, and who does not acquire reading ability at the expectancy level, is generally identified properly if placed in the corrective group. However, there is a fine line between the emotionally disturbed corrective reader and the remedial reader with an emotional problem. The main difference is that the emotionally disturbed child had an adjustment problem prior to the reading disability; the emotional problem caused the reading disability. The situation is reversed with the remedial reader; a remedial disability may cause an emotional adjustment problem.

The type of emotionally disturbed child that will develop a reading problem is as varied as the number of types of adjustment problems that may exist. There really is no classical type. However, the syndrome can be exemplified.

A child has an emotional problem, that is, he is afraid to be separated from his mother. The child is forced to attend school and develops school phobia. He does not, or cannot, attend to instruction. He cannot attend to the material he is supposed to read. He does not achieve.

If and when the emotional condition changes, the pupil will be ready for instruction. The cause must be removed, or the child must learn to cope with the situation, before the instruction can be effective.

Typically, the emotionally disturbed individual displays serious comprehension problems. This usually is the result of an inability to concentrate on the task at hand. However, a word of caution: being emotionally disturbed does not necessarily imply that the individual will have a reading problem. The reference here is to the corrective reader with an adjustment problem, not to all children who are emotionally disturbed.

Remedial Reader

The remedial reader is truly an example of the handicapped learner. The primary cause of the reading problem is physiological and seldom can be corrected. The reading disability results from dysfunction within the central nervous system. The individual is not mentally retarded. He has sufficient intellectual capacity to learn but, because of a dysfunction within the processing system, is unable to perform adequately when decoding written language. The condition has many labels. It sometimes is referred to as dyslexia, primary reading retardation, or a specific learning disability.

The diagnosis is based on a cluster of behaviors. Assuming the reader is remedial, the evaluator may wish to determine if the cause is endogenous or exogenous. Endogenous refers to a condition that has been inherited. The gene or inherited tendency is received most commonly by male members of the family but may manifest itself in or be carried by the female. Case histories reveal that several members of a family have reading problems. It is not uncommon to learn that the child's grandfather, uncle, and several cousins have been unable to learn to read. The problem may be evident in consecutive generations or scattered in no apparent order.

Exogenous refers to conditions that affect learning and that occur during the prenatal stage, at the time of birth, or any time thereafter. The most frequently identified probable causes are anoxia and trauma. The word "probable" is used advisedly because the cause can only be assumed from signs and is not absolutely verifiable. Conditions that frequently are indicated as the cause of anoxia are prolonged or difficult delivery, prolonged and high fevers, and accidents. Trauma is the result of injury or insult to the brain.

Complications are more frequent in male births than in female births. This may be because the average male fetus is somewhat larger than the average female, and the skeletal structure of the male may be larger and broader. The male also is more apt to suffer cranial injury with resulting brain damage than is the female. This situation is related to cultural customs. Little boys are encouraged to climb trees and play equipment, ride bicycles and minibikes, and participate in body contact sports. These customs and birth complications are contributors to the learning problems of the male and are responsible in part for the fact that more males than females are identified as having specific learning disabilities.

Childhood diseases and high fevers are suspected of causing brain injury, with resulting learning problems. Illnesses and high fevers are not sex related and can affect the female with equal frequency.

Specific types of written language problems common to the remedial reader include the following: inadequate sight vocabulary, reversals, figureground confusion, visual discrimination, visual closure, sequencing, and abstract comprehension. Sight vocabulary deficits may occur in the absence of other deficits or concomitantly with one or more related problems.

Reversals may be static or kinetic, or both. Static reversals are the rotation in place of a symbol. The rotation may be from left to right, as in *b* for *d,* or from top to bottom, as in *p* for *b.* The child may read *pat* for *bat.* Kinetic reversals are the transposition of a letter or letters. The child may read *tap* for *pat* or attempt to pronounce *athe* for *hate.*

Reversals frequently are associated with early directionality learning and the establishment of brain hemisphere dominance. When the condition persists beyond a normal developmental age of six or seven, it may be indicative of mixed dominance or perceptual dysfunction.

Visual figureground and visual discrimination are important aspects of the decoding process. The reader must be able to see words as letter units, differentiate meaningful stimuli from the background, and note differences in size, shape, and direction of letters and words. The reader who demonstrates problems in these areas may view the written page as a confusing mass of symbols without order or meaning. Clearly defined word forms are necessary for the acquisition of a sight vocabulary.

Visual closure, described previously, facilitates word recognition, reading rate, and rhythm. Without this skill, the reading process is slowed considerably; the need to look at each and every unit also may affect comprehension.

The remedial reader may have comprehension problems because of insufficient sight vocabulary; however, in many cases, the understanding surpasses word recognition. The types of reading comprehension that are most difficult for the disabled reader are those dealing with time (or sequence) and inferences.

Problems in understanding time, order, and sequence may be demonstrated in both auditory and visual modes or may be confined exclusively to written language. The child may have confused order in retelling story facts or be unable to determine cause and effect in relation to which happened first.

Individuals with central nervous system dysfunctions can be concrete in their thinking processes. They may lack the ability to abstract or to see the relationship of one statement to another. This behavior is noted in the remedial reader, particularly in relation to inferential comprehension. The child may be able to identify words in a passage but be unable to relate to ideas that are not stated specifically. The problem may not affect the ability to read basic instructional material. It can affect reading for enjoyment and can limit the scope of material that can be comprehended and appreciated.

EVALUATING READING ABILITY

The type of evaluation tool used to determine reading ability is selected on the basis of the type of information to be obtained. There are informal measures and standardized tests that will yield word recognition and comprehension scores indicative of grade level achievement. Other measures are designed to identify specific skills or educational objectives to be included in the child's instructional program.

Teacher-Prepared Informal Reading Inventory

The Informal Reading Inventory (IRI) is an instrument that can help the evaluator in determining the child's word recognition, oral and silent reading comprehension, and hearing comprehension grade achievement. In addition, it can be used to identify specific strengths and weaknesses. Because this version is teacher prepared, the material can be planned to answer questions relevant to a specific reading program.

Contrary to the suggestions of others, the author of this text believes that the inventory should be taken from the reading instruction material that will be used for teaching the child. If the questions are "At what level should the child be taught in the ABC series?," and "What skills from the third level workbook does the child know?," then they can be answered best by using that series.

Preparing an IRI

An IRI is an individually administered measure. It can be used in part to answer specific questions, or in its entirety for an overall picture of the child's performance.

To prepare the word recognition test, use a random sample of words from the vocabulary list of a graded reading series. For a series that uses a linguistic approach, a random sample of words from each pattern is recommended. For a complete IRI, one that spans kindergarten through eighth grade, or higher, it may be necessary to use subject matter texts at the upper levels. If the basal series being used has more than one book per grade level, the list should include words from all books, or separate lists should be made for each book.

Print or type the words in a column. If possible, use a primer typewriter for lists up to and including grade one. Leave sufficient space between words so that the list can be used for timed presentation. Be sure the student's copy is printed clearly. It can be prepared on ordinary paper and then permanently fastened to a stronger product to increase durability. On the examiner's copy, make two additional columns of lines for scoring space (Appendix B).

Word recognition in an IRI also is measured in context. This is accomplished by scoring word errors in the oral passage.

Comprehension is evaluated in three ways: oral reading comprehension, silent reading comprehension, and hearing comprehension. Three separate selections at each grade level are needed for this purpose. When using a traditional basal for the reading selection, it is helpful to open the book to about the middle and find a selection near that point. The middle of the book usually contains grade level material; other selections may be review.

The length and type of selection depends on the reading level. At the primary level (primer) a twenty-word story may be sufficient. The number of words in the selection increases as the grade level rises. A selection at the eighth grade reader level may contain as many as several hundred words.

Label each selection as to its purpose. Count the number of words in both the oral and silent selections and indicate them on the page. Triple-space the oral selection on the examiner's copy. In this way there is ample space to note reading behavior.

Prepare a set of questions for each selection. Type the questions under the selections on the examiner's copy. At the lower level, four or five questions are used. Factual recall and vocabulary questions are typical at this level. As the selections increase in length, expand the number of questions. Suggested types of questions involve vocabulary, inferential, sequence, analogies, cause and effect, and factual recall (check under Directed Reading Activity examples).

Be certain the student's copy is printed clearly. This is not a test of visual closure ability per se. The examiner's copy can be prepared on a Ditto so that many copies will be available.

Administering and Scoring an IRI

An IRI can be used to determine a child's independent, instruction, and frustration reading levels as well as hearing comprehension level. Levels are computed on the basis of the child's ability to recognize words in context and to comprehend the material read. Suggested criteria are as follows:

Word recognition accuracy percent	Comprehension accuracy percent
Independent level above 96 percent	90–100
Instruction level 91–96	75
Frustration level 90 or below	below 75
Hearing comprehension	75

The word recognition lists are administered first. They are easier and faster to use. An independent level score, or the highest level correct for a severe word recognition case, can be used as a starting point for the selection reading.

Scores from the timed recognition test will indicate the child's sight vocabulary level. The untimed presentation yields information on word analysis ability. The examiner's copy has the column of words on the left and an equal number of spaces to the right for scoring or indicating the child's responses.

The instructions are, "I am going to show you some words. I'm going to show them rather quickly. You will need to be ready and to look closely. If you know the word, say it. If you have trouble with it, I'll give you a chance to look at it a little longer, and then you see if you can sound it out. Some of the words probably will be easy for you. Some of them are difficult (hard). I'm going to show you words that I don't expect you to know. I need to do this to help you learn them later."

For primary grade children, or for those suspected of having a reading problem, begin with preprimer words. For older children, or for those whose grade level approximation is known, begin at the appropriate level for independent reading.

Place the copy directly in front of the student. Keep the words covered until ready for testing. If the examiner is right-handed, it is best to sit at the right of the pupil. In this way the scoresheet can be placed to the right of the examiner and out of the direct visual line of the student. The seating arrangement is reversed for the left-handed examiner.

Show the first word. The time of exposure is approximately the slow silent count of 1,000, 2,000. Score the child's response. If the child did not respond, remind him that you are flashing the words and that he must be ready to look and think. Expose error words for analysis. Record the answer in the untimed column. Your own version of phonetic transcription can be used to note incorrect responses. Allow a reasonable length of time for this portion of the test, but do not allow the process to drag.

Continue exposing each word for about the same time period. When the response is correct, move to the next word. Do not expose known words for an untimed presentation. Untimed is used for incorrect identification or no response.

Attempt to find the level at which the child recognizes 100 percent of the words. Continue upward until the error level reaches 50 percent. (See Appendix B for an example of scored responses.)

When the testing is completed, you may want to return to error words to determine how the child analyzed or what he recognized. For example, the child was inconsistent in identifying words with *ed* endings. Go back to an error example and ask the child to look at the word. Check to see if he recognized the number of syllables, or how the word ended. If necessary, cover the *ed*. In this fashion, you can determine specific knowledge and problem areas.

Begin the paragraph reading at the highest level at which the child scored 100 percent correct in word recognition. In the case of a pupil with severe word recognition deficits, use the lowest level possible.

The directions are, "I'm going to ask you to read some paragraphs and some short stories. Some of them are to be read aloud. Others you will read silently (to yourself). At the end of every selection I will ask you questions about what you have read. If you do not know a word, I will tell you what it is."

The order of presentation is not important. Oral selections are read first as this gives the examiner time to score and count errors while the pupil is reading silently. The computed score is used in making the decision to continue or end the testing.

Oral selections are scored for omissions (The child could ~~not~~ read), substitutions (The child could ~~not~~ read), additions (The child could not read), and words supplied by the teacher (The child | | | | | could not read). When a child pauses, a stroke is placed in front of the word, one stroke per second. After the fifth second the word is supplied; *t.h.* indicates teacher's help.

Other types of notations are made for qualitative information. Word by word reading (The | child | could | not | read.) is indicated by vertical lines. Repetitions are underscored for every repeat (He could not read!). Reading through punctuation is indicated by an "x" (The child could not read × He). Incorrect inflection is marked by either an arrow pointing up ↑ or one pointing down ↓. (The child could not read. ↑). Run-togethers are

---

Note: The last two paragraphs on this page and sections of pages 184 and 249 were double spaced to allow for hand-written notations.

marked with a͜ to show which words are run together (The͜ child does͜ not͜ want to.).

The number of words in a passage (125) is divided into the number of errors (4) to arrive at the percentage of errors (3.2). This is subtracted from 100 percent to determine percent correct (96.8).

Qualitative information is used in analyzing the quality of the child's reading and in determining possible causes of comprehension difficulty. For example, ↑ indicates that the sentence was read with rising inflection, or as a question, not as a declarative statement.

Hearing comprehension testing is optional. However, it does have several uses that can be valuable in planning an instructional program. The directions are as follows: "I'm going to read you some stories. When I finish each one, I will ask you questions."

The stories are read in grade sequence, beginning at a level equal to the child's instructional comprehension level. Testing upward continues until the child scores under 75 percent.

Information from this test, when compared to reading comprehension, will help determine the discrepancy between the child's oral language understanding level and his ability to comprehend written language. The hearing comprehension score is sometimes a better indicator of a child's potential than an IQ score.

On rare occasions a silent reading comprehension score will exceed the hearing comprehension. When this occurs, the examiner can suspect that the individual is a visual learner, and modality testing is suggested.

An IRI can be used with all types and ages of learners. For older children with severe reading disabilities, the material can be high interest, low readability. In this way they are not insulted by the content of the material. When used with developmental readers or gifted individuals, the silent selection can be timed to determine reading rate. To compute the rate, convert the number of minutes to seconds (1½ minutes = 90 seconds). Count the number of words in the selection (800). Divide the number of seconds into the number of words (90 into 800 = 8.9). Multiply the answer by seconds in a minute 8.9 × 60 = 534). The rate is 534 words per minute.

The IRI described above can be prepared easily by teachers or a paraprofessional. Similar instruments are available commercially.

Commercial Tests

Basic Education Skills Inventory (1973)
  Gary Adamson, Ed.D., Morris Shrago, Ph.D., and Glen Van Etten, Ed.D.

B. L. Winch and Associates
Select-Education, Inc.
P.O. Box 1185
Torrance, California 90505

Purpose: Assessment of multiple areas of word recognition.

Population: Kindergarten–grade 6.

Description: The BESI is an inventory that determines reading and mathematics expectancy. In the reading test, 22 areas are assessed. Subtests range from auditory memory to structural analysis of words. The measure also can be used for determining problems and abilities in manuscript writing. The grade range information varies according to the skill, such as Direction in Space: grades K–6, Suffixes: Grades 2–6. The material is easy to use; directions are clear. It is a useful inventory for assessing specific skill areas.

DART, Diagnostic Analysis of Reading Tasks (1976)
Ethel Steinberg
Slosson Educational Publications, Inc.
P.O. Box 280
East Aurora, New York 14052

Purpose: Test of decoding skills.

Population: Test I, below grade 2.5; Test II, above 2.5.

Description: DART was devised as a rapid means of diagnosing decoding problems but not comprehension problems. Skills assessed are phonics, structural analysis, and recognition of useful word parts. Nonsense words are used to determine knowledge of sound-symbol relationships and auditory discrimination. The information from the scoresheet is interpreted easily and transferred to the Student Reading Record Sheet. Problem areas are checked on the sheet and can be used in planning an Individualized Education Program. The test is not timed and can be readministered to check progress.

DST: Reading, Diagnostic Screening Test (1976)
Thomas D. Gnagey
Facilitation House
Box 611
Ottawa, Illinois 61350

Purpose: Diagnostic screening test.

Population: Grades 1–12.

Description: This test is designed to be used as a quick diagnostic tool that can be translated readily into practical individualized instructional programs. The resulting scores yield information on three word recognition levels and comprehension. In addition, the teacher can identify specific knowledge of linguistic patterns such as *cvc, vr,* and silent *e.* Each of the eight subtests yields a grade level proficiency. A time-saving pretest helps the examiner determine which subtests are appropriate and where to begin actual testing.

Fountain Valley Teacher Support System in Reading (1971)
   Richard L. Zweig, et. al.
   Richard L. Zweig Associates, Inc.
   20800 Beach Boulevard
   Huntington Beach, California 92648

Purpose: Word analysis, vocabulary, comprehension.

Population: Grades 1–6.

Description: The tests are prepared on audiotapes and may be used for individual or group administration. Tests are self-scoring for immediate feedback. The manual includes learning alternatives to reteach or reinforce. The progress profiles can be used to keep continuous records. Tests may be used in part or with older children who are remedial. The manual sets instructional objectives for specific test parts and can be used in planning a program or writing IEPs.

Handbook in Diagnostic Teaching (1974)
   Philip H. Mann and Patricia Suiter
   Allyn and Bacon, Inc.
   470 Atlantic Avenue
   Boston, Massachusetts 02210

Purpose: Reading test plus guide for preparation of testing material.

Population: Levels primer through 6.

Description: This is a set of inventories for reading, spelling, and related developmental areas. The inventories can be used as presented; however, the text includes directions for preparing similar material. Scoring and interpreting are discussed in terms that are understandable by anyone with a basic knowledge of language. It is a very compact set of materials for testing and understanding deficit language skills.

Individualized Criterion Referenced Testing (1976)
Educational Development Corporation
Learning Resources Division
P.O. Drawer 3709
202 Lake Miriam Drive
Lakeland, Florida 33803

Purpose: Criterion-referenced testing, all areas.

Population: Primary–intermediate levels.

Description: This measure can be used individually or in small groups. As in all criterion-referenced testing, it is not normative; objectives are written on a continuum. The child does or does not meet an objective. Scoring can be completed with a template. One of the advantages of this test is that unsuccessful objectives become instructional objectives or IEPs. Early level materials are consumable. The examiner must understand criterion-referenced testing, or the directions will be overwhelming on first reading. Once the principle is understood, the procedure is easy to use.

Prescriptive Reading Inventory, P.R.I., Levels I and II (1976)
CTB/McGraw-Hill, Inc.
Del Monte Research Park
Monterey, California 93940

Purpose: Diagnosis of learning behaviors.

Population: Beginning grade 1.

Description: P.R.I. Levels I and II are criterion-referenced tests that identify individual behaviors as stated in objective terms. There are nine components in all. If used in its entirety, this material is a test, intervention, and reassessment package. *Prescriptive Reading Inventory, P.R.I.* (1972) is a criterion-referenced test that assesses common reading objectives, grades 1.5 through 6.5. It also is a complete program that can be used for identifying skills, writing behavioral objectives, and retesting to determine if goals have been met.

Slosson Oral Reading Test (1963)
Richard L. Slosson, M.A.
Slosson Educational Publications
P.O. Box 380
East Aurora, New York 14052

Purpose: Word recognition.

Population: Grade 1–high school.

Description: This is perhaps the fastest to administer of the quick tests—an average of three minutes individually. It is simply a list of graded words to be read aloud and is not a diagnostic tool. It can be used for determining approximate reading levels for initial grouping or as a starting point for more in-depth testing. Correlation with other measures is surprisingly high.

Stanford Diagnostic Reading Test III (1974)
   Bjorn Karlsen, Richard Madden, and Eric F. Gardner
   Harcourt Brace Jovanovich, Inc.
   757 Third Ave.
   New York, New York 10017

Purpose: Group test to diagnose reading problems individually.

Population: High school–college.

Description: This test assesses four components of the reading process: comprehension, vocabulary, decoding, and rate. The test is organized like previous Stanford tests. It is included here because it can be group administered to adults. Tests that are applicable to adults are rare. Information from this test can be used to determine mature readers who need additional help. It is particularly helpful at the college level for study skills programs.

Woodcock-Johnson Psycho-educational Battery (1977)
   Richard W. Woodcock and M. Bonner Johnson
   Teaching Resources Corporation
   100 Boylston Street
   Boston, Massachusetts 02116

Purpose: General assessment.

Population: Grades 1–12.

Description: This covers many academic areas and is easy to use. If properly administered, it yields information that is normative and diagnostic. Subtest time takes from 15 to 25 minutes, depending on the subject's age and cooperation. It is an especially helpful instrument for itinerant diagnosticians because it is an all-in-one measure.

TEACHING READING

Teaching reading to an exceptional learner does not necessarily mean that the child has a reading problem. Therefore, teaching methods that can be used with developmental readers, the gifted, or those with reading deficits are included here.

The Language Experience Approach (LEA)

There is no best way to teach reading. However, one method that can be used with all age groups and types of learners is the Language Experience Approach (LEA). The LEA is eclectic in that the procedure can encompass all aspects of language learning from listening skills through and including written expression.

The context of material used for reading can be as broad in scope as the interests of the learner. Basal readers and workbooks are not required. The approach can be highly individualized while being used for group instruction.

The steps in the LEA include the following:

Developing the Language Chart

The chart (at the primary level) or the story (at the more advanced level) is written by the learners with the teacher's guidance. (Teacher is used generically here; a teacher may be a trained professional or any interested person who understands the method.) The pupils tell a story; it is recorded by the teacher. The content of the story may relate to a recent experience, a make-believe person, a description of a sporting event, paraphrased material that has been read to the learners, or anything that is developmentally appropriate and of interest.

A primer story written after a walk on a late September day may be as follows:

The Walk

"I saw a tree with red and yellow leaves," said Paul.
"Me too," said Claudette.
Jenny said, "I saw a Christmas tree, and it was all green."
"When can we go for another walk?" asked Willy.

The children's names were included to motivate them to want to read and because name recognition and writing are among the first written language skills acquired. The story was not written as a paragraph so it could be shown more clearly that a sentence is a grouping of words that expresses a thought, and that capitals and punctuation marks are used in written language. As the children develop in knowledge of written language, the form and complexity of structure is used appropriately.

Writing on the chalkboard and then copying onto chart paper allows for story changes and corrections. Older children dictate longer stories; these are written on paper and copied on the chalkboard or typed for reading.

When a child gives a sentence that is grammatically incorrect, it should be written as stated but with correct spelling. *Me don't wanna go* should be written as *Me don't want to go*. *Wanna* is not a word that the child will find in written material and is useless as a visual experience. After the story is written, the teacher discusses each sentence, and suggestions for grammatical changes are offered. If the child has a good teacher model, the sentence will become *I don't want to go,* and it will be the child's idea to make the change.

Reading

Chart stories are read when they are completed. The teacher reads the entire story to determine if the children approve it as written. Changes are made when appropriate. The teacher then reads the first sentence, moving a hand from left to right under the words while reading. The hand moves in a continuous motion, not word by word. The pupils read with the teacher, then one child is asked to read. The process continues on until every pupil has had an opportunity to read.

For older children, or on an individual basis, the teacher does not read sentence by sentence. Once the story is in acceptable form, the reading is done by the child. The teacher supplies help when needed. Phonic analysis is not suggested, but context clues are pointed out.

Developing Sight Vocabulary

Several methods can be used for developing sight vocabulary. The most frequent is to underline specific words. As the child reads the story, any word that presents a problem is underlined. These words are reviewed at the end of the lesson. Later they are placed on flash cards for practice drill.

Several words learned in this fashion are grouped together, and the child is tested for recognition. When a word is recognized with 100 percent accuracy, it is filed for inclusion in a writing or spelling lesson. The child also may keep a vocabulary notebook. In that event, the word is entered in the appropriate alphabetical space for study and independent use.

Developing Word Analysis Skills

Lessons are planned using the child's sight words. The method of introduction is determined by the child's need or obvious readiness. For example, the pupil has used several words that have a common spelling in a story. With these words, the teacher uses the procedure discussed under phonic analysis earlier in this chapter. The child is guided to see and hear the similarity until the generalization is formed. New words using the spelling are included in the follow-up activity.

Instruction in structural analysis follows the same order. For both phonic and structural analysis, the teacher must be cognizant of the child's developmental level and the logical order of teaching word analysis skills.

Developing Comprehension

Comprehension of word, sentence, and paragraph meaning is part of the Language Experience Approach from the first step on. Initially the teacher might ask a child to tell what a word means, or ask the pupil to read a sentence supplied by another student and restate it in his own words. Asking children to read a sentence or a paragraph and then say it in another way is an excellent means of checking comprehension for all reading material.

Controlling Vocabulary

One of the complaints against the LEA is that vocabulary is not controlled. Words are not repeated enough to be learned, or words that are too difficult may be included. Children do not use or learn words that are too difficult for them. When a polysyllabic word from a child's speaking vocabulary is learned as a reading word, it is within the pupil's ability or he would not have learned it in the first place. If the child uses a word once and never refers to it again, it may not be a word that is needed at that time. Repetition is not difficult to bring about; using the words from the child's story, the teacher constructs another story. The reading material is still the child's vocabulary; it simply is restructured.

If there are words the teacher wants the child to learn, a lesson in which the pupil will use those words is planned. For example, the word *basket* is to be learned. The teacher and the children discuss the word. The teacher suggests they write a story naming as many uses for, or kinds of, baskets that they can imagine. The word is introduced and repeated in this fashion. Planning is the key to the Learning Experience Approach.

For additional information on this approach, the reader is directed to Stauffer (1970).

Directed Reading Activity (DRA)

If used properly, the Directed Reading Activity (DRA) is what the name implies: it is a reading lesson in which the teacher directs the children's learning. There are five interrelated steps or activities in the DRA:

1. readiness and motivation
2. guided silent reading for a purpose
3. comprehension check and rereading
4. development of word analysis skills
5. follow-up and reinforcement

As an example, a short passage that is geared to an adult population is used here. With this material, a DRA is planned that will exemplify the steps and processes involved in a reading lesson. These steps are applicable to a paragraph in a preprimer or a science lesson in a junior high textbook.

Readiness and Motivation

This step introduces new vocabulary in context, develops concepts needed to understand the material, and arouses interest for reading the material.

Vocabulary: *prognosis* as a new reading word
terminal as a new meaning
Teacher: Did you ever help someone who was ill? What did you do? What had the prognosis been? (Write the question on the board. Guide response to include word prognosis, and write it on the board.) What happened to you after the person recuperated? Have you ever helped someone who was terminal? (Discussion should include understanding of the word.) Have you ever heard of someone who was put on trial because the person took care of someone who was ill? (It is hoped that discussion will elicit story of malpractice suit.)

Guided Silent Reading

Purposes for reading are established in this part of the procedure.

Teacher: The story we are about to read is entitled *The Trial.*

Considering what we have been discussing, what do you think the story is about?

Students: A doctor was put on trial for killing a patient. The doctor went to jail or paid a fine.

Teacher: You said the doctor was on trial. Read to find out who was on trial; see if you are correct. You also said the patient died. Read to find out what happened to the sick person in this story and what happened to the person who helped the patient.

This lesson is for adults, and is short. Therefore, the entire passage should be read before comprehension is checked. For readers with severe comprehension problems, guide statements and comprehension questions should be used with very short passages such as two or three sentences. The story:

The Trial

A little over 200 years ago in Salem, Massachusetts, the townsfolk gathered at the shore to await the outcome of a trial. The accused was a blonde, blue-eyed girl of nineteen.

Her crime had been that of saving the life of a cabin boy from the schooner Sea Witch. The medical prognosis had been terminal. The lad had been abandoned by his shipmates. The people of the town feared his malady.

The outcome of the trial was innocent by death.

Classroom Follow-up

Teacher: Who was put on trial? (Factual recall question referring back to guide statement.)

What happened to the patient? (Factual recall referring back to guide statement.)

If he lived, why was the girl on trial? (Inference and background knowledge of that period.)

Did the sick boy have a family in Salem? (Inference)

What word did the author use in place of illness? (Vocabulary)

Why didn't the townspeople help the boy? (Factual recall, background knowledge of the plague, and inference.)

How did the author give you a clue to the beliefs of the townspeople? (Symbolism)

How was the girl proved innocent? (Background and cause and effect)

Word Analysis

This lesson deals with structural analysis, specifically, the meaning of *mal.* The word malady is written on the chalkboard.

Teacher: This word was in the story we read. What did it mean?

I am going to say a sentence in which there is a missing word. See if you can fill in the blank with a word that begins the same way as malady.

He does not behave like the well-adjusted people in his class; he is _____ . (maladjusted)

What does maladjusted mean? (Word is written on board under the word malady.)

Can you think of other words that begin the same way? (Other words are listed and discussed.)

What do all of these words have in common? (They mean something not good—bad or evil.)

When you look at the words, can you see something that is the same? (*mal*)

When you see a new word that begins with *mal,* what is one of the things you can remember that might help you understand the meaning? (Students state generalization.)

Follow-Up and Reinforcement

The activity for this lesson is in two parts:

1. Discuss the word *prognosis* as to meaning and ending. Assign the task of finding other words with the same ending. This will be discussed in another lesson.

2. Assign students the task of researching the topic of Salem witches. Material from research can be used for a reading unit on the history of myths and customs in America.

Word-Learning Technique

VAKT is the acronym for visual, auditory, kinesthetic, and tactile. The letters have become synonymous with a remedial word-learning technique described by Fernald (1943). She suggested the method for learning to spell. In more recent years it has become the tool of the remedial reading teacher. Briefly, the steps are as follows:

1. The word to be learned is discussed as to meaning and syllables. The student is to explain the meaning and to tell how many parts, or syllables, are in the word. The dictionary is used to verify the response and to discuss further, if needed.
2. The teacher places a strip of paper (3" × 9") in front of the student, or in a direct visual line. The teacher says the whole word, says the word in syllables while writing the word, and repeats the word when it has been written. It may be written in manuscript or cursive form.
3. The teacher demonstrates how to trace the word using two fingers. The procedure is the same as with writing. The word is said, said in syllables as it is traced, and repeated as a whole word after the tracing. The demonstration continues until the student indicates that he is ready to try.
4. The student traces the word following all of the demonstrated steps. Should an error be made, the student is stopped immediately. The teacher demonstrates the correct procedure and continues to do so until the student is ready to try again. (Prompting to motivate is acceptable.)
5. When the student feels able to write the word correctly, the tracing sample is removed from sight. The student writes the word using all of the steps as in the tracing. If an error of any kind is made, the writing is stopped and the partial word is erased. The student returns to the tracing for additional practice. When the word has been written correctly, it is compared to the sample.
6. When the child writes the word correctly on three consecutive trials, the word is presumed to have been learned, at least for the moment.
7. The sample word and the practice material are filed in a word box or word file. The material can be reused if needed, and the word becomes part of a vocabulary or analysis lesson at some future date.

As described, the technique must be used on a one-to-one basis. The theory behind the method is that the involvement of four modalities increases the probability that the learning will be effective. The child is distracted less easily, and improved attention facilitates learning.

However, the reader must be cautioned that this method is not a panacea. Even with the best clinician teaching, it does not always work. In fact, it is not the best technique for some modality impaired children. When this method is used with some children who, for example, have impaired auditory perception, the pairing of the good input (VKT) with the impaired input (A), the product may be totally distorted or irretrievable in the future. In other words, combining modalities may not be helpful. Determining which children can and should use this technique often is a trial-and-error situation.

LEA + VAKT + DRA = RP

The LEA, the DRA, and VAKT have been discussed. It is time now to combine the three into a Remedial Program. With modification, this program can be used with young children or adults, the mentally retarded, the disadvantaged, or the learning disabled.

1. The student tells a story. The source can be original or paraphrased from another source such as a newspaper or textbook. The teacher writes the story as dictated.
2. The story then is read back to the student, word by word, or sentence by sentence, depending on the ability of the student. When appropriate, language skills such as grammar, sentence structure, and punctuation can be taught as part of the lesson. The student writes as the teacher dictates.
3. When the student misspells a word, the writing is stopped. The word then is learned through VAKT, or a modification of the technique that is appropriate for the student. When the word is learned, it is written in the story and underlined.
4. The story is typed for a future reading lesson. All words learned are placed on cards for flash presentation and drill.
5. At the time of the next reading lesson, the flash cards are used to check word recognition and review.
6. The typed story is presented for reading using the DRA procedure. The story is discussed, and the child may be asked to recall parts of the material. The student is asked to read the story silently to find specific answers, identify vocabulary words, or to locate statements

for oral rereading. Comprehension is checked using a variety of types of questions.

7. Words from the story and the file box are used to teach word analysis skills.

8. The follow-up and reinforcement activities involve independent work such as a worksheet relating to the word analysis skill just taught. The material in this section can be teacher prepared or a commercial product.

A Sequential Learning Method

This method can be used in its entirety or at any level appropriate to the needs of the learner.

To teach the names of the letters of the alphabet, group them into sets of five letters. X is seldom used and can be taught separately. Make four columns of 25 letters. Place the letters in random order. For example, to teach the names of *b, f, g, t,* and *u,* the column might be as follows: *b, f, g, t, u, f, t, b, u, g, t, u, b, g, f, f, b, u, g, t, u, t, b, g, f.*

Make a tachistoscope slide the width of the column, plus space on either side. Make a small window that will clearly expose the letter to be viewed. Place the slide over the first column. Say to the child, "I am going to show you some letters. I will say the names of the letters on this page and when I am finished, it will be your turn." Say the names of the first five letters, which are the letters to be learned. After you have named the letters, cover them. Move the slide down to expose the first letter. If the child names it correctly, say, "Good," and go to the next letter. If the pupil is incorrect or does not respond, supply the correct answer. Then go to the next, and so on.

If the child scores 95 percent correct, go to another set of five. After the second set, or when the child has learned ten letter names, combine the two sets for a review lesson.

As the child progresses through the alphabet, review lessons should be used every third lesson for reinforcement as well as testing. Letters that are not known with 100 percent accuracy should be relearned.

To teach the sounds attached to consonants, use the same procedure. Group the consonants, make columns, use the same directions, and substitute the letter sound for the name.

Vowels should be taught in spelling patterns. For example *at, ut, it, et, ot, am, im, om, um, em,* and so on. For long vowels use *ite, ate, ote, ute, ete* or *ide, ade, ude, ode,* and *ede.*

When the consonants and some vowel patterns have been learned, combine them into one syllable words such as *pat, cut, mit, bet,* and *not.*

To teach other words, particularly those that must be learned as wholes, the same method is applicable. Select any five words. Place them in random order in the columns. Demonstrate the correct response and proceed as before. This approach is much faster than flash cards and can be scored for accuracy.

A scoresheet can be made for any of the steps by using one sheet for student and one for instructor. If an error is made, draw a line through the appropriate stimulus. This will help determine accuracy level to comply with Individualized Education Program (IEP) stated criteria.

THE GIFTED READER

Children who are reading above grade level can be as frustrated as disabled readers. The classroom teacher who must cope with the bored, above-average reader also may suffer feelings of frustration.

Following an individualized instructional period on applying cloze procedure, the gifted student may find this activity challenging. Give the student the grade level basal reader. Tell the person to rewrite a story, or stories, using missing elements. The pupil is to omit words that can be dropped without losing the meaning of the passage. No more than ten words per hundred can be omitted. The omitted words may not be articles or conjunctions.

Developing the gifted reader's vocabulary while sticking to a grade level basal can present a problem. The following idea keeps the gifted learner working from the same text as the others but does not limit this student to material that is too easy.

Give the child a list of vocabulary words from the grade level placement basal. Assign the task of making a crossword puzzle using these words. The written clues must come from the second meaning as stated in the dictionary. Reading the dictionary can stretch the mind and improve the vocabulary of anyone who can understand or read at that level.

The wise teacher keeps a sample of the materials made in these activities. In subsequent years the puzzles and missing element stories become reinforcement exercises for the average reader.

COMMERCIAL PROGRAMS AND MATERIALS

Children's Press Reading Program (1972)
  Regensteiner Publishing Enterprises, Inc.
  Children's Press
  1224 West Van Buren Street
  Chicago, Illinois 60607

This is a series of high interest, low reading level books with tapes that present the story to be read, page by page, and then straight through. Each book introduces a specific occupation to the student. Comprehension questions are provided, as well as supplementary activities including language arts, mathematics, social studies, research, and art projects. The titles of some of the books in this series are:

> *I Want to Be a Baseball Player*
> *I Want to Be a Service Station Attendant*
> *I Want to Be an Architect*
> *I Want to Be a Secretary*
> *I Want to Be a Musician*

Minisystem: Fact, Fiction, and Opinion (1974)
George W. Bond, Lois K. Nichols, and George J. Smith
Susan L. Helman, story author
Learning Systems Corporation
D.C. Heath and Company
125 Spring Street
Lexington, Massachusetts 02173

This program is designed for intermediate level students. It consists of a cassette tape, activity sheet, and story card. Its purpose is to teach students to distinguish among the concepts of fact, fiction, and opinion and to recognize specific words and phrases that introduce opinion. The material can be used for independent learning and to develop discussion skills with the gifted.

Pal Reading Games (1977)
George Bratton
Xerox Education Publications
245 Long Hill Road
Middletown, Connecticut 06457

This material is designed for students working two or more years below grade level, but can be used for developmental readers. The games deal with phonic and structural analysis, sight words, and word meanings. It is suggested that the games be used sequentially and that the vocabulary words be incorporated into spelling and writing lessons.

Reading Skills in Action: Words We Use (1976)
Leon Bewley, Florence Devine, and Dorothy Snowman
Benefic Press
10300 W. Roosevelt Rd.
Westchester, Illinois 60153

This selection is composed of a workbook and six cassette tapes. It is designed to develop phonics skills by providing an understanding of the skill to be developed in the workbook, then giving taped examples as models. There is an introduction to each skill, reinforcement, and review. The intent of the program is to help learners become successively more independent in each skill as they progress.

Reading-Thinking Activities (1979)
   Mary Jane Cogan, M.Ed.
   Media Materials, Inc.
   2936 Remington Avenue
   Baltimore, Maryland 21211

The material consists of a workbook with reproducible pages and a cassette tape that accompanies the first page of each new unit. It provides the student with activities in the skill areas of vocabulary, cause and effect, analogies, factual information, and other fundamental reading skills needed for passage comprehension. The material is interesting and is particularly helpful with the corrective reader who has comprehension problems or has difficulty abstracting.

Recipe for Reading (1975)
   Nina Traub
   Educators Publishing Service, Inc.
   75 Moulton Street
   Cambridge, Massachusetts 02138

Designed for disabled readers, this program includes phonics, linguistics, sight vocabulary, spelling, and writing. It has appeal to a wide range of children. The manual gives very clear directions as to use and the reasons for its appropriateness. It is a multisensory approach. The materials include reading booklets, duplicator masters, and sequence charts.

The Ideal Wordshop Reading Cassette Program (1969)
   Roberta La Coste, Alvera B. Meighan, and Dorothy Craig
   Ideal School Supply Company
   11000 South Lavergne Avenue
   Oak Lawn, Illinois 60453

This program is composed of a workbook with reproducible pages, cassette tapes, and reading charts. Its intent is to develop almost every reading and listening skill; it can be used at any level from primary to secondary remedial. The materials supplied allow older students to work independently. Both introduction and reinforcement of skills are provided.

The New Specific Skill Series: Programs for Individualized Instruction
(1978)
Barnell Loft, Ltd.
958 Church Street
Baldwin, New York 11510

The material is composed of 14 levels of booklets, from prereading to grade twelve, with work in the following skill areas: sounds, directions, content, factual information, locating answers, conclusions, main ideas, and sequence. Placement tests are available to determine the level at which the student should be working. The program can be used with older students who can work independently. Tests are provided to check achievement following each selection.

Using Your Reading Skills Series (1977)
Guidance Associates
757 Third Avenue
New York, New York 10017

This series is four two-part sound filmstrip programs designed to improve comprehension in the content areas. Titles are: *Getting the Main Idea; Finding Work Clues; Skim, Scan, or Study?; Charts, Tables, Maps and Graphs.* This is for use with children at the intermediate level who have basic skills but need work in understanding textbook material.

REFERENCES

Adamson, G., Shrago, M., & Van Etten, G. *Basic education skills inventory*. Torrance, Calif.: Select-Education, Inc., 1973.

Bewley, L., Devine, F., & Snowman, D. *Reading skills in action: Words we use*. Westchester, Ill.: Benefic Press, 1976.

Bond, G. W., Nichols, L. K., Smith, G. J., & Helman, S. L. *Minisystem: Fact, fiction, and opinion*. Lexington, Mass.: D.C. Heath and Co., 1974.

Bratton, G. *Pal reading games*. Middletown, Conn.: Xerox Education Publications, 1977.

Children's Press reading program. Chicago: Children's Press, 1972.

Cogan, M. J. *Reading-thinking activities*. Baltimore: Media Materials, Inc., 1979.

Fernald, G. M. *Remedial techniques in basic school subjects*. New York: McGraw-Hill Book Co., Inc., 1943.

Gnagey, T. D. *DST: Reading*. Ottawa, Ill.: Facilitation House, 1976.

Individualized criterion referenced testing. Lakeland, Fla: Educational Development Corp., 1976.

Karlsen, B., Madden, R., & Gardner, E. F. *Stanford diagnostic reading test III*. New York: Harcourt Brace Jovanovich, Inc., 1974.

La Coste, R., Meighan, A. B., & Craig, D. *The Ideal wordshop reading cassette program*. Oak Lawn, Ill.: Ideal School Supply Co., 1969.

Mann, P. H., & Suiter, P. *Handbook in diagnostic teaching*. Boston: Allyn and Bacon, Inc., 1974.

Prescriptive reading inventory, PRI, Levels I and II. Monterey, Calif.: CTB/McGraw-Hill, Inc., 1976.

Slosson, R. L. *Slosson oral reading test*. East Aurora, N.Y.: Slosson Educational Publications, 1963.

Stauffer, R. G. *The language-experience approach to the teaching of reading*. New York: Harper and Row, Publishers, Inc., 1970.

Steinberg, E. *DART, Diagnostic analysis of reading task*. East Aurora, N.Y.: Slosson Educational Publications, Inc., 1976.

The new specific skill series: Programs for individualized instruction. Baldwin, N.Y.: Barnell Loft, Ltd., 1978.

Traub, N. *Recipe for reading*. Cambridge, Mass.: Educators Publishing Service, Inc., 1975.

Using your reading skills series. New York: Guidance Associates, 1977.

Woodcock, R. W., & Johnson, M. B. *Woodcock-Johnson psycho-educational battery*. Boston: Teaching Resources Corp., 1977.

Zweig, R. L. *Fountain Valley teacher support system in reading*. Huntington Beach, Calif.: Richard L. Zweig Associates, Inc., 1971.

Chapter 8

Handwriting

PENMANSHIP: THE VANISHING ART?

The skill of writing legibly may be a vanishing art, at least in this country. If legibility of written language were to be included in United States literacy statistics, the rate undoubtedly would drop drastically. This is not a reference to the ability to produce legible material but to the applied practice.

Far too many people say, "When my writing cools, even I can't read it." The probable cause for this is that their handwriting instruction was geared to conformity, not legibility. To be effective, handwriting should be taught in such a way as to develop the individual's own, unique style. Effective in this sense refers to legible written language.

The objective of a handwriting program—manuscript, or cursive—should be to produce legibility. To achieve this, the learner should be encouraged to use personal abilities and characteristics in writing legibly at all times. Teaching should be geared toward developing the strengths within the individual's physical abilities and personality patterns.

Penmanship can be a personal accomplishment, a thing of quiet pride. The exceptional learner needs every opportunity to develop skills and abilities that will foster self-acceptance. Handwriting is a personal reflection of one's self-worth.

HANDWRITING VOCABULARY

Before beginning a program to develop handwriting, the instructor should be familiar with the meanings of terms used in most systems. It is not essential that students use the correct word to describe a stroke or skill; however, it is helpful if the teacher uses the descriptor label in explanations. Knowing terms will help the instructor in selecting material from commercial programs.

Alignment refers to letter position. Uphill or downhill writing are examples of alignment problems. It can affect legibility if the alignment is irregular, with the tops of some words written over the bottoms of others. The problem may be caused by poor eye-hand coordination or body position.

Backward oval is the motion or stroke in forming round letters in a counterclockwise direction. In cursive writing, the letters, *a*, *o*, *d*, and *D* employ this motion. In manuscript it is a suggested stroke on all oval letters but need not be used: the direction should be optional.

Beginning stroke is the movement from the point of contact with the paper. In some styles of cursive writing a beginning stroke is used to begin flow, but it is not an essential element of the letter.

Checkstroke, also referred to as short retrace, is the small point on cursive letters *r*, *s*, *b*, *v*, and *w*.

Descenders are letters that extend below the baseline. In manuscript they are lower case *g, j, p, q,* and *y*. Cursive descenders are lower case *f, g, j, p, z, y,* and *z*; the capitals are *G, Y,* and *Z* .

Downcurve is the portion of a round or oval letter that is produced from top to bottom. *A, a, c, d, g, o,* and *q* are cursive examples; *a, c, d, e, g, o, q,* and *s* are manuscript letters made with this motion.

Downstroke is any motion from top to bottom. It is the stroke used in forming the vertical lines in all manuscript letters except the second half of *U*. It also is used to describe the outer curved line in cursive letters such as *t* and *a*.

Forward oval is used to describe the closed or partially closed circular motion in forming letters such as *B* and *P*. Directionally, it is clockwise.

Headroom refers to the space from top line, or bottom of written words in preceding line on unlined paper, and the tallest letter, *I*. Understanding the need for headroom greatly helps legibility. Maximum letters should not touch the top line.

Intermediate letters are those that are approximately three-quarters the height of maximum letters. In cursive writing they are *t, d,* and *p* However, *p* may be produced as a minimum letter.

Loop refers to cursive letters such as *l* and *g* . Cursive *l* and *e* are upper loop letters; *j, g, q,* and *z* are lower loop. A horizontal loop is sometimes used in uppercase cursive letters *L* and *F*.

Maximum letters are those that extend to the highest point. In manuscript they are all of the capitals and *b, d, f, h, k, l,* and *t* in lowercase. Cursive lowercase maximum letters are *ℓ*, *f*, *ℎ*, *ℓ*, and *k*.

Minimum letters do not extend above the midline. Lowercase letters such as *a, c, e, i, m, n, o, r, s, u, v, w,* and *x* are in this group.

Overcurve is an indirect oval motion producing the rounded tops in letters such as *m* and *n*. In the reverse, or *undercurve*, it is the upward motion or forward curve as in the bottom part of *u* and *w*.

Retrace is the motion back over a line, as in the checkstroke or in closed cursive letters *t, d, p, B, P,* and *R*. Retrace is essential for legibility. The amount of retrace may help distinguish between *cℓ* and *d*, as in *cℓ* for *d*, and *é* for *i*.

Rhythm refers to evenness or the stops and slows in writing. Poor rhythm may produce jerky lines, pointed curves, and line quality.

Slant refers to the angle from the absolute vertical or perpendicular. Traditionally, using cursive slant to the right or forward was believed to be *the* only way. In the last several decades, backward slant has become acceptable for the left-handed writer. The absence of slant was a requirement in manuscript. In some systems, slant is being suggested as a more natural way of forming letters because it leads into a cursive style.

Eventually direction of slant will be recognized for what it is, an artificial criterion for judging performance. The direction of the slant does not affect legibility. As long as the slant is consistent and all letters are produced in the same direction, to the left, straight up and down, or to the right, legibility is not involved. It is when slant is mixed or letters lean into each other that decoding may become difficult.

Vertical line is the basic stroke in manuscript letters. All uppercase letters except *U* are made with a downward vertical line.

MANUSCRIPT VS. CURSIVE

For the last four or five decades parents and teachers have asked the question, "Should I teach my child (children) to write or to print?" The choice was not questioned until the mid-20s. At that time cursive writing was the only method taught. The answer is not simple; it depends on the child and his abilities and disabilities.

Printing is manuscript writing. The plain script used today is derived from the more ornate style of the scribes of centuries ago. Manuscript has advantages, particularly as a beginning form of handwriting.

Most children learn to write at about the same time they learn to read the printed page. Manuscript more closely resembles the print used in books. Using a written symbol that resembles reading material simplifies the process. Children learn one new symbol form at a time. Reading and writing act as readiness and reinforcer; writing a sight vocabulary word is using meaningful material, and the reading learning is reinforced. In addition, printing usually is easier to align and space. Each letter is formed separately, giving the beginning writer time to prepare mentally and physically for symbol production.

The disadvantages are that it is slower, takes more precise eye-hand coordination, and may present problems for individuals who have directionality deficits. A letter such as *A* in manuscript requires three separate strokes. To form the letter correctly, the writer must have the ability to produce downward diagonals that intersect or join at exactly the proper point. The third line, the horizontal, must begin at a point touching the left vertical slant and end touching the right vertical slant line. The horizontal should be neither too high nor too low in relationship to placement within the angle. In other words, printing a capital *A* is a difficult procedure, especially if eye-hand coordination is not well developed.

Confusion with letters such as *b* and *d* is an example of what can happen to individuals who have directionality problems. When printing, they may reverse the direction; this reinforces incorrect learning.

Cursive writing, as previously suggested, is a more rapid form of recording. It takes less coordination and decreases the probability of static reversals. However, many of the letters are quite dissimilar from their printed counterparts. Learning to read and write cursive words requires the acquisition of a third language symbol system. For the mentally retarded or those with a specific language disability, this task may be too difficult.

The decision as to which symbol system to teach should be determined on the basis of the learner's abilities and needs. Either form will serve the same purpose and communicate ideas in writing, and both are legally acceptable. Employers seldom require a specific form; what they do require is legibility. Either or both forms are of value if, and only if, they can be read easily.

WRITING READINESS

A child is ready to begin instruction when he is physically ready to use fine motor skills and when he sees a need to learn. The development of physical abilities can be aided through gross and fine motor activities that are not related to language. Understanding the need to know how to write is a matter of motivation. Showing the importance of being able to write is one of the easier tasks in education. Sustained motivation may become crucial when legibility is stressed.

The physical requirements for writing readiness are as follows: the ability to sit comfortably in a chair for periods of reasonable duration, adequate motor control to move the arm across the writing surface from left to right and to grasp a writing tool with flexible fingers, and adequate visual sensitivity, particularly at near point. There are, of course, exceptions to these conditions. The requirements refer to most learners.

The physically impaired who function from a prone position should not be excluded from instruction, nor should the cerebral palsied if other levels of readiness are indicated. Procedures should be modified or a mechanical device should be used. Learning to type with a head pointer may be the cerebral palsied child's equivalent to manuscript instruction.

Writing Readiness Activities

The following are examples of activities that can be used at various levels of readiness.

Activity 1. Landing on the Moon is a revision of the old Pin the Tail game. Make a large picture of the moon. Color the moon spots different shades or colors. Give each child a spaceship with an adhesive on the back. The ships are in colors to match the moon spots.

Explain to the children that they are going to land on the moon. They are to find their spot; it is the same color as their ship. To make it more fun, they are coming in blind until the moment of impact. (Children who watch television will have no difficulty with the language.)

When it is their turn, have them close their eyes and lead them to the moon. Turn them around just before they reach the target. Say, "Land." Have them open their eyes and in one motion find their spot and land.

Their aim will improve with practice, as will their ability to place their writing instruments on target. The activity is much like looking up and then down at the paper in the copy practice exercises.

Activity 2. Finger Painting is fun; it is kinesthetic and tactile learning. Initially allow the children to create anything they desire. When you are ready to develop specific movements, give the children paper and paints. Have them make big circles, downward vertical lines, horizontals from left to right, and so on. Begin with big forms; decrease the size until the children are able to make good two-inch forms.

When they actually are learning letter forms, allow them to practice in the paint. You can't make a mistake when finger painting; anything goes; the children know this. The tension from the writing situation is removed, and practice is fun in color.

Activity 3. Finger tapping may seem unrelated to writing; however, it may help determine laterality, and it does aid in developing small muscle control.

Have the children tap on their desks. Use the index finger on the dominant hand. For children who have not developed handedness, have them use one hand and then the other. Observe if there is a difference in speed and rhythm. The hand that produces the most taps with the best rhythm is probably the side to train.

Play a record with a strong beat. Have the children listen until they learn the rhythm, then have them tap out the beat.

A variation is to put a dot on each child's desk. Have the children touch the dot as they tap. To do this they will look at, or glance at, the spot; this aids eye-hand coordination.

Commercial tappers also are available. These devices count taps and can be used for laterality testing. Old telegraph keys make good tappers, too.

Activity 4. Left-to-right movement begins by placing a one-inch strip of tape across each child's desk. The tape should be sectioned off into one-inch colored squares, each a different color.

Have the children place their arms comfortably, but flat, with fingers pointing to the first square on the left side. They are not to raise their arms but are to practice gliding across the surface. The purpose is to train them in left-to-right eye and hand movement. This will produce smooth movement across the writing surface. If the left-handed child becomes used to holding the wrist straight, it may prevent hooking when instruction is started.

Initially call out each color in the order they appear from left to right. As the children become accustomed to the exercise and crossing the body midline, consecutive calls are not needed. The directions are, "When I say the name of a color, find it with your eyes, move your pointing finger to the correct square, and wait for the next color."

You can add auditory sequential memory to the exercise by asking them what colors they touched.

Activity 5. Chalkboard practices are a must as writing readiness. Writing on the chalkboard also is a good motivator. Children usually want to do what the teacher does, and writing on the chalkboard is definitely a teacher activity.

Begin with large scribbles. Allow the children to make whatever marks they wish. When they become accustomed to using chalk, begin the exercises. Incidentally, chalk works best if it is not held like a pencil. Resting it on the thumb and guiding with the fingers works best.

The strokes used in manuscript are circles, curved lines, downward vertical lines, and horizontals from left to right. Exercises should contain motions to develop these strokes.

Begin with very large circles, as big as the children can make, some clockwise and some counterclockwise. Push-pulls with really tall strokes come next. Left-to-right horizontals with slight diagonal returns help left-to-right eye and hand movement.

Descending separate lines, horizontals, and descending diagonals follow in logical progression. When line control is good, begin connecting. Have the children draw circles, squares, triangles, and other geometric forms. All activities are nonlanguage, with the exception of directions. It is readiness, not writing, at this point.

When the children (or a child) can make good productions of about 6 to 10 inches, they should be ready for letter instruction.

MANUSCRIPT INSTRUCTION

Teaching children to write should begin with the formation of large letters. Letters should be practiced at the chalkboard. When a child has difficulty with an element, it should be discussed and remediation exercises used. For example, the child makes a misshapen *O* with poor closure. Practice with scribble circles and tracing a sample are appropriate steps.

The steps in letter introduction, or which letters to teach first, are a matter of the instructor's choice. Letters that are meaningful improve motivation. One way of deciding what to teach is to determine the letters that appear most frequently in the names of the children.

Assume that in the group of children who are ready for writing instruction the letter *e* appears most frequently in their names. A lesson might be as follows:

Print the names of the children in a column on the far side of the board, then say:

"Boys and girls, I've written your names on the board. Let's look at them and read them."

After the names have been read aloud say,

"There are some letters that are used more than others. The letter *e* appears most often. Let's count and see how many names have an *e*."

The words are studied for the letter, and the purpose for learning is established. The teacher then says,

"Because we use *e* so often in our names, we will learn to write it. Tomorrow we will pick another letter to learn."

When a specific letter is needed, it may come from a reading word. The word is written on the board. The teacher may explain:

"Today you are going to learn a letter from one of your reading words."

Point to the word and have the children identify it, then say, "The letter we are going to work on is _____ ."

Instruction on the strokes, direction, height, and so on is given. The children are afforded the opportunity to practice at the chalkboard. Letters should be introduced in context and practiced at the board before being attempted on paper.

Initially, writing should be on unlined paper. Newsprint paper is still the least expensive, and if a sheet is scrapped, it is no loss. Also, unlined paper prevents alignment problems that can make a child feel inadequate. Writing through a line is impossible if there are no lines.

Guides to develop alignment and spacing can be achieved by folding the paper. The horizontal folds can be from two inches to one inch apart. When spacing guides are required, vertical folds of about one inch are good. This forms squares, and the child learns to write a letter in each square and to leave one blank between words.

Folded papers are not as pretty in a pile as flat sheets. However, this is a crutch that is discarded soon, and the feeling of accomplishment as witnessed by smiling faces makes up for untidy stacks of papers.

When a child consistently demonstrates good letter formation ability, he should move directly to primer paper. Primer paper has widely spaced solid lines with broken midlines. Midline markers aid in developing size control.

The length of time a child remains at any one stage depends on rate of accomplishment. It is far better to keep a child at the chalkboard or on unlined paper than to push him to keep up with the other children. Similarly, a child who brings highly developed skills to beginning instruction should not be subjected to practices on skills already mastered. Overlearning may cause negative results.

Writing practices should be meaningful and fun if possible. Printing pages of *e*'s does little to stimulate interest. Letters should be used in context. The words may be the children's names, labels for personal objects, titles for stories they have dictated, dates, and captions for pictures they have drawn.

Copying is one of the best practices. However, the children should be able to read the material to be copied. They should not be required to copy words, sentences, or stories that have no meaning to them. The sentences from their story chart are good copy, especially if they contain the child's name; this makes it a very personal learning experience.

Figure 8-1 is an example of a teacher-prepared checklist to evaluate manuscript writing.

Figure 8-1 Sample Writing Checklist

	Manuscript			Cursive		
	M	P	R	M	P	R
Alignment						
Backward oval						
Check stroke						
Clozure						
Corner						
Descenders						
Down stroke						
Forward oval						
Headroom						
Letter size						
maximum						
intermediate						
minimum						
Loop						
upper						
lower						
horizontal						
Over curve						
Under curve						
Retrace						
Slant consistency						
right						
left						
straight						
Spacing						
letters						
words						

M, has mastered; P, needs more practice; R needs remediation.

CURSIVE INSTRUCTION

Readiness

When a child is ready for instruction in cursive handwriting depends on reading ability, physical coordination, and interest in learning the form. "Yes" answers to the following questions are excellent indicators:

1. Does _____ have an interest in learning to write in the cursive alphabet?
2. Can _____ read at least a few simple words in cursive form?
3. Does _____ have sufficient motor control to produce legible cursive writing?
4. Will cursive writing help _____ overcome reversal and/or spelling problems?
5. Has _____ mastered the manuscript alphabet?

Questions 1 and 2 are perhaps the most relevant. "No" to the second question means that learning to read words in cursive must be part of the beginning instruction.

The fourth question may be appropriate to consider when the implementation of cursive writing can serve a remedial function. The last question was listed in that position on purpose. Mastering the production of the manuscript alphabet may never occur with some exceptional learners. It should be considered for those who are developmental in the area of written language.

Teaching Strategies

By the time children are ready for cursive instruction, they will have acquired an understanding of written language and developed motor skills to manipulate the writing tool adequately. However, they still may need some readiness activities.

To begin the introduction of cursive writing, place examples on the chalkboard. Use the material that you ordinarily would place on the board, such as the individual seat work assignments. Before writing, decide which cursive words appear to be the most like the manuscript form or which could be supplied easily by cloze procedure. Print as much of the instructions as necessary; use the cursive form wherever possible. Have the children read the instructions aloud. Discuss the cursive words. From this point, instruction follows much like that for learning manuscript.

Air writing can replace chalkboard exercises. Have the children stand and make circles in the air. Follow this with up-and-down movements.

Begin with arms pointing to the left. Move the arm up with a swing, down, and then up. The arm should move slowly across the body.

If the children think this activity is silly or baby stuff, remind them that a warm-up is a sensible part of any physical activity. A professional baseball player would never take a swing at a ball before getting his muscles loose. Air writing helps relax the arm.

The actual introduction of letter formation should be in context. Write a word containing the letter, then have the children read the word and name the letters if possible. Indicate the letter to be learned; underline it. Make the letter in isolation, then make it again, but slowly. Describe the production as to direction, size, retrace, and so on.

Most cursive letters are used in a connected form; practice with single letters also should be connected, such as *iii*. Keep such practice to a minimum. Have letters written in meaningful words as much as possible.

As with manuscript instruction, order of presentation depends on need, interest, or in some cases the commercial program being used. Begin with letters used most frequently. Letters that form the children's names and short words are a good idea. Salutations and closings are of interest; names and addresses can be put into use, and therefore have a purpose.

Letter formation is described under handwriting vocabulary at the start of this chapter.

At the end of every lesson the children should be encouraged to compare their writing with a model. They may find it helpful to state what is good and what needs improvement. If they can see their problems, have them decide what other letters require the same strokes. Plan their next lesson with them. This may help sustain interest and keep them on target.

There are some do's and dont's that make writing instruction meaningful:

Do have the children practice the traditional oval motion and push-pulls. *Don't* have them do pages of these exercises. They help develop good writing technique, but when they become a drag, the outcome may be a developing dislike for writing.

Do have them trace a model if they are confused. *Don't* embarrass a mature student by requiring such practice in front of peers.

Do allow all learners to develop their own, unique legible style. *Don't* attempt to force conformity. Remember, the objective is legible handwriting.

TEACHER-PREPARED METHODS AND MATERIALS

Activity 1. Sandbox writing can be used for manuscript and cursive instruction. Take a large cookie sheet with a one-inch edge. Fill the tray with fine sand. It can be used for letter and word practice. For children who are having difficulty with specific letters or strokes, cut a template in the form of the problem letter. The children then can trace the form in the sand.

Activity 2. Clay letters help teach the alphabet and can be used for tracing manuscript forms. Give the children enough clay to form the letter to be learned. Show them how to form the clay into a rope, then into the instructional letter. It can be pressed into place in the corner of the desk and used as a model for copying or tracing.

Activity 3. For beginning manuscript learners, prepare a worksheet of objects and figures that are made from strokes used in writing letters. The lines should be broken. Have the children complete the lines by tracing. When the picture is complete, it can be colored. For example, Humpty Dumpty is made of broken lines to form a large oval. His lips are curled into a smile; this is an undercurve. His bow tie is diagonal and vertical lines. The wall is made of vertical and diagonal lines. Arrows may be used to guide direction.

Activity 4. Hidden letters improve visual closure and are fun. Make a worksheet that has a picture with hidden letters. The letters may be complete or only partially visible. For example, draw a tree with lots of leaves. The leaf lines can be any number of different letters. Have some animals looking at the tree. Parts of the animals can be circles, *e*'s, and so on. The possibilities are limitless.

Tell the children they are to find the hidden letters; when they see one, they can trace over it with a crayon or pencil. The number of letters can be posted on the chalkboard so that the children will know if they have found them all.

Activity 5. Uniformity of space and slant can be difficult for beginning cursive writers, particularly those with spatial problems. To help overcome this problem, take a sheet of ⅜" lined paper. Place it on an angle under a sheet of unlined white paper. The angle should be the degree of desired slant. The lines of the bottom sheet should show through; trace them with a bold black thin-line marker.

Place the dark-lined paper under the child's practice paper. The two pieces of paper should form a grid of evenly spaced diagonals. The lines underneath provide a guide for spacing and slant.

Activity 6. This technique and material have many uses. It is an adaptation of that used for teaching writing to the blind.

Take a flat-surfaced board such as a piece of ¼" plywood or firm linoleum. Place a sheet of paper over the surface. Secure the paper with two strong horizontal rubber bands. The space between the rubber bands should be even and the desired distance for word writing. The bands act as the lines on the paper. Because they are raised, they become barriers for alignment, and because they are flexible, they will stretch for below the line letters.

To produce letters or words for tracing, place a piece of screening on the board surface. The rubber bands may be positioned vertically to hold the paper in place. Using a crayon, write the letter or word to be traced. When the paper is removed, the word will have texture from the small deposits of crayon left from the screen's impression.

Adding machine paper rolls are excellent for this device. It is inexpensive and can be cut to any length.

COMMERCIAL PROGRAMS AND MATERIALS

A Writing Manual for Teaching the Left-handed (1967)
Mildred B. Plunkett
Educators Publishing Service
75 Moulton Street
Cambridge, Massachusetts 02138

Purpose: Aid teacher in proper instruction.

Population: All left-handed who need instruction.

Description: This manual is one of the few designed specifically to instruct the left-handed writer. The author clearly states the principles on which handwriting should be based. By following her instructions, the teacher can develop programs for beginners or for those who need remediation because they have learned improperly. The classroom teacher who never has experienced writing with the left hand may find that this material will bring new insight to the problem and greatly improve instruction.

Basic Handwriting Series (1978)
June E. Herr, Ethel L. Sammet, and Eugenie Fernandez
The Continental Press, Inc.
Elizabethtown, Pennsylvania 17022

Purpose: Introduction of penmanship, manuscript, and cursive.

Population: Kindergarten—Grade 3.

Description: The series is divided into levels or stages of development. Readiness is for use in kindergarten and grade one. The development of manuscript letters and numerals is presented at this level. Grade two is designed to help children make the transition from manuscript to cursive writing. Grade three is designed to develop cursive skills. The material includes duplicator worksheets and practice sheets. The instructions to the teacher are clear and easy to follow. Tracing letters precedes the actual writing. At the lower level, key pictures are used to help children learn letter names.

Creative Growth with Handwriting (1975)
  Walter B. Barbe, Virginia H. Lucas, Clinton S. Hackney, and
    Constance McAllister
  Zaner-Bloser, Inc.
  612 North Park Street
  Columbus, Ohio 43215

Purpose: Make good penmanship meaningful through interesting lessons.

Population: Upper primary and intermediate levels.

Description: The Zaner-Bloser handwriting programs and materials have been used for many years. This material, as the title suggests, is creative. Letter formations are taught in combination with contextual writing. The topics cover letter practice, book reports, foreign countries, poetry, and much more. Learning to write legibly need not be boring using these ideas. It is especially good for the intermediate level exceptional child who has an imagination.

D'Nealian Handwriting (1978)
  Donald N. Thurber
  Scott, Foresman and Company
  99 Bauer Drive
  Oakland, New Jersey 07436

Purpose: Produce legibility with ease and speed.

Population: Readiness through intermediate.

Description: This program is rather unusual in that manuscript letters are slightly slanted. The goal of the program is to produce legible handwriting with as much ease and speed as possible. The material covers everything from readiness to reading and producing cursive writing. The teacher's guides are well thought out and good for use by the inexperienced teacher or the veteran who needs a new approach to teaching penmanship. For a resource room teacher or itinerant, the completeness and applicability of this material for the exceptional learner may make this one extremely helpful.

Groovy Letters (1972)
   Ideal School Supply Company
   11000 South Lavergne Avenue
   Oak Lawn, Illinois 60453

Purpose: Practice or remedial letter learning.

Population: Primary levels.

Description: This material consists of letters on durable cards. On each card the letter to be learned is cut out or grooved. The letter also is printed in blue beside the cutout, and additional space is provided for writing this letter. The cards can be used for multisensory learning.

Handwriting I (1970)
   Cynthia D. Buchanan
   Sullivan Associates
   Behavioral Research Laboratories
   Box 577
   Palo Alto, California 94302

Purpose: Total expressive written language program.

Population: Primary through intermediate.

Description: This consists of a 64-page text and a 279-page teacher's manual. The program is presented step by step, beginning with visual discrimination of curved and straight lines through sentence writing. Sentence structure, capitalization, and punctuation are included; these elements can be used to reinforce other instruction. Because of compactness, this is another good source for resource room and itinerant teachers.

Handwriting (1972)
   Forrest D. Fernkopf
   Ealingfilms
   2211 Michigan Avenue
   Santa Monica, California 90404

Purpose: Develop interest through audiovisual handwriting instruction.

Population: Primary through intermediate.

Description: This is a video program divided into two parts, manuscript and cursive. Each of the kits contains 24 super 8mm film loops to be used with 25 suggested lessons. Spirit masters are supplied for reproducing practice material. It can be used as a supplement to an existing handwriting program or can be used alone. It can be used for whole classes, small groups, or individualized because of the media presentation. The projector can be set up in a learning station or library, and the program can be used for practice and reinforcement. It is different and may appeal to the learner who is bored or is repeating the process.

Manuscript Animated Alphabet (1973)
  Photo Motion Corporation
  Morrison Building
  King of Prussia, Pennsylvania 19406

Purpose: Develops letter formation step-by-step through animation.

Population: Primary.

Description: This material is designed for use in beginning instruction. It consists of 32 transparency booklets, a guide, and mask. The letters and numerals are presented in movement or shape groups. The letters are in pairs for visual comparison. The whole letter is shown, and as the teacher flips the pages of a booklet, the letter develops, stroke by stroke, or is animated. A tabletop projector is available for use with the program. Group instruction is with the projector; the transparencies also can be used for individual instruction.

Peter Possum's Practice Papers for Perfect Penmanship (1975)
  Susan Ryono
  Frank Schaffer
  26616 Indian Peak Road
  Palos Verdes Peninsula, California 90274

Purpose: Creative way of teaching or reteaching letters.

Population: Primary level or remedial older students.

Description: This material is presented in black-and-white line drawing cartoons. It is a manuscript program that can be used with older children. To teach circles, the drawings depict race cars with round wheels. Pages are removable from the teacher's activity book, and material is reproducible; it can be used in learning centers and as group assignments.

SRA, Lunchbox (1977)
Science Research Associates, Inc.
P.O. Box 4924
Chicago, Illinois 60680

Purpose: Big program in small package.

Population: Primary through intermediate.

Description: The program is packaged in yellow plastic lunchboxes, one for manuscript and one for cursive. The material consists of durable cards with the letter to be learned and lines for practice. Clear plastic covers are provided to extend the life of the material. Guides, or progress sheets, are used for assessing the child's developing skill and for noting items mastered. The material can be used during instruction or as an independent practice.

The Johnson Handwriting Program (1977)
Warren T. Johnson
Educators Publishing Service, Inc.
75 Moulton Street
Cambridge, Massachusetts 02138

Purpose: Cursive program to develop fine motor control.

Population: All age levels.

Description: This is a cursive program, designed for use by any age level. It includes exercises referred to as neurological track patterns intended to aid in the development of eye-hand coordination and fine motor control. The workbooks contain the letters to be learned, explanations of letter formation, letters in context for practice, and interesting information on the history of the adaptation of the Roman cursive alphabet.

REFERENCES

Barbe, W. B., Lucas, V. H., Hackney, C. S., & McAllister, C. *Creative growth with handwriting*. Columbus, Ohio: Zaner-Bloser Inc., 1975.

Buchanan, C. D. *Handwriting I*. Palo Alto, Calif.: Sullivan Associates, Behavioral Research Laboratories, 1970.

Fernkopf, F. D. *Handwriting*. Newton, Mass.: Ealingfilms, 1972.

Groovy letters. Oak Lawn, Ill.: Ideal School Supply Co., 1972.

Herr, J. E., Sammet, E. L., & Fernandez, E. *Basic handwriting series*. Elizabethtown, Pa.: The Continental Press, Inc., 1978.

Johnson, W. T. *The Johnson handwriting program*. Cambridge, Mass.: Educators Publishing Service, Inc., 1977.

Manuscript animated alphabet. King of Prussia, Pa.: Photo Motion Corp., 1973.

Plunkett, M. B. *A writing manual for teaching the left-handed*. Cambridge, Mass.: Educators Publishing Service, 1967.

Ryono, S. *Peter Possum's practice papers for perfect penmanship*. Palos Verdes Peninsula, Calif.: Frank Schaffer, 1975.

SRA, lunchbox. Chicago: Science Research Associates, Inc., 1977.

Thurber, D. N. *D'Nealian handwriting*. Oakland, N.J.: Scott, Foresman and Co., 1978.

Chapter 9

Written Language

SPELLING

The purpose of learning to spell words is to communicate thoughts in writing. Requiring correct spelling on first consideration may appear artificial. There are many words that are as easy to decode if misspelled as if written correctly. However, there are words that are so similar in spelling that an omission or substitution of a letter transforms the meaning. *A*ffect and *e*ffect is an example of meaning change with a single letter. Therefore, correct spelling is important, in fact necessary.

Several factors make learning to spell American English difficult. Granted, there are regular spellings; however, many words do not fit a spelling pattern nor can they be sounded out to determine the correct letters. The alphabet has 26 characters; American English words have at least 44 phonemes. To complicate matters, words from other languages have been assimilated into the vocabulary. These words may not have an equivalent translation, so the foreign spelling is retained.

In addition to the lack of phoneme-grapheme relationship, there are sounds or word parts with variant spellings, such as *door* and a*dore*, wr*ite* and l*ight*, and alth*ough* and kn*ow*. There are spelling patterns, or letter groups with variant sounds, as in th*ough* and en*ough*.

The spelling system of American English, because of the inconsistent letter-sound relationship, is the most difficult aspect of written language to learn. To master the system requires intelligence, good visual memory, and applied auditory skills. It is necessary to give serious consideration to these factors when planning a spelling program for exceptional learners.

READINESS FOR SPELLING

As in all learning, certain abilities help in acquiring a spelling vocabulary. Intellectually, the learner must have the ability to retain and retrieve

201

visual and auditory sequences. Visual discrimination and visual memory are essential elements. Auditorily the learner must be able to discriminate sound differences and word parts. To be meaningful, spelling words should be in the learner's speaking and reading vocabulary. In addition, the learner should have the ability to communicate this knowledge, either by writing the words or by some mechanical means.

For the exceptional child who may have a deficit in one or more of these abilities, alternate strategies for learning are necessary. A mentally retarded child may not have good recall or discrimination but may need to write survival words. Readiness in this case is determined by need and at least minimal potential.

At the opposite range of intellectual ability, the relevant readiness factor may be desire to learn. It is not unusual to hear a gifted three-year-old ask, "How do you spell aardvark?" To such children, learning to spell is a natural part of knowing. They may acquire a spelling vocabulary at the same rate as their reading vocabulary. Some gifted children learn to read by asking adults how to spell a word, then practice writing it until it becomes a visually known word.

For the most part, spelling is memorization. The extent to which individuals can remember depends on intent to learn, in this case desire to remember the spellings of words. A child may have above-average intelligence; an excellent listening, speaking, and reading vocabulary; motor skills for writing; and know the alphabet—all of which are supposed to produce a good speller—yet lack the desire to conform to correct orthographic sequences. The child lacks motivation and does not care about spelling correctly; close is good enough. Until the child sees a need to spell words in the traditional letter sequence, all other readiness factors are of little consequence. Readiness criteria must be as individualized as is the individual.

Several academic skills are necessary if spelling instruction is to be successful. The child should know letter names. Although it is possible to reproduce a sequential pattern from visual memory, learning the sequence of letters is easier if a label is attached to the symbol.

Children should be able to read the words they are required to spell. This is extremely important when considering readiness of severely impaired readers. They should have sight vocabularies as their spelling words. On occasion, children might be expected to learn new words as part of their developing writing vocabularies, but not at the beginning level. The one exception to this occurs when using a technique that combines learning to read with spelling in a kinesthetic approach.

TEACHING SPELLING

The selection of the words to be learned is as important as the method used for studying spelling words. In most cases the words should be known reading words. Using a commercial graded program is no guarantee that the children are familiar with the words in the spelling lists.

Checking word recognition is not difficult. At the beginning of the semester, make a Ditto master containing the spelling words. Give each child a copy. At appropriate times have each child read the words on the page. Mark the unknown words.

If for some reason the children must learn the unknown words from the lists, the words first should become part of their reading instruction. The child who is reading below grade level should not be required to learn the same words as classmates who are several levels higher.

Commercial spelling programs develop word lists based on various criteria. The consequence is that what are considered spelling words for second-grade children in one program may be third-grade words in another. If children are transfers, or if a new program is initiated, the lists may contain words the children already know. In some cases the children are precocious spellers and have learned grade-appropriate words much earlier.

To make spelling instruction as interesting and meaningful as possible, eliminate the words that children can spell from the lists. Pretesting is the best way to determine such known spelling words.

There are two procedures for pretesting. One that is used most often is that of administering a weekly test before assigning words. Children then are required to study the unknown or misspelled words. While this is far better than having children practice words they can spell already, there are shortcomings to the method.

The most important problem that may arise from weekly pretesting is that it may leave some children with no new words. The second method, unit or monthly testing, may solve the problem. Many commercial programs are divided into units; if not, take several lists or those that would constitute a month's lessons. Administer the unit lists. Make certain the children know this is not a test that will be graded for a mark. When the children who know the words have been identified, alternate spelling lessons can be prepared for them. It is unfair to the proficient speller to mark time while peers are learning. If the school system provides a list of required words for every grade level, the preceding procedure can be applied.

Occasionally an instructor will have neither a basal speller nor a curriculum guide, so other sources must be found. Having the child decide what words to learn is a good alternate to a prepared list. The words may be selected from the reading sight vocabulary or from the *Dolche List of the Two Thousand Commonest Words for Spelling* (1942).

To make the selection have the child read the words orally. The child then indicates words to be learned. It also is a good idea to give the problem speller an opportunity to decide on the number of words per lesson. If the number suggested is unrealistic, the teacher applies guidance.

When the spelling words have been identified and the first group has been assigned, the teacher should attempt to identify the child's most efficient way of studying. To accomplish this, suggest various study methods.

One method is the study team. Two children are teamed. Their words need not be the same. Words are studied visually. When one member is ready to be tested, the other reads the words. The child being tested then corrects his own work by comparing it with the study list.

Team partners should be chosen by the children themselves. It may be very unwise for the teacher to select partners. If one child is an excellent speller and the other a disabled speller, the situation may be unbearable for both members of the team, unless it is by their own choice.

For children with low mental capacity or for those with specific language disabilities, a list of five or more new words may appear overwhelming. To avoid this situation, the words may be assigned one at a time. A word is presented on Monday and studied. Another word is given on Tuesday, and the first word is reviewed. On Wednesday, the two words are tested, reviewed if necessary, and a third is assigned. The procedure is continued until the five words have been mastered.

If spelling words have been selected from the child's reading vocabulary, they can be used in a follow-up activity. The child is assigned the task of rewriting the story from which the words were taken. This will make it possible to check reading comprehension, work on sentence structure, and help the child practice the spelling words all in one lesson.

One of the best ways to help children is to encourage correct spelling at all times. Make it clear that when they are writing, you are available to help them. If a child asks for the spelling of a word during a writing assignment, be willing to help. Place a piece of paper in a position that is clearly visible to the child. Say the word. As you say it, write the letters or syllables, depending on the developmental level of the child. When the word has been written, repeat it.

If the child is mainstreamed or the school is departmentalized, an agreement should be reached with all teachers. Correct spelling should be required in all subjects. A child who is unable to spell a science word should not have the answer marked incorrect. However, the spelling error should be indicated. When the paper is returned, the child should be expected to practice the correct spelling for future use.

When an instructor knows that a child has a spelling problem, a list of words for possible choice should be used. For example, the science teacher is using a completion test with 25 questions. A list containing 50 science terms is included. The student then may select the correct response from many choices. This reduces the element of chance while providing an opportunity to produce a paper without spelling errors. It may foster pride in accomplishment and motivate the child to improve his spelling.

There also are ways to ensure that children will learn to dislike spelling, especially those with spelling deficiencies. Three of the most noteworthy are traditional practices. The first is needless written repetition of words. Research shows that beyond three consecutive writings, the positive effect decreases proportionately. Several negative effects are possible.

Children who are working in manuscript often write columns of letters: *c*'s are written under *c*, *a*'s under *a*, and *t*'s under *t*. The word *cat* as a unit is not practiced. A child in a special education class was given the assignment of writing each word 25 times. The pupil was known to have reversals and had been taught to use cursive to remediate the problem. Among the words was *their*. The child wrote it correctly the first two times, and thereafter wrote *thier*. Incorrect learning was reinforced and the transposition problem was not remediated.

The group success chart is another means of producing a dislike for spelling. Children who spell without error should be rewarded for admirable accomplishment. However, children who try but cannot learn to spell need not be reminded continually of their inadequacies. This is exactly what may happen when a large progress chart, complete with stars or other reward symbols, is displayed. The child with 100 percent correct moves ahead rapidly in glowing fashion while the child with a spelling problem learns self-rejection because of his failure.

Individual progress charts solve this dilemma. Token rewards can be issued for small progress steps and for perfect papers. In this way every child can learn with a positive attitude.

The third way to develop negative behavior toward spelling is the curse to the poor speller, the spelling bee. Hurt and humiliation are the products of peer rejection and public display of spelling errors. The child who cannot spell is always the last team member chosen. If this child is the captain and gets to select the team, this pupil is the first to miss and have to go to his seat. In either case, a spelling bee is not fun for special pupils and is a lesson in humility they do not need.

TEACHER-PREPARED METHODS AND MATERIALS

Activity 1. Using the spelling words, construct a crossword puzzle. If a word has more than one meaning, it should be used as many times as meanings. The children should use a copy of the spelling words to complete the puzzle. At this point they should not be expected to spell from memory unless the words are for review from previous lessons.

Activity 2. Spelling squares is an easily prepared independent activity. Cut oak tag squares of approximately one inch. Make a letter holder by cutting one-inch slits in cardboard or other sturdy material.

Using the child's spelling words, print a letter on each square. Make as many squares as there are letters in the words. Put the letters in an envelope labeled with the child's name. The child is given the envelope and the letter holder.

The object is to use the letter squares to form the words. The spelling list can be used as a study assignment. For review purposes, words from several previous lessons can be used; spelling from memory then is required.

Activity 3. A spelling bingo game can be used as a group learning experience with the children working from lists of different words.

Each child receives a card marked into 25 squares. The child picks five words from his spelling list, then prints the words into the squares, one word on each line. If a word contains fewer than five letters, the remaining space is marked free.

Using the 26 letters of the alphabet, the teacher (leader) calls one letter at a time. If the letter appears more than once, it is marked in all positions.

The first child to get X on all letters in the five words calls bingo. To check the correctness of the call, the child says the word, spells it aloud, and repeats the word. While the teacher is checking, the other children watch their boards to find errors or missing letters.

Bright children may want to play more than one card. Cards may be increased in size to provide for longer words.

Activity 4. This is recommended for the gifted learner or one who is a capable speller. The learner is given a copy of the phonetic alphabet, and the individual's spelling words, which are written in phonetic transcription. The student is to transcribe them into regular orthography. A short paragraph containing the spelling words written in the phonetic alphabet can be used instead of the list.

COMMERCIAL PROGRAMS AND MATERIALS

I Can Spell (1977)
Jean A. Lucken
Love Publishing Company
6635 East Villanova Place
Denver, Colorado 80222

Purpose: Alternate to spelling basal.

Population: Upper primary through secondary.

Description: The material is designed for use with students who cannot function in a basal spelling program. It is an individualized approach that allows the learner to select words from reading material; this ensures that the child can read at least his own spelling words. Material is on spirit masters. There are 22 lessons that go from spelling drill through story writing. They are very helpful in planning remedial programs for older children. The students contract for the amount of work to be accomplished. This may improve motivation.

TMI-Grolier Self-Tutoring Programs (1970)
Lyn Sandow
Grolier Inc.
575 Lexington Avenue
New York, New York 10022

Purpose: Remedial programmed instruction.

Population: Intermediate levels.

Description: This material is programmed for independent learning. The written language area contains three programs: First Steps in Reading, Spelling, and Punctuation. The material to be learned is viewed through a MIN-MAX teaching machine, which actually is a tachistoscope that allows frame-by-frame viewing. The material is not difficult, but the presentation looks grown-up and can be used by a wide age range.

Write to Spell (1976)
Judith M. Schifferle
Curriculum Associates, Inc.
Department AR
6 Henshaw Street
Woburn, Massachusetts 01801

Purpose: Combined spelling and writing self-paced remedial program.

Population: Intermediate levels.

Description: This material is designed to improve the student's ability to spell while learning to write. There are 80 picture/activity cards in the kit. Each student receives a Student Directions Sheet, Writing Forms, and Testing Forms. The student chooses a topic, then selects a card from the kit. When the activity is completed, the teacher and the pupil identify and correct grammatical and spelling errors and writing style. The student records errors, or marks all correct for the activity if appropriate. The program is designed for individual instruction but can be modified for group instruction. It is particularly good for adolescents who are mainstreamed and attend a resource room for written language instruction.

SPELLING DISABILITIES

Spelling problems range in severity from mild to nearly complete inability to write even simple words. Causes may be lack of attention to detail, poor teaching, lowered mental capacity, or neurological dysfunction.

Lack of motivation to spell correctly has been suggested as a primary cause for minor spelling deficits. The problem of misspelled words is not confined to the retarded nor to the uneducated. Spelling errors among this group often are attributed to disinterest or to the irregularity of the language. The problem increases as the person grows less involved with formal education. The conformity to correct spelling that is required in school is discarded and is replaced with rationalizations and circuitous tactics to hide errors. Meaningful instruction at the elementary level may prevent the poor spelling that afflicts many.

A common error is omitting silent letters. Before assuming the cause or planning remediation, the teacher must ask the child to compare the spelling error with a correct sample. If the child can see the error, a lesson or lessons on the spelling pattern is in order.

When words are spelled as they sound, it may be because of too much phonics. Reading vocabulary words with nonphonic spellings should form a major part of spelling assignments until new understandings are formed.

When the phonic speller omits vowels, which is not uncommon, it usually is because the individual does not understand the value of the missing letter. A child who has learned that *c* says *ca* and *b* is *ba* adds a *g*, which to the pupil is *ja,* and has spelled the word *cbg* or *cabbage.* This is a problem of incorrect learning and may involve poor visual memory as well.

The learner with a specific language problem may have the most severe spelling problem. The condition sometimes is referred to as dysgraphia.

The cause is associated with dysfunction of the central nervous system. It may be an inability to organize the word perceptually into correct letter sequence, to store the information in correct order, to retrieve the information as it was received, or to control motor movements to produce the letters in correct sequence.

Remediation is long and laborious. Repeated multisensory experiences are required. VAKT (visual, auditory, kinesthetic, tactile) is the best remedial technique. In some cases the handicapped individual profits from oral instruction. That is, the person is taught to say each letter of the word and produce the letter immediately after hearing himself speak. This technique may be helpful if visual recall is affected.

The problem of correcting or remediating spelling problems is complex. The teacher should select a technique that is helpful in most cases, believe in it, and give it ample time to work. The process is slow and, as stated earlier, is compounded by the language system.

TEACHER-PREPARED EVALUATION METHODS AND MATERIALS

Teacher-prepared evaluation of spelling can be accomplished through two standard procedures. The first is used for either the test-study method of instruction or for testing only. The second involves cloze procedure.

In the first method, the teacher states the word, uses it in a sentence, then restates the word. Pronunciation should be distinct, syllables should be easily recognizable, and, to avoid ambiguity, the sentence should clearly designate meaning.

Evaluating spelling ability should be a personal learning experience. The scoring should be completed by the student and the teacher. Papers should not be exchanged among students. If errors are to be known by other students, it should be by choice—information willingly shared by peers. It should not be common knowledge gleaned through indiscriminate paper grading activities. Records of progress also should be confidential.

The second method, the cloze procedure, makes it possible to administer tests to groups. The individuals within the group may be tested on different words.

Sentences are constructed using the spelling words. A word to be spelled is omitted in each sentence on the student's copy. The student reads the sentence and completes it, or fills in the blank.

Immediately upon completion of the task, the student takes the teacher's copy and checks for correctness. Student and teacher discuss any errors as to type or cause. Ideas for remediating or studying are planned. The teacher should record words in error for inclusion in a later lesson.

COMMERCIALLY AVAILABLE TESTS

DST: Spelling, Diagnostic Screening Test (1976)
　Thomas D. Gnagey
　Facilitation House
　Box 611
　Ottawa, Illinois 61350

Purpose: Spelling screening.

Population: Grades 1–5.

Description: This is a flexible instrument that can be used with a group to determine placement or individually to determine phonics orientation for spelling instruction, efficiency of written test procedures, analysis of gross visual and auditory memory, and as a predictor of spelling potential. The 78-item word list is developmentally sequential. Only appropriate words need be administered. Both phoneme-grapheme regular words and irregular or nonphonic words are used. Testing time is five to ten minutes. Itinerant diagnosticians will find this a helpful measure.

TWS, Test of Written Spelling (1976)
　Stephen C. Larsen, Ph.D., and Donald D. Hammill, Ph.D.
　Pro-Ed
　333 Perry Brooks Building
　Austin, Texas 78701

Purpose: Determination of grade level achievement.

Population: Grades 1–8.

Description: This test is designed to yield a measure of written spelling ability. Words from thirteen basal spellers were used in arriving at the graded lists. The authors suggest that the results may be used to suggest general areas to be included in future teaching. Two lists of words, labeled predictable and unpredictable, are used. There are 35 words in the first list and 25 in the second. Where to test, or which words belong to a grade level, are indicated in the administration section. The traditional format is used: say the words in isolation, in sentence, and in isolation.

WRITTEN EXPRESSION

Teaching Written Language

In years past the aim of a liberal education was to provide students with skills to express themselves in writing. Society still holds to the belief that a person who cannot write is not truly educated. It is a fact that in many vocations, as well as colleges and universities, the applicant comes unprepared in the writing skills necessary to see the individual through the job or course work. Yet every teacher, with the exception of the mathematics instructor, could be a teacher of writing. Science requires student laboratory reports, and social studies students must describe past events. All reports should be graded, not only for content but also for grammar, spelling, and style. This section is designed to provide the teacher with a means by which contextual writing can be taught.

It is unnecessary for the exceptional student to spend the many years sitting in English class learning grammar. The teaching of grammar has no relevance unless the student writes, and grammar should be taught only when the student errs in writing or speaking. Knowing the parts of speech does not a writer make; practice plus imagination do.

Students should be taught writing skills as soon as they have a reading vocabulary. In the early grades simple sentences are all that is necessary. Many acceptable sentences in American English consist of only one or two words, such as, "Go!" "Men work." "Girls dream." and "Boys play." To help the instructor in teaching the exceptional child, this book includes a glossary of terms related to written language (Appendix C). This information is intended for the instructor's review and is not necessarily for the direct instruction of the children.

Teacher-Prepared Methods and Materials

Activity 1. One way to stimulate sentence writing is to construct a mobile from which several different objects hang. Students are to select five objects and write a short sentence, using the name of the object in the sentence. Using the same mobile, in another lesson the student writes down two or three describers of the objects.

Activity 2. As children progress from two-word sentences to longer ones, show them a simple picture. Discuss the picture as a group, then ask the students to write three or four sentences describing the picture. At the end of the writing exercise, introduce the concept of the *topic sentence* (main idea or general statement summing up the paragraph). Ask the students to rewrite their paragraphs using a topic sentence as one of their sentences.

Activity 3. To introduce students to writing stories, prepare a filmstrip depicting the parts of a one-paragraph story. Each picture of the filmstrip shows only one action, thus yielding one sentence. Discuss each picture separately. At the end of the discussion on each picture, students should write one sentence. When the students have assembled their sentences into paragraphs, ask them to rewrite their paragraphs and include a topic sentence. As an independent exercise, each student should write a second paragraph and include a topic sentence.

Activity 4. Functional writing may be the goal of written instruction for exceptional students, particularly those of working age. This should include filling out job applications, letter writing, completing order blanks, and describing a process. The following suggestions can be used to teach each one of these tasks.

Contact the local Chamber of Commerce for job applications for local businesses and industries. Have students select applications for jobs that interest them. Completion of several different forms will improve their feeling of confidence when seeking employment.

Have students write a resume letter to a prospective employer describing their skills and experience in their particular field. Learning to write letters serves a purpose when taught this way.

Ask students to bring in an order blank from a catalog received in the mail. Help them complete the order blank, listing addresses to which the order should be sent, amounts, code numbers, prices, tax, mailing cost, and total.

Have students describe a process in step-by-step fashion. Processes may include how to change a tire, make a pizza, refinish an antique, or build a model airplane. After their oral description have them write the same material. Guide them through each step. When they become comfortable with the process, initiate independent assignments on topics of their choice.

Activity 5. To develop student use of figures of speech and poetic devices, play a tape or record of music, preferably without lyrics. Discuss the music as a group. Ask the students to write about their emotional reaction to the music, or how they felt when they heard it. Showing a work of art, an original or a print, can have the same effect for the visual learner.

Activity 6. Punctuation, spelling, and grammatical errors that students make in their writing can be dealt with in the following ways:

In reading each paper, the teacher should list the errors on a separate piece of paper. Budding young writers can be discouraged by too many red marks on their papers. Individual errors by only one student should be reviewed by pupil and teacher.

At this point, specific rules should be introduced and discussed. The student should create five sentences using the rule, be it for punctuation, spelling, or grammar. The teacher should check to see that the student has mastered the rule.

If a group of students makes a common error or errors, compose a story involving those errors. Make a Ditto and a transparency of the story. Review the transparency first. Explain the errors and the rules that apply. After the review, give each student the Ditto of the story and ask the individual to find the errors. Then each student should write sentences using the rule. Again, check to see that the student has applied the rule.

Activity 7. After students have become accustomed to writing paragraphs and stories and can accept constructive criticism of their errors, allow them to write independently but provide the guidance of correction and praise. A good story, regardless of its errors, should be read to the class.

Activity 8. Students may have difficulty getting started. They cannot zero in on a subject. Story starter titles provided for the students are limited only by the teacher's imagination. The following is a list of story starter titles that has proved successful:

So, You Think You're Flat!
The Eye
Roaches Arise! Take Over the World
Life in a Drainpipe
How to Create Your Own Corpse
Let Me Out of the Mirror
Spots on the Ceiling
I'm Tired of Standing, but Chairs Are for People
What Was that Noise?
How Green Was My Envy
Full Moon

Commercial Materials and Programs

Basic Writing Skills (1976)
    Robert Burleigh
    Society for Visual Education, Inc.
    1345 Diversey Parkway
    Chicago, Illinois 60614

Purpose: Provides audiovisual material reinforcement for basic skills.

Population: Intermediate levels.

Description: This program is a series of six sound filmstrips (filmstrip and audiocassette). The presentations are mature enough to be used with older children. The content builds from individual words to sentences and includes punctuation.

CHILD (1974)
> Donald E. Strommer, Eugene Medvedeff, Ph.D., and Beverly Dearth, Ph.D.
> Westinghouse Learning Corporation
> P.O. Box 30
> Iowa City, Iowa 52240

Purpose: Screen, test, remediate, a total multisensory approach.

Population: Primary and low level intermediate.

Description: *CHILD* is a complete program that includes materials for early identification through screening, in-depth perceptual motor diagnosis, prescriptions, curriculum development, and grouping. The user's manual is self-instructional with twelve steps that guide the reader through each phase of the program.

The instructional ideas are multimodality, using VAKT processes to develop oral and written language skills. Specific skills developed include reading, spelling, vocabulary, phoneme-grapheme relationships, syntactical structures, letter formation, alphabetizing, and dictionary skills.

Included are suggestions for total class instruction, stations for self-contained programs, individual and small group instruction, and resource room application. The program is packaged in one rather small box, making this a good source for the itinerant.

Individual Cassette Learning Package (1974)
> Media Materials, Inc.
> 2936 Remington Avenue
> Baltimore, Maryland 21211

Purpose: Put interest into learning sentence structure and more.

Population: Intermediate levels.

Description: The program is packaged in six separate units. Each unit has an audiotape, teacher's guide, student work booklet, and posttest. The teacher's guide is a small two-page booklet that gives the title, author, approximate time for the lesson, performance objectives, notes for instruction, and follow-up activities. Each unit has a different story author.

Titles include *Tell Me More* (adjectives); *Every Sentence Has A Purpose* (four kinds of sentences); the *Apostrophe Act*; *Suffixes, able, ion, and Friends*; *No More Run-on Sentences!*, and *Recognizing Complete Sentences*.

Our Living Language (1970)
    Kathleen Wall and Eyelyn Riddle
    Milliken Publishing Co.
    1100 Research Boulevard
    St. Louis, Missouri 63132

Purpose: To cover all aspects of expressive written language program.

Population: Grades 4 through 8.

Description: This consists of ten full-color transparency duplicating books with 12 transparencies and 28 duplicating masters in each book. The transparencies are for group instruction, the duplicating pages for the child's individual worksheets. Every aspect of written language is covered. It can be used as a basis for a program, as a supplement to a program, or for review and remediation. The company also produces three levels of similar material for work with creative writing and two for library skills and reference work.

Parts of Speech Rummy (1973)
    General Learning Corporation
    P.O. Box 2188
    Morristown, New Jersey 07960

Purpose: To use game format for learning parts of speech.

Population: 8 through 15 years depending upon mental age.

Description: This is a language game played like rummy. There are five identical decks of cards. The object is to get sets of three-of-a-kind parts of speech and a run of different parts. Parts of speech include nouns, pronouns, adjectives, verbs, adverbs, prepositions, conjunctions, and interjections. The game can be used to improve recognition of parts of speech, develop sentence structure, and create interest in writing. It is recommended for use with children ages 11 to 15, but graphics may be inappropriate. It is fun for gifted younger children ages 8 or 9.

Practice in Dictionary Skills (1974)
    The Instructor Publications, Inc.
    P.O. Box 6108
    Duluth, Minnesota 55806

Purpose: Improve understanding of words and their spellings.

Population: Primary gifted through intermediate levels MR and LD.

Description: This duplicating master series is self-directing and suitable to use with intermediate level elementary students. As horizontal learning for the gifted, it can be used at a lower grade. The student uses cursive writing so it becomes more than just dictionary work. There are twenty lessons, ranging from alphabetical order through word histories and spelling hints. This is an excellent supplement to a basal speller.

Putting Words in Order—Sentence Structure (1973)
    Troll Associates
    320 Route 17
    Mahwah, New Jersey 07430

Purpose: To teach sentence structure and parts of speech.

Population: Upper primary and intermediate levels.

Description: This is an audiovisual program that combines filmstrips and audiocassette tapes to teach sentence structure and parts of speech. Topics include: What Is a Sentence?, Subjects and Predicates, What Is a Noun? What Is a Verb?, Adjectives and Adverbs, and Subject and Predicate Agreement. Each topic is presented on a filmstrip and audiotape. Additional activities for reinforcement are suggested.

Tutorette Audiocard System (1974)
    June S. Heinrich
    Educational Systems
    Audiotronics Corporation
    P.O. Box 3997
    North Hollywood, California 91609

Purpose: Individualized program to improve reading and written expression.

Population: Intermediate through remedial high school levels.

Description: This is a multisensory approach to individualized instruction. Each program consists of 96 prerecorded audiocards, four experience sheets that can be used for testing, and an answer sheet. The student inserts the card, watches the visual material, and listens to the teacher's explanation. The material is prepared in levels. For example, the program on prefixes, suffixes, and combining forms can be used at the intermediate level or for remedial work at the high school level. It is both a reading and writing program.

WRITTEN LANGUAGE DISABILITIES

Written language errors usually are reflections of oral language deficits. A child who has not learned to use plurals correctly when speaking will display the same error in writing in most cases. Other verbal errors are produced with equal frequency when writing.

The possibility of written language deficits is multiplied by the complexity of the process. A child who has learned to pause when speaking must learn that such oral cues are noted by punctuation. Apparently the sustained pause at the end of a sentence is realized easily, and punctuation usually is attached. However, shorter pauses can present problems. The most common error of punctuation is misuse of the comma (Appendix C).

Word omissions are another common problem. This situation can be the result of the brain which is formulating thought for writing at a rate greater than the motor process can produce. Learning to proofread with careful attention to details may overcome the problem.

The most severe writing problems are those caused by central nervous system dysfunction. Specific language disabilities related to encoding written language may be referred to as written expressive aphasia or dysgraphia (see Chapter 5). The condition may manifest itself as the inability to formulate thought for writing, the inability to record thought, confused word order when writing, or an inability to perform motor functions. Severe penmanship and spelling errors are included in this category of disabled learners.

As a developmental condition it is relatively unusual. It appears most frequently as a partial or complete loss of language ability following an illness with prolonged high fevers, drug induction, or trauma to the brain such as a skull fracture or severe concussion.

The extent to which the written language deficits can be remediated depends on the degree of impairment. If oral language is intact, and if the person has motor capacity, the individual occasionally can be taught to communicate in simple written sentences. The procedure is to teach the individual to form the thought into a sentence, say the sentence aloud, and write the sentence one word at a time as each word is spoken. Recording on tape can help the person recall the words intended to be written.

When the problem is the inability to produce letter forms, a typewriter may be used. If letter order (reversals) is part of the problem, cursive writing may be necessary. The Orton method as described by Gillingham and Stillman (1966) uses kinesthetic learning of cursive writing and can be helpful in these cases.

Determining the cause of written language problems is not as essential as finding the right method to correct or remediate the condition. The instructional program must be tailored to specific abilities and needs. There is no panacea for the problem. Remediation often is based on trial and error. Progress is slow because expressive written language is the last and most complex of the language processes.

Teacher-Prepared Evaluation Materials

A three-part written language test can be prepared with little effort. The purpose of the measure is to determine errors as displayed on the three types of writing: copying, writing from dictation, and spontaneous writing.

Select a paragraph or very short story. Have the individual copy the material in either manuscript or cursive. In some cases, a sample of both is useful.

Use another selection that is within the learner's reading level. Tell the child that you are going to tell a story and that the pupil is to write it. Read the material slowly. Repeat words if necessary. This is not a speed test, it is a writing test.

The spontaneous sample may be on any topic. The use of a picture and discussion can help motivate the pupil. For example, the child is a 10-year-old who is interested in race cars. Show a picture of a stock car. Discuss racing and cars. Have the pupil write a paragraph about race cars.

Use a checklist that records errors. The penmanship checklist (Chapter 7) and the writing glossary (Appendix C) may help in constructing the list. The list should include all aspects of written language such as penmanship, spelling, and syntax.

Compare the types of errors made on each sample. If the same errors are noted on all three samples, they obviously are of a more critical nature. Remediation of problems should begin with the lowest level ability and progress developmentally. The fact that the person may have some higher level skills is not indicative of total need level.

For an in-depth presentation on written language problems and determining needs, Myklebust (1965) is useful.

Commercial Written Language Tests

There are relatively few measures of written language available commercially. For the most part, evaluation in this area is included as a subtest in a complete battery. Previous chapters listed several tests in this category. *The Brigance Diagnostic Inventory of Basic Skills* (1977) and the *Slingerland Screening Test for Identifying Children with Specific Language Disabilities* (1970) are examples of measures with subtests for evaluation of writing abilities.

REFERENCES

Brigance, A. H. *Brigance diagnostic inventory of basic skills.* Woburn, Mass.: Curriculum Associates, Inc., 1977.
Burleigh, R. *Basic writing skills.* Chicago: Society for Visual Education, Inc., 1976.
Dolch, E. W. *Better spelling.* Champaign, Ill.: Garrard Press, pp. 257–270, 1942.
Gagney, T. D. *DST: Spelling, diagnostic screening test.* Ottawa, Ill.: Facilitation House, 1976.
Gillingham, A., & Stillman, B. *Remedial training for children with specific disabilities in reading, spelling, and penmanship* (7th ed.). Cambridge, Mass.: Educators Publishing Service, 1966.
Heinrich, J. S. *Tutorette audiocard system.* North Hollywood, Calif.: Educational Systems, Audiotronics Corp., 1974.
Individualized cassette learning package. Baltimore: Media Materials, Inc., 1974.
Larsen, S. C., & Hammill, D. D. *TWS, Test of written spelling.* Austin, Texas: Pro-Ed, 1976.
Lucken, J. A. *I can spell.* Denver: Love Publishing Co., 1977.
Myklebust, H. R. *Development and disorders of written language* (Vols. 1 & 2). New York: Grune & Stratton, Inc., 1965.
Parts of speech rummy. Morristown, N.J.: General Learning Corp., 1973.
Practice in dictionary skills. Duluth, Minn.: The Instructor Publications, Inc., 1974.
Putting words in order-sentence structure. Mahwah, N.J.: Troll Associates, 1973.
Sandow, L. *TMI-Grolier self-tutoring programs.* New York: Grolier Inc., 1970.
Schifferle, J. M. *Write to spell.* Newton, Mass.: Curriculum Associates, Inc., 1976.
Slingerland, B. H. *Screening test for identifying children with specific language disabilities.* Cambridge, Mass.: Educator's Publishing Service, Inc., 1970.
Strommer, D. E., Medvedeff, E., & Dearth, B. *CHILD.* Iowa City, Iowa: Westinghouse Learning Corp., 1974.
Wall, K., & Riddle, E. *Our living language.* St. Louis: Milliken Press, 1970.

Chapter 10

The Language Learner, the Family, and Society

LANGUAGE AND EMOTIONAL ADJUSTMENT

Learning language is of little value if it is not put to use, particularly if it does not help the learner develop a mentally healthy and socially acceptable personality. The importance of language to the learner and to interrelationships with family and society can be understood clearly when considered in relation to emotional and social adjustment.

In today's society, social and emotional adjustment are measured by an individual's ability to conform to a set of behaviors. Learning the acceptable behavior of a society begins very early in a child's life. For example, learning to smile to please an adult may occur as early as three months. While such conforming behavior may be as pleasant for the infant as it is for the adult, the fact remains that the child that learns to smile is accepted more readily by the family or the social group in which he is reared.

Language is the major tool by which individuals learn acceptable behavior. The normally developing child hears a reproachful "no," which may be accompanied by an unpleasant physical experience, and soon learns that to avoid the unpleasant, the individual does not perform the act that caused the "no." As the child matures and acquires specific vocabulary such as "please," "thank you," and "I'm sorry," he also learns that these words generally yield positive results. By using such words, the child's total existence can be made more enjoyable.

When a child fails to perform acceptable or expected behaviors, the deviance in development may be viewed as maladjustment. In the case of a child with delayed language or a specific language disability, the manifestation of seemingly antisocial behavior may be the direct result of the inability to communicate, or it may be the product of self-rejection. The self-rejection may have had its beginnings in actual rejection by individuals in the child's environment, or it may have been affected by frustration or shame.

Actual manifested behaviors may be aggressive, destructive, passive, or withdrawn. In fact, the list of possible causes of maladaptive behavior and the list of the behaviors themselves, when presented in various combinations, is nearly endless. Discussion of the many possible social and emotional ramifications of a language deficit is impossible in a text of this nature. However, to help the reader understand the seriousness and the scope of effect, four actual case histories are presented next. They clearly illustrate how children and their parents may react to specific language problems.

Case History 1: The S. Family

Mr. and Mrs. S. were college graduates. Mr. S. was an accountant and Mrs. S. a full-time housewife. They had two children, Janet and Steven. Janet was a healthy, normal infant. Her delivery was uncomplicated, and she was born a chubby six pounds. Her eating and sleeping habits were those of a model child.

Her mother, inexperienced at child care, confided to a friend that she would be glad when Janet talked. It seemed that at two weeks Janet cried when she was hungry, had gas, needed diapering, or just wanted attention. To the new mother the cries all sounded the same.

Several months later Mrs. S. told her friend that she could understand Janet; they were talking. She explained that when Janet was mad at her mobile, she cried short "wahs." When she was hungry she sounded like discontentment personified. Mrs. S. described several other cries, including a special sound directed to Mr. S. at their evening playtimes.

What had occurred in the period of several months was the not uncommon miracle of communication. The child had cried. An adult had smiled and spoken to the child. The needs of the child had been met with pleasant visual, auditory, tactile, and gustatory experiences. The child had experimented with sounds, and the parents had experimented with caring behaviors. The child had learned to match specific experiences with her crying sounds, and the parents had learned to perform specific acts in relation to those sounds. One behavior reinforced the other. They were communicating, and good healthy social and emotional development was occurring for all concerned.

By the age of nine months, Janet was crawling all over the apartment. She was thrilling her proud parents with her vocabulary of "da da," "ma ma," and "bye bye," which was performed with a tiny waving hand. She walked at one year, and her expanded vocabulary included "no," "yes," "can do," "eat," and several essential words such as "Mam Mam" for grandmother.

When Janet was three, the family moved. She was enrolled in a private preschool program. She was a chatterbox and loved to tell her favorite fairy tales to anyone who would listen. By mid-year her teacher reported that she was well liked by the other children and that she had the lead role in the school play.

It was fortunate for the parents that Janet had developed as she had because they soon were to discover that some children are slow learners.

At age 27, Mrs. S. gave birth to her second child, Steven. His arrival had been awaited with great expectations. He was born after 20 hours of difficult labor. Instruments were used for delivery. According to the obstetricians, Stevie had had difficulty with respiration, but with the aid of oxygen he soon gained normal color and appeared to be fine. His birth weight was just over eight pounds. When mother and child went home, everything seemed quite normal.

For all intents and purposes the S. family appeared to be the typical American family. They resided in a small suburb of a metropolis. Their three-bedroom ranch home was furnished in new early American style furniture. The garage housed two cars—a station wagon for Mrs. S. and an economy car for Mr. S. They had dreams of Janet's being a teacher or a nurse; Steven would play football as had his father and would go to college and become a medical doctor or an attorney.

Six months after Steven's birth, Mrs. S. was concerned about his development and behavior and asked his pediatrician to give him an extra thorough examination. She explained that although he didn't cry much, he always was fussy. He would scream for no apparent reason. His sleep patterns were irregular. He was large for his age but didn't seem to want to sit up or attempt to crawl. He liked to be held, but talking to him seemed to make him restless. The doctor assured her that Stevie was fine. He was a healthy child, just a little slower developing because he was a boy.

At one year Stevie could sit alone and hold his bottle. He made some sounds that Mr. and Mrs. S. believed to be "da da" and "ma ma," although they admitted that he didn't always use them for the correct parent.

Mr. and Mrs. S., on the advice of a friend, had Stevie evaluated at a nearby college language clinic. At the first parent conference Mr. S. informed the clinic staff that he and Mrs. S. would adjust their way of life to Stevie's slowness. They preferred to accept the doctor's earlier assurance that he was fine, just a little slow.

One year later when Mrs. S. took Janet to the kindergarten screening, she was carrying a very big two-year-old, nonverbal Stevie. The speech therapist who was to screen Janet was interested in Stevie. When questioned, Mrs. S. indicated that he had just begun to walk and that he made sounds, but they did not sound like real words. She also told the speech therapist that he would cry and put his hands over his ears as though he were in pain.

Unfortunately, Mrs. S. was not interested in the therapist's suggestions that she place Stevie in a preschool language program operated by the Easter Seal Society. Mrs. S. felt that Stevie was too young to leave her.

Three years later when Stevie began a language program operated by a nearby college, Mrs. S. told the interviewer that he was nearly totally dependent upon her. She said that understanding Stevie was difficult. For the most part communication was a guessing game; he would point, and she would touch things until she found what he wanted. This often led to frustration, and Stevie would end the session in a screaming, kicking, temper tantrum.

Mrs. S. indicated that Stevie did have a communication system worked out with his father. It was a special code that they knew, and sometimes they would let the women know what they were talking about. With the code Mr. S. taught Stevie to play baseball and to enjoy watching baseball and football on television. She said that when alone, Stevie never used the volume on the set, he just watched. Stevie and Mr. S. also attended the local high school games.

In the five years following Stevie's birth, Janet had undergone some radical personality changes. Mrs. S. had been so involved in caring for the nonverbal Stevie that she spent less and less time with her daughter. In addition, as Janet grew older and more capable, Mrs. S. expected help in caring for Stevie. Mrs. S. desperately needed rest from the overdependent child.

Janet, once a pleasant, outgoing child, began to withdraw. She was disobedient, to gain attention. Punishment usually was in the form of restriction to her bedroom, which added to the withdrawal behavior. In school, the teacher reported that she was a good student but didn't seem to want friends.

The summer before Stevie was to begin his first public school experience, the S. family decided to take separate vacations. As they tell it, the men went camping and the women went shopping.

Mrs. S. and Janet became friends again. Thereafter, Janet returned to the delightful, pleasant child of before. Mr. S. spent the evenings of his vacation writing down Stevie's words, which he later shared with Mrs. S. and Janet.

In mid-year of kindergarten, the school authorities asked for permission to test Stevie. The psychologist recommended a class for trainable mentally retarded. He had found Stevie to be functioning in the mid-40s on the Wechsler Intelligence Scale for Children. The family voiced a unified objection to the placement. They could not accept the fact that he was retarded. He was transferred to another private preschool program for the remainder of the school term.

The following September Stevie entered a primary educable mentally retarded class which was part of the public school system. In the teacher's opinion, he still didn't talk. She objected to his presence in her class. Stevie developed a dislike for school and refused to attend whenever possible. To make the situation more complicated, he suddenly began running an above-normal temperature and often was unable to retain his breakfast. The family once again was in a turmoil. This situation continued for nearly two years.

When Stevie was eight, his family traveled more than 500 miles to a language clinic for one more evaluation. The staff recognized his problem as that of an auditory perceptual deficit.

Although his auditory sensitivity was well within normal limits, he was enrolled in a class for hard-of-hearing and deaf children. He was taught a few signs to make communication possible. At the same time he was taught to read and to write with a visual-visual approach. His speech therapist taught him to produce appropriate sounds through speech reading and isolated sound matching. The following year he was integrated into a regular third-grade class.

Stevie now is in middle school. He plays football to please his father but prefers tennis and golf. Both are sports that do not require language among players. For the most part, his speech development has caught up with the rest of him. He still has difficulty learning through the auditory channel and maintains his grades by using a tape recorder. Fortunately he enjoys reading and learns rapidly through written language.

He has few friends and still prefers his father's company to that of his peers. Children in school describe him as quiet and a bookworm. He was tested recently for part-time placement in a program for the gifted. His most recent IEP included five hours of accelerated education.

He continues to have moments of difficulty understanding oral language, particularly when under stress. This may be a lifelong condition, but for Stevie there is another way to learn. He is an exceptional learner and has developed a personality that fits his learning style.

Janet is on the debating team in senior high school. She jokes about herself and the family problem. She says she does all the talking and in that way compensates for the quiet one.

Case History 2: Beth

Beth was the fifth child in a family of six siblings. She didn't have much chance to talk; someone else always had the floor. When she was three, she was a very self-reliant little girl who could do battle with the best of them. She seldom spoke, and when she did, it wasn't clear what she was saying.

When Beth was five, Mrs. M. took her to register for kindergarten. Beth did not pass the screening and was enrolled in the summer program for immature children. A speech evaluation disclosed more than the normal number and types of misarticulations.

The speech therapist asked Mrs. M. to have a complete evaluation, including a neurological test. Testing revealed minimal cerebral dysfunction. The cause was unknown.

Beth entered kindergarten in September. The teacher reported that she was cooperative but that her speech was unintelligible. Mrs. M. agreed to have Beth taken to a local clinic, where she began individual therapy. The following year she attended a junior first grade, and the public school speech therapist began daily sessions of programmed instruction.

Beth's speech did not improve. She began to talk even less than before. She did not withdraw; she became aggressive. The school psychologist became involved. After three years in school, she was placed in a class for socially and emotionally disturbed students. Her mother reported that her siblings hated her and that she and Mr. M. were embarrassed by her behavior.

When Beth was ten, she was placed in a resource room for all academic subjects and integrated into a regular class for art and physical education. She became friends with her new special education teacher. At the end of the first marking period, her grades in the resource room indicated average achievement. The teacher told Mrs. M. that as far as she could see Beth was a very good child. She said Beth was difficult to understand, but if you listened, you could learn her substitutions, most of which were vowel sounds. Mrs. M. agreed to have Beth reevaluated. A speech therapist, a new school psychologist, the resource room teacher, and the regular class teacher were included in the study team. The label was changed from socially and emotionally disturbed to learning disability. Counseling, which included the parents and the other siblings, was initiated.

Therapy for the family continued for nearly two years. Beth became an accepted member of the family, and today when someone laughs at the way Beth sounds, her older brother becomes the aggressor, ready to protect his little sister. She has learned to avoid specific sounds whenever possible. Except in her own family group or with her few close friends, she speaks in single words or very short sentences. The high school guidance counselor is helping her to prepare for a vocation that will allow her to lead a normal life.

Case History 3: Peter

Mr. and Mrs. J. had three children. Peter was the middle one. Both parents were employed in a small factory, each working a different shift so that the children always were cared for. Mr. J. had dropped out of school when he was sixteen because he just hadn't learned to read and wasn't getting much out of the assignments that he could do. Mrs. J. had become pregnant in her senior year and had not returned for her diploma. Her grades had been average, but school wasn't important to her then.

Developmentally, Peter was normal in all respects. His problem was noted initially in grade one when he failed to learn a single reading word in the first three months of school. By June his sight vocabulary consisted of "I," "elephant," and "jack-o'-lantern." He was retained in grade one.

Repeating the grade was of little help. He still was struggling with a primer at the end of the second year. During grade two he began to demonstrate negative behaviors. He didn't complete workbook assignments and refused to write spelling words.

Mr. and Mrs. J. consented to a psychological evaluation. The results indicated average intelligence. The teacher was certain that the problem was his attitude. The parents began to take away privileges for academic failures.

When Peter was thirteen, he was placed in a special education class. He had earned the reputation of being a bad boy who wouldn't do his work. He was convinced that he was worthless. He chose friends with equally bad reputations. One afternoon he and two other boys decided to go for a ride. The boys were unlicensed and the car was taken without permission. This action resulted in Peter's being placed in a correctional institution for one year.

The following year Peter returned home and to a new school. He was tested for class placement. His reading level was grade two. His IQ had dropped nearly 20 points. He did not qualify for special class placement.

Two years later he withdrew from school. He had refused to make friends and, to avoid trouble, became a complete loner. He took a job in the same factory that employed his parents.

When Peter was eighteen, he tried to join the Army. He was functionally illiterate and therefore was rejected. He was a six-foot-tall, handsome youth who was completely void of hope for his future. As he put it, "I couldn't even read the comics; the best I could do was look at the pictures."

At 23 he still is a loner but regularly attends an adult class for remedial reading and is working on his high school equivalence degree. The ending of Peter's story has yet to be written.

Case History 4: Leah

Leah's case history begins when she was twelve. Until that time she had been a very normal and happy girl. Her school grades were above average and she was on the honor roll most marking periods. Her parents were divorced but she was able to see her father regularly and was only mildly upset when he remarried. If she had any complaints about her life they were voiced lovingly about her pesky five-year-old brother Mike, whom she adored.

On July Fourth she awoke to a beautifully sunny day. She arose early and immediately began helping her mother get ready for the family picnic. While her mother prepared breakfast and the basket lunch, Leah packed swim clothes, towels, and even an extra set of shorts for her little brother. It promised to be a great day.

Mrs. P., Mike, and Leah left the house shortly before noon. Within the hour Leah was lying unconscious in the emergency room of the local hospital. There had been an auto accident and Leah had suffered a severe head injury.

When she regained consciousness 76 hours later, she was unable to recall what had happened. Mrs. P. quickly gave her the necessary details and quieted her fears. She slept peacefully for the remainder of the day. The following day she was talking to the nurses and ready for a short walk when her mother arrived.

The doctors were extremely pleased with her recovery. Her head injury appeared to have had little or no effect on her mental capacity. Her motor abilities and balance were fine. She remained in the hospital for three weeks and had minor cosmetic surgery on facial scars. By mid-August she was home and enjoying the freedom of summer vacation and planning her fall wardrobe in anticipation of returning to school in September. When the first day of school arrived, the only signs of the accident were the very thin red lines of healing tissue and an occasional headache that was controlled easily with aspirin.

After the usual first-day routine of checking-in, seat assignments, and material distribution she was ready to go to work. Her homeroom teacher was new to the school and had decided that a writing project about summer vacation would be a good way to get to know her pupils. When the teacher announced that they were to write a story entitled *My Summer Experience,* Leah smiled and thought to herself this one will be easy. She decided to write about the accident and her favorite doctor.

As she placed the new ball-point pen on the paper, she had what she described as "a really bad pain in my head." She tried to write but the marks she was making didn't make any sense. She couldn't write her name. She tried several times. The harder she tried, the more her head hurt. Finally she went to the teacher and tried to explain. The teacher misunderstood what the confused child was saying and reacted in a negative fashion. Leah began to cry and several children ran to her aid. This added to the new teacher's distress and fear of losing control of the situation.

Eventually, one of the students was able to help the teacher understand what Leah was crying about. The student and Leah went to the school nurse's office; by this time she had become physically ill. Mrs. P. was summoned. Following a brief consultation with the principal, Leah and her mother left for the hospital, where Leah was readmitted.

Over a period of two weeks, Leah was seen by a neurologist, a school psychologist, and an educational diagnostician. It was obvious that she was dysgraphic; the problem was that the school did not have anyone trained to work with her specific language disability.

Leah returned to her regular sixth-grade class. The teacher, who did not know how to help her, began to avoid Leah. Leah misinterpreted the teacher's behavior as rejection. She decided that the accident had made her a dummy and that no one really wanted her any more.

The problem was compounded by several added family conditions. Mr. P. and his new wife moved from the area and withdrew child support. Mrs. P. was forced to take a second part-time job. Leah saw less of her mother and nothing of her father. In addition, she was forced to accept the responsibility of caring for her brother while Mrs. P. worked.

Mrs. P. reported that by midsummer the family situation was impossible. She sought help at a nearby county mental health clinic. The psychologist assigned to work with the family had been trained as a special educator and aided Mrs. P. in getting proper class placement for Leah. The following September she was transferred to a middle school with a class for brain-injured children. With special class placement and applied remedial techniques, the situation began to improve.

At sixteen, Leah is an expert touch typist and earns money to help ease the family's financial situation. She has mastered writing her signature but does not attempt manual writing for anything other than the briefest of notes. Her plans for the future include going to a business college to become a computer operator.

CONCLUSION AND DISCUSSION

The language elements are more than auding, speaking, reading, and writing. They are intricate aspects of everyday living that make life enjoyable and successful. A child, or an adult, who cannot use language in the usual way may be handicapped to such an extent that the person's personality is unable to develop normally. In many cases, the personality problem, which may be more evident than the language disability, may affect the entire family, causing absolute disruption in daily living.

The cases presented here are indicative of situations where either the family, or the language learner, sought and received help. However, this is not always the situation. What makes this so unfortunate is that most, if not all, language problems can be remediated. That is not to say that total language is available to all learners; it does mean that most cases, even the severely impaired, can be improved or taught an alternate communication form.

The average, or normal, language learner takes years to master the four elements of the system. Therefore, the exceptional learner should be given as much time and opportunity as is needed to reach the fullest potential. Teachers working with the exceptional individual find that successful language teaching and learning is not an easy course but one that is well worth the effort.

When teaching language, expect the most and you will get more. Ask for less and that is surely what you will accomplish.

Sweep Test Screening: A Programmed Instruction Method*

INTRODUCTION

This program is self-instructional and is intended for use by persons other than hearing testing specialists. The material includes procedures for familiarization with the audiometer and screening for possible hearing loss. Findings from the screening can be helpful in making referrals for audiological evaluation but should never be considered conclusive evidence of hearing loss.

An explanation of various types of hearing testing is found in Chapter 1 of this volume. If that material has not been read, please do so before undertaking this program.

EQUIPMENT NEEDED

1. One pure-tone audiometer with its components preset to the following:
   a. POWER SWITCH: "off"
   b. TRANSDUCER SELECTOR: "left earphone"–earphones plugged in
   c. INTERRUPTOR SWITCH: "normally off"
   d. ATTENUATOR: $55dB_{HL}$
   e. OUTPUT SELECTOR: 1KHz
2. An AC power outlet. *Audiometer should NOT be plugged in.*

---

*Revised from *Sweep Test Screening—Programmed Text,* unpublished paper by Joseph Curry, M.Ed., by permission of the author.

PART I

Objectives

The purpose of this program is to teach you the five basic components of a pure-tone audiometer and their functions. After completing the program you will be able to name each component in statements of its functions. In addition, you will be able to demonstrate a thorough understanding of the function of each component by manipulating the controls of a pure-tone audiometer to satisfy each of the four conditions presented in a test at the end of the program.

Instructions

Cover all statements following item 1 with a sheet of paper or book. Read statement 1 and fill in the blank. Uncover statement 2 and check your answer to statement 1 with the word in the right-hand column. Read statement 2 and respond in the same fashion. Continue this procedure through the program.

1. The _____ of this program is to teach you to operate a pure-tone audiometer.

2. Before you can learn to _____ a pure-tone audiometer, you should know what it is used for.

   purpose

3. A _____ _____ _____ aids in evaluating a person's hearing.

   operate

4. This device is called a _____ _____ _____ .

   pure-tone audiometer

5. A person's _____ can be evaluated with the aid of a pure-tone audiometer.

   pure-tone audiometer

6. To _____ a pure-tone audiometer properly, you must first understand its five components and their functions.

   hearing

7. A pure-tone audiometer has _____ components.

   operate

8. The first _____ permits an electric current to flow into the audiometer.

five

9. When the POWER SWITCH is set to the "on" position an _____ current will flow into the audiometer.

component

10. When the _____ SWITCH is in the "off" position no current will enter the audiometer and it will not work.

electric

11. One reason why an audiometer may not be working is that the POWER _____ may be in the "off" position.

POWER

12. If the POWER SWITCH is "on" and the audiometer still does not work, the cause may be that the power cord is _____ plugged in.

SWITCH

13. The first basic component of a pure-tone audiometer is the _____ _____ .

not

LOCATE THE *POWER SWITCH* ON THIS PURE-TONE AUDIOMETER AND TURN IT TO THE "ON" POSITION.

14. An electric current is now flowing into the audiometer (provided it has been plugged in) because you have turned the POWER SWITCH to the _____ position.

POWER SWITCH

15. You have just learned that the first basic component of a pure-tone audiometer is the _____ _____ .

on

CONGRATULATIONS!

16. You also have learned that the function of the POWER SWITCH is to permit an _____ _____ to enter the audiometer.

POWER SWITCH

17. The second basic _____ of   electric
    a pure-tone audiometer is the   current
    TRANSDUCER SELECTOR.
18. The _____ SELECTOR   component
    determines whether an electric signal
    will be sent to the right (red) or left
    (blue) earphone.
19. When   the   TRANSDUCER   TRANSDUCER
    _____ is set at "R" (or
    "right") the electric signal will be sent
    to the right (red) earphone.
20. When the TRANSDUCER SELEC-   SELECTOR
    TOR is set at "L" (or "left") the elec-
    tric signal will be sent to the
    _____ (blue) ear-
    phone.
21. The right earphone is designated by   left
    the color _____ .
22. The left earphone is designated by the   red
    color _____ .
23. The blue earphone should be placed   blue
    over the _____ ear.
24. The red earphone should be placed   left
    over the _____ ear.
    LOCATE THE *TRANSDUCER*   right
    SELECTOR AND SET IT TO THE
    "RIGHT" POSITION.
25. When a sound is presented it will be
    heard in the right (red) earphone be-
    cause you have set the transducer
    selector to the "_____"
    position.
    PROPERLY PLACE THE EAR-   ("R", "Right")
    PHONES OVER YOUR EARS—
    RED: RIGHT EAR, BLUE: LEFT
    EAR (NOTE: REMOVE EYE-
    GLASSES, EARRINGS, AND
    PREVENT HAIR FROM FALLING
    BETWEEN EARPHONE AND
    EAR.)
26. Since you have set the TRANS-
    DUCER SELECTOR to the "R" or

"Right" position and have placed the red earphone over your right ear, the sound, when it is presented, will be heard in your _____ ear.

right

27. You have just learned that the second component of a pure-tone audiometer is the _____ _____.

TRANSDUCER SELECTOR

28. Now you know two basic components, the _____ SWITCH and the TRANSDUCER SELECTOR.

POWER

29. The function of the _____ _____ is to permit an electric current to flow into the audiometer.

POWER SWITCH

30. The function of the _____ _____ is to select the earphone (right or left) to which the sound will be presented.

TRANSDUCER SELECTOR

IF YOU HAVE COMPLETED THE LAST FOUR STATEMENTS CORRECTLY, YOU'RE DOING VERY WELL! IF YOU MISSED #29, REVIEW #s 9 AND 10. IF YOU MISSED #30, REVIEW #s 18, 19, and 20.

31. The _____ basic component of the audiometer is called the INTERRUPTOR SWITCH/ TONE PRESENTATION BAR (or BUTTON).

third

32. The _____ SWITCH/TONE PRESENTATION BAR (BUTTON) actually is two components in one—the interruptor switch and the tone presentation bar or button.

33. The INTERRUPTOR SWITCH and the _____ PRESEN-

INTERRUPTOR

TATION BAR are combined because they function together.

34. The INTERRUPTOR _____ has two positions—normally off and normally on.

TONE

35. If   the   _____ _____ is set to the "normally off" position, a tone will be heard in the earphones when the TONE PRESENTATION BUTTON is depressed.

SWITCH

LOCATE THE *INTERRUPTOR SWITCH* ON THE AUDIOMETER AND SET IT TO THE "NORMALLY OFF" POSITION.

INTERRUPTOR
SWITCH

36. Since the INTERRUPTOR SWITCH is set to the "normally off" position you should hear a tone in the right earphone (you already have set the TRANSDUCER SELECTOR to the "right" position) when you depress the _____ PRESENTATION BAR (BUTTON).

LOCATE THE *TONE PRESENTATION BUTTON (BAR)* ON THE AUDIOMETER, PUSH IT DOWN, AND HOLD IT DOWN.

TONE

37. You are now hearing a tone because you are _____ the TONE PRESENTATION BUTTON.

38. If you release the _____ _____ BAR (BUTTON) the tone will stop.

depressing

RELEASE THE *TONE PRESENTATION BAR.*

39. The _____ SWITCH is set to the "normally off" position and so you hear a tone in the earphone when you depress the TONE PRESENTATION BAR.

TONE
PRESENTATION

DEPRESS THE *TONE PRESENTATION BUTTON.*

INTERRUPTOR

40. You are now hearing a _____
    in the right earphone.

    RELEASE THE *TONE PRESENTA-*   tone
    TION BUTTON.

41. Since the INTERRUPTOR SWITCH
    is set to the "normally off" position,
    you do _____ hear the
    tone since you are not depressing the
    TONE PRESENTATION BUTTON.

    DO NOT DEPRESS THE *TONE*   not
    PRESENTATION BUTTON.

42. You do _____ hear a tone in the
    right earphone.

43. The _____ SWITCH   not
    and the TONE PRESENTATION
    BUTTON function together.

44. If you hear a tone when you depress   INTERRUPTOR
    the _____ _____
    BUTTON (or BAR), you know that
    the INTERRUPTOR SWITCH must
    have been set to the "normally off"
    position.

45. You will hear a tone when you depress   TONE
    the TONE PRESENTATION BUT-   PRESENTATION
    TON if the INTERRUPTOR
    SWITCH is set to the "normally
    _____" position.

46. The INTERRUPTOR SWITCH and   off
    the TONE PRESENTATION BUT-
    TON _____ together.

47. Therefore, if the INTERRUPTOR   function,
    SWITCH is set to the "normally   work
    on" position the _____
    _____ BUTTON will
    function in the *opposite* way from
    when the INTERRUPTOR SWITCH
    was set to the "normally off" posi-
    tion.

48. If   the   _____   TONE
    _____ is set to the "nor-   PRESENTATION
    mally on" position and if you depress

the TONE PRESENTATION BUT-
TON you will not hear the tone.
DEPRESS THE *TONE PRESENTA-*
TION BUTTON AND HOLD IT
DOWN. SET THE *INTERRUPTOR*
SWITCH TO THE "NORMALLY
ON" POSITION. CONTINUE TO
DEPRESS THE *TONE PRESENTA-*
TION BUTTON.

INTERRUPTOR
SWITCH

49. You are ＿＿＿＿＿ hearing the
tone because you are depressing the
TONE PRESENTATION BUTTON
while the INTERRUPTOR SWITCH
is in the "normally on" position.
CONTINUE TO DEPRESS THE
TONE PRESENTATION BUTTON.

not

50. Since the INTERRUPTOR SWITCH
is set to the "normally on" position
you will hear the tone when you
release the ＿＿＿＿＿
＿＿＿＿＿ BAR (BUT-
TON).
RELEASE THE *TONE PRESENTA-*
TION BUTTON.

TONE
PRESENTATION

51. You are hearing the tone because you
are ＿＿＿＿＿ depressing the
TONE PRESENTATION BUTTON
while the INTERRUPTOR SWITCH
is in the "normally on" position.

52. Without depressing the TONE PRE-
SENTATION BUTTON, the tone is
on when the INTERRUPTOR
SWITCH is set to the "normally
＿＿＿＿＿" position.
SET THE INTERRUPTOR SWITCH
TO THE "NORMALLY OFF" PO-
SITION.

not

on

53. Now you are ＿＿＿＿＿ hearing the tone.

54. Without depressing the TONE PRE-
SENTATION BUTTON, the tone is
off when the INTERRUPTOR

not

SWITCH is set to the "normally
_____" position.

55. The INTERRUPTOR SWITCH and the _____ _____ _____ function together.

off

56. The INTERRUPTOR SWITCH determines the condition (button down or button up) under which a _____ will be heard.

TONE
PRESENTATION
BUTTON

57. The TONE PRESENTATION BUTTON presents the tone under the condition set by the _____ _____ .

tone

58. The INTERRUPTOR SWITCH/ TONE PRESENTATION BAR is the _____ component of the pure-tone audiometer.

INTERRUPTOR
SWITCH

CAN YOU ANSWER THESE? IF NOT, REFER TO THE STATEMENT NUMBERS THAT ACCOMPANY THE ANSWER.

third

59. That basic component of the pure-tone audiometer that permits an electric current to flow into the audiometer is the _____ _____ .

60. The component that selects the earphone (right-red or left-blue) to which the sound will be presented is the _____ _____ _____ .

POWER SWITCH
9, 10, 29

61. The third basic component you have learned is called the _____ _____ / _____ _____ _____ .

TRANSDUCER
SELECTOR: 18-
20, 30

62. If the INTERRUPTOR SWITCH is set to the "normally off" position, a tone will be heard if the TONE PRESENTATION BAR is _____ .

INTERRUPTOR
SWITCH/TONE
PRESENTATION
BAR: 31
DEPRESSED: 36-55

63. If the INTERRUPTOR SWITCH is set to the "normally _____" position, no tone will be heard when the

TONE PRESENTATION BUTTON
is not depressed.

64. If a tone is heard and the TONE PRE-
SENTATION BUTTON is not depressed the INTERRUPTOR
SWITCH must have been set to the
"normally _____" position.   off: 36-55

65. If the TONE PRESENTATION
BUTTON is depressed and no tone is
heard, the INTERRUPTOR SWITCH
must have been set to the "normally
_____" position.   on: 36-55

66. The _____ _____ determines the condition (bar down or bar
up) under which a tone will be heard.   on: 36-55

67. The _____ _____
_____ presents a tone   INTERRUPTOR
under the condition set by the IN-   SWITCH
TERRUPTOR SWITCH.

IF YOU HAVE ANSWERED   TONE
#59-#67 CORRECTLY, EXCEL-   PRESENTATION
LENT!!   BAR OR BUTTON:
                                                      52, 54, 57

68. Since there are _____
basic components of a pure-tone audiometer and you already know three,
you only have two to go!

69. The fourth component of the   five
_____
_____ is called the
ATTENUATOR.

70. The _____ of the   PURE-TONE
ATTENUATOR is to vary the inten-   AUDIOMETER
sity or loudness of the tone.

71. The intensity of a _____   function,
is measured in dB (decibels).   purpose

72. The ATTENUATOR has several dB   tone, sound
settings or positions varying usually in
5dB steps from 0dB to 110dB or from
−10dB to 100 _____ .

LOCATE THE *ATTENUATOR* ON   dB
THE AUDIOMETER.

73. The ATTENUATOR is set at
_____ dB.

74. Therefore, the tone you hear when   55
you depress the _____
_____ BUTTON is presented
at the 55dB level of intensity.

75. You may increase or decrease the   TONE
_____ of a tone by   PRESENTATION
turning the ATTENUATOR to successively higher numbers (to increase
intensity) or to successively lower
numbers (to decrease intensity).

WHILE DEPRESSING THE *TONE*   intensity
PRESENTATION BUTTON, GRAD-
UALLY INCREASE THE INTEN-
SITY OF THE TONE BY TURNING
THE *ATTENUATOR* TO SUCCES-
SIVELY HIGHER NUMBERS.
NEXT, DECREASE THE INTEN-
SITY. NOW, GO BACK TO 55dB.

76. As the intensity or loudness of the
tone increased, the dB settings on the
ATTENUATOR also _____

_____ .

77. The dB settings on the AT-   increased
TENUATOR decreased as the intensity or loudness of the tone

_____ .

78. Setting the _____ to 0dB   decreased
or –10dB does not mean there is an
absence of sound (tone) at this level.

79. The 0dB or –10 _____ level repre-   ATTENUATOR
sents the lower limit of intensity for
normal hearing.

80. Under ideal conditions, only a person   dB
whose hearing is normal may hear a
_____ presented at these lower
limits of intensity.

81. One whose hearing is not within the   tone, sound
normal range will _____ hear a tone
presented at the 0dB or –10dB level.

82. The _____ is the
    component of the audiometer that var-
    ies the intensity or loudness of a
    sound or tone.

not

83. CONGRATULATIONS! You have
    learned the _____ of the
    fourth basic component of the pure-
    tone audiometer—the ATTEN-
    UATOR.

ATTENUATOR

84. The _____ and final component is
    the OUTPUT SELECTOR.

function

85. The _____ SELECTOR
    selects the kind of sound (pure tones,
    speech, noise) that will be heard in the
    earphones.

fifth

86. The OUTPUT _____ on a
    pure-tone audiometer selects one of
    several pure tones.

OUTPUT

87. The _____ _____
    selects pure tones having frequencies
    (or pitches) ranging from very low to
    very high.

SELECTOR

88. The average _____ tone
    audiometer has frequencies ranging
    from 250Hz (Hertz) or 500Hz to 8KHz
    (K=1000).

OUTPUT SELECTOR

89. Other frequencies available may be
    1KHz, 1500Hz, 2KHz, 3KHz, and
    4K_____ .

pure

90. 1500Hz also may be expressed as
    _____ KHz.

Hz or Hertz

91. This is so because K= _____ .

1.5

92. To write 4KHz in longer form you
    would write _____Hz.

1000

93. The frequencies on the audiometer
    may be indicated in long or
    _____ form.

4000

94. Therefore, 1000Hz may be indicated
    as 1KHz or _____ Hz.

short

95. _____ (or Hertz) refers to the units
    in which frequencies are measured.

1000

96. Another name for these units is cycles per second (or cp_____).

Hz

97. Therefore, 1000Hz may also be written: 1000 _____ _____ _____ .

s

98. Thus, the _____ SELECTOR will have frequencies designated in one of four ways: 1000Hz, 1000 cps, 1KHz, or 1K cps.

cps

99. The frequencies selected by the _____ _____ probably will range from 250Hz or 500Hz to about 8000 Hz.

OUTPUT

LOCATE THE *OUTPUT SELECTOR* ON THE AUDIOMETER.

OUTPUT SELECTOR

100. It is set to _____ Hz.

DEPRESS THE *TONE PRESENTATION* BAR AND NOTE THE PITCH OF THIS 1000Hz PURE TONE. NOW SWEEP THROUGH THE FREQUENCIES (TURN TO HIGHER AND LOWER NUMBERS), NOTING THE CHANGES IN PITCH. RETURN THE *OUTPUT SELECTOR* TO 1000Hz.

1000 or 1K

101. A pure _____ that is low in pitch has a low frequency.

102. A pure tone that has a high pitch has a _____ frequency.

tone

103. As you were sweeping through the frequencies from low to high, the tones varied from _____ to high.

high

104. On the pure-tone audiometer, the lowest frequency capable of being _____ by the OUTPUT SELECTOR usually is 250Hz or 500Hz.

low

105. The highest frequency capable of being selected by the _____ _____ usually is 8KHz.

selected

106. The _____ of the OUTPUT SELECTOR on a pure-tone audiometer is to select one of several available pure tones, usually ranging from 250Hz or 500Hz to 8KHz.

OUTPUT SELECTOR

107. Now you can name the _____ basic components of the pure-tone audiometer.

function

five

You should be able to name the correct audiometer component in these statements of their functions. Cover each statement as before.

1. The _____ _____ permits an electric current to enter the audiometer.

2. The _____ _____ selects the earphone (Right or Left) in which the tone will be heard.

POWER SWITCH: 9, 10, 29

3. The _____ _____/ _____ _____ _____ has two interrelated functions.

TRANSDUCER SELECTOR: 18-20, 30

4. The _____ _____ sets the condition (button down or button up) under which a tone will be heard.

INTERRUPTOR SWITCH/TONE PRESENTATION BAR

5. The _____ _____ _____ presents a tone under the condition set by the INTERRUPTOR SWITCH.

INTERRUPTOR SWITCH: 52, 54, 58

6. The _____ varies the intensity or loudness of the tone, usually in 5dB steps from 0dB to 110dB or from −10dB to 100dB.

TONE PRESENTATION BUTTON: 52, 54, 57

7. The _____ _____ selects one of several pure tones (usually varying from 250Hz or 500Hz to 8000Hz) that will be heard in the earphones.

ATTENUATOR: 70, 72, 82

OUTPUT SELECTOR: 85-87, 105

PART II

Now that you are familiar with the pure-tone audiometer, you are ready for Step 2, the screening procedure. Practice on a friend or someone who also wishes to learn the procedure. Practice the procedure until you are thoroughly comfortable with the operation of the audiometer and the settings to be used. DO NOT PRACTICE ON THE CHILD OR CHILDREN YOU PLAN TO TEST.

Instructions

1. Select a room or place that is as free of noise and distractions as possible. Make sure the audiometer is working properly.
2. Seat the child in such a way that he cannot see the hands of the operator. (This tends to eliminate the possibility of visual clues.)
3. Tell the child that he will hear some tones (beeps, noises, etc.). Some will be loud and some soft. Some of them will be high pitch sounds and some low pitch.
4. Tell the child that he should raise a hand as soon as he hears the tone and put his hand down when the sound stops. The right hand should be raised for the tone in the right ear, and the left hand for the tone in the left ear. Young children may need practice in raising right and left hand.
5. Remove objects that would interfere with proper fit of earphones (glasses, earrings, and hair from around the ear). Face the child and bring the earphones around from behind his head, permitting the cord to fall behind the pupil. Place the grid of the earphone directly over the concha so the sound is delivered directly into the ear canal. It may be helpful to have a second person place the earphones because adjustments are needed occasionally during the testing.

Testing

1. *Awareness Tone*
   a. transducer selector—"right earphone"
   b. output selector—1000 Hz
   c. attenuator 50 dB_{HL}
   d. interruptor switch—"normally off"
   e. tone presentation—hold the bar down for approximately 2-second intervals, being sure to vary the time between intervals.

If the child raises and lowers his hand correctly, proceed through the screening steps. If the child does not respond correctly, reinstruct the pupil.

2. *Screening*

    a. attenuator–25 dB$_{HL}$ _____ present tone

    b. output selector   2 K Hz   _____ present tone

                      4 K Hz   _____ present tone

                   500   Hz   _____ present tone

                   250   Hz   _____ present tone

    c. transducer selector–"left earphone"

    d. output selector 1 K Hz   _____ present tone

                  2 K Hz   _____ present tone

               500   Hz   _____ present tone

               250   Hz   _____ present tone

3. *Failure Criterion*

The child fails screening if he fails to respond correctly to more than one tone in one or both ears. If this failure criterion is met, stop the test immediately. A child who fails this test should be referred for threshold evaluation as soon as possible.

Sample Informal Reading Inventory

RECAPITULATION SHEET

Grade Level	Word Recognition			Comprehension		
	Timed	Untimed	Context	Oral	Silent	Hearing
Preprimer						
Primer						
1.						
2.						
3.						
4.						
5.	88	96	96	80	100	86
6.						

Independent Level _____

Instruction Level _____

Frustration Level _____

Hearing Comprehension Level _____

Strengths:

Problem Areas:

EXAMINER'S COPY
Word Recognition List
Grade Level 5

Stimulus	Timed Response	Untimed
1. rememberance ✓	remember	✓
2. selection	✓	
3. surprisingly	✓	
4. randomly	✓	
5. multiplication	✓	
6. frightening ✓	frighten	✓
7. avalanche	✓	
8. habitat	✓	
9. refrigerator	✓	
10. foreign	✓	
11. igloo	✓	
12. tundra	✓	
13. weatherman	✓	
14. prairies	✓	
15. escalator	✓	
16. ambulance	✓	
17. rigid	✓	
18. disposable	✓	
19. harvesting	✓	
20. depend	✓	
21. disaster	✓	
22. frigid	✓	
23. Appalachian ✓	d.k.	d.k.
24. wonderous	✓	
25. forestry	✓	

-4 per error

3 errors
88%

1 error
96%

EXAMINER'S COPY

Reading Grade Level *5*   Word Count *84*

Oral Selection
Flying

I can't remember the time in my life when I have not dream(ed) of flying.
My first flight happened as a result of a *Penny a Pound* |||| ^{T.h.} charity
event.

The idea was simple; The person was weighed and then paid a penny for every pound. My flight cost 82¢ and lasted about ten minutes.

Last week I found another ~~aviation~~ bargain, flight lessons at half price. It will take more than pennies to fly this time, but it will be worth it.

Oral Comprehension Questions

1. Was the author a pilot? (inference)   no
2. How much did the author weigh at the time of the first flight? (inference)   82 lbs.
3. What are the future plans of the author? (inference)   To learn to fly.
4. How long has the author wanted to be a pilot? (factual recall)   Always
5. What is a charity event? (vocabulary)   don't know

           Word rec. 3 errors—96%
           Comp. 1 error—80%

STUDENT'S COPY

Word Count *84*

Oral Comprehension Selection
Flying

I can't remember the time in my life when I have not dreamed of flying. My first flight happened as a result of a *Penny a Pound* charity event.

The idea was simple; the person was weighed and then paid a penny for every pound. My flight cost 82¢ and lasted about ten minutes.

Last week I found another aviation bargain, flight lessons at half price. It will take more than pennies to fly this time, but it will be worth it.

EXAMINER'S COPY

Reading Grade Level *5*   Word Count *128*

Silent Comprehension Selection
Flight Check

   Some people think that flying isn't safe, especially in a single-engine plane. Of course there are risks; however, if they knew about the safety regulations and precautions a pilot takes, their attitudes might change.

   Did you ever see a person about to drive away in a car check the tires, the brakes, the power systems, or, for that matter, the gas gauge? Pilots do all of those things—and more.

   They begin at the propeller and check for big nicks and cracks, then the wings, tires, tail assembly, rudders, struts, flaps, and so on. After they start the engine, they check the radios, engine, and other equipment. In fact, they have a checklist fastened on the instrument panel. It's put there by the manufacturer. Without a flight check, a good pilot will not take off.

Silent Comprehension Questions

1. How does the author feel about flying? (inference) *Likes it*
2. What are the precautions a good pilot takes before flying? (factual recall) *Checks it over*
3. What parts of the airplane were mentioned? (sequence and factual recall) *tires, brakes, engine, and gas gauge.*
4. Why does the author feel that flying is safer than driving? (inference) *Pilots fly only safe planes*
5. What do pilots use to be sure they have not forgotten anything? (vocabulary and factual recall) *Use a checklist*
6. Where is it kept and why? (factual recall and reasoning) *On the instrument panel so they won't forget*
7. Do all pilots do a preflight check? (inference) *The good ones do.*

100%

STUDENT'S COPY

Word Count *128*

Silent Comprehension Selection
Flight Check

   Some people think that flying isn't safe, especially in a single-engine plane. Of course there are risks; however, if they knew about the safety regulations and precautions a pilot takes, their attitudes might change.

Did you ever see a person about to drive away in a car check the tires, the brakes, the power systems, or, for that matter, the gas gauge? Pilots do all of those things—and more.

They begin at the propeller and check for big nicks and cracks, then the wings, tires, tail assembly, rudders, struts, flaps, and so on. After they start the engine, they check the radios, engine, and other equipment. In fact, they have a checklist fastened on the instrument panel. It's put there by the manufacturer. Without a flight check, a good pilot will not take off.

EXAMINER'S COPY

Hearing Comprehension Selection
Sunday Solo

I had a little less than 30 hours of flight instruction on that memorable Sunday afternoon. The flight instructor had had me flying some figure eights and 360s around a marker. He turned to me and said, "Take the plane back to the field." I was surprised. We had only been up about 30 minutes and we were scheduled for an hour.

The landing was smooth, hardly a bounce, and on grass that's a good trick. I taxied around toward the hangar, but he said to keep going. Just before the turn onto the runway, I was told to stop. He opened his door, got out, and said, "Go fly."

Hearing Comprehension Selection Questions

1. What happened on that memorable Sunday? (inference and factual recall) The person soloed
2. What events had led up to the solo flight? (sequence) Flying figure 8's and circles
3. What is a 360 around a marker? (vocabulary and background) Circle around something
4. At what kind of airfield did the student pilot take instruction? (inference, factual recall) didn't say
5. Had the student pilot expected to solo that day? (inference) No
6. What does the word taxied mean in this story? (vocabulary, reasoning, and background) driving the plane on the ground
7. Was it the student pilot's first solo? (inference) Probably

86%

Glossary of Terms for Written Language

PARTS OF SPEECH

Noun

A noun is the name of a person, place, or thing. Boy is a noun. A *common noun* is a word with general characteristics, such as table. A *proper noun* is the name of a specific person, place, or thing and is capitalized. For example, Bloomsburg is the name of a certain place. All of the parts of speech can become nouns, depending upon their use in the sentence. For example, in the sentence, *Work is hard,* work is a noun because it acts as the subject of the sentence.

Pronoun

A pronoun is a word that takes the place of a noun. Some types of pronouns are *personal pronouns,* such as he and they; *interrogative pronouns,* such as who? and what?; and *relative pronouns,* such as this and that.

Adjective

An adjective is a word that describes or modifies a noun or pronoun, such as *blue* dress or *old* person.

Verb

A verb is a word that shows action or state of being. *Action verbs* are classified into two types, *transitive* and *intransitive complete.* A transitive verb takes an object. For example, in the sentence, *Mark bounces the basketball,* bounces is a transitive verb that has an object, basketball. The intransitive complete verb shows action, but does not have an object. For example, *Mark walked into the school.* Walked shows action but does not have an object.

State-of-being verbs show no action, but are followed by a noun or adjective that is the same as or describes the subject noun. They are called *intransitive linking* verbs. For example, *Mark is a man.* In this sentence *is* is an intransitive linking verb. All of the *to be* verbs, *is, are, was, were,* etc., as well as the following verbs, *smell, taste, feel, look, sound, become, appear,* and *seem,* are intransitive linking verbs.

Tense

There are six *tenses* of verbs in American English: *present* tense, I walk; *past* tense, I walked; *future* tense, I shall walk; *present perfect* tense, I have walked; *past perfect* tense, I had walked; *future perfect* tense, I shall have walked. The past and perfect tenses usually are formed by adding *ed* to the present tense form. However, American English is rife with irregular verbs, such as *drink,* whose past tense is *drank,* and whose present perfect tense is *have drunk;* or *go,* whose past tense is *went,* and whose present perfect tense is *have gone.*

Verbs can act as other parts of speech. These usually take three forms: the infinitive, which is the word *to* plus the verb, and the gerund and participle, verbs with an *ing* ending.

Infinitive

An infinitive can act as a noun, an adjective, or an adverb. For example, *To hope was her last chance.* In this sentence, *to hope* is the subject, and therefore is a noun. In, *This is the house to buy,* the words *to buy* form an adjective describing house. In, *We listen to learn,* the *to learn* is an adverb describing listen.

Participle

A participle is a verb form ending in *ing* and acting as an adjective, such as, *Jumping up for the rebound, Mark caught the ball and made the basket.* In this sentence, the participial phrase is an adjective because it describes the noun *Mark.*

Gerund

A gerund is a verb form ending in *ing* that acts as a noun. *Swimming is Joy's favorite sport.* In this sentence, *swimming* is a noun that acts as the subject of the sentence.

Adverb

An adverb is a word that describes a verb, an adjective, or another adverb. In the sentence, *Joy spells poorly,* the word *poorly* is an adverb that describes *spells.* In the sentence, *Joy spells rather poorly,* the word *rather* is an adverb that describes *poorly.* In the sentence, *She is a very poor speller,* the *very* is an adverb that describes *poor,* which is an adjective.

Preposition

A preposition is a word that connects a noun, pronoun, or noun phrase to another word in the sentence, such as a verb. In the sentence, *Mack walked through the front door,* the word *through* is a preposition. Some common prepositions are *about, above, across, against, among, at, behind, beside, between, by, except, for, from, in, into, of, on, over, through, to, toward, under, upon,* and *with.*

Conjunction

A conjunction is used to connect words, phrases, clauses, or sentences. Conjunctions may be coordinating, such as *and, but, or;* subordinating, such as *if, when, because, through;* or correlative, such as, *either . . . or, both . . . and,* etc. In the sentence, *Mary and Mark are mother and son,* in both cases *and* is a coordinating conjunction connecting two nouns. In the sentence, *Tell him if you want to go,* the word *if* is a subordinating conjunction connecting two clauses. In, *Either you clean up or I shall punish you,* the *either . . . or* is a correlative conjunction connecting two clauses.

Interjection

An interjection is an exclamatory word or phrase such as *Oh!* or *Heavens to Betsy!* In American English, as in most languages, oaths in nonstandard language are considered interjections.

Sentence

A sentence is a group of words that expresses a complete thought. Sentences are classified according to intent and structure. Depending on the intent, a sentence may be *declarative* (making a statement), *interrogative* (asking a question), *imperative* (giving a command), or *exclamatory* (making an outcry). Declarative and imperative sentences end with periods, an interrogative sentence with a question mark, and an exclamatory sentence with an exclamation mark.

When sentences are classified by structure, they can be *simple, compound, complex,* or *compound-complex.* The following are examples of each type:

> *I went to the store.* (simple)
> *I went to the store and I bought some bread.* (compound)
> *When I went to the store, I bought some bread.* (complex, adverbial clause)
> *I bought some bread that Mario baked.* (complex, adjectival clause)
> *When I went to the store, I bought some bread and I saw my friend.* (compound-complex)

PUNCTUATION

Punctuation in American English is relatively consistent and can be done easily and correctly if a few rules are kept in mind. It is not the purpose of this book to list all kinds of punctuation or all of the rules. The following are included because they appear to be rules that students break frequently.

1. A colon (:) introduces a series, such as, *The listing of animals is as follows: aardvark, horse, dog, cat (Persian), and gazelle.* Colons are *not* to be used before what would be the direct object or predicate nominative, such as, *The following are: dog, cat, gazelle, etc.*
2. A comma (,) is used when a natural pause is indicated, such as, *There are, in fact, many like this one.*
3. A comma is used after an introductory subordinate clause, such as, *If you want to go, then you must be on time.*
4. A comma is used to separate two independent clauses in a compound sentence, such as, *He will ask for that privilege, or he won't get it.* If a coordinating conjunction is not used, then a semicolon (;) is the correct form of punctuation, as in, *She ate most of the peaches; I had some, too.*
5. Titles of books and other publications under separate cover are underlined. Titles of stories in magazines or anthologies are set off by quotations.

FIGURES OF SPEECH AND POETIC DEVICES

Simile

A simile is a comparison of two dissimilar elements using the words *like* or *as*. For example, *The lights of a Mack Truck at night are like the eyes of an electrified monster from outer space.*

Metaphor

A metaphor is a comparison of two dissimilar things without the use of *like* or *as*. For example, *The sound of a Mack Truck at night is the cacophony of a herd of injured elephants.*

Personification

Personification is the application of human characteristics to a thing or an action. *The falling leaves whispered their lament of summer past* exemplifies personification.

Hyperbole

Hyperbole is exaggeration, such as, *His heart was as big as the world and as pure as solid gold.*

Onomatopoeia

Onomatopoeia is the use of words that sound like the natural sound associated with the action or object involved. The following words are onomatopoeic: *crash, clang, coo coo, buzz, tinkle, zip,* and *slither.*

Alliteration

Alliteration is the repetition of similar initial sounds in two or more words. *The ragged rabbit ran rapidly* is an example of alliteration.

Index

About the Author

DR. MARGARET S. WEBBER began her undergraduate work in elementary education at Bridgewater State College, Bridgewater, Mass., and received the Bachelor of Science in Education degree from Oneonta State University College, Oneonta, N.Y. She completed courses for certification in special education at Newark State College, Union, N.J. She received the degrees of Master of Science in Reading and Doctor of Education in Psychology from Temple University, Philadelphia.

She has taught elementary students, the educable mentally retarded, and remedial reading, and has been a clinical diagnostician. In higher education she supervised graduate students and was an instructor of English education at Temple. For the last twelve years, Dr. Webber has been a professor in the Department of Special Education at Bloomsburg State College, Bloomsburg, Pa. Her responsibilities have included teaching both undergraduate and graduate courses in learning disabilities and language arts.

She is an active member of and has held offices in numerous professional organizations. Most recently, she has served as president of the Pennsylvania Federation Council for Exceptional Children.